BY THE E

COMPUTER BUYING GUIDE
RATING THE BEST
Computers, Peripherals & Software

More Big Laughs from SIGNET

(0451)

1985 COMPUTER BUYING GUIDE

CONTENTS

5

INTRODUCTION

Shopping for computers, peripherals, and software isn't an easy task. Whether you're looking for your first computer or looking to upgrade your current system, there are an overwhelming number of possibilities to choose from. Luckily, there is an easy way to make sure you're buying the equipment that's right for you, even if you don't have time to investigate all of the possibilities yourself. **The Computer Buying Guide** can help you make the right decision, because we've already done the comparing for you.

In this book, you'll find head-to-head comparisons of all the major brands and models of computers, peripherals, and software. Detailed comparison charts answer such specific questions as "Which dot matrix printers are faster than the Epson?" and "How does the IBM Portable PC compare to the Compaq?" To answer these questions yourself would require many hours of research, and you could never be sure you've checked every option. But with the information provided in these charts, you can quickly narrow your options down to those specific products that answer your needs.

In addition to the comparison charts, you'll find detailed reviews of dozens of computers, peripherals, and programs. These reviews provide the type of information that you'll need to make a final selection, by answering such questions as "Exactly what can I do with this program?" and "How easy is it to use?" Only by reading these hands-on evaluations will you know whether the hardware and software lives up to the manufacturers' claims.

The reviews are written in clear and simple language that anyone can understand; you don't need to understand computer jargon and buzzwords to use this

Prices may vary; shop for discount prices.

book. In fact, contrary to what many people believe, you don't need to understand computer jargon to use a computer.

SCOPE OF THE BOOK

We have tried to offer as much variety as possible in this book, so that computer users with different needs will find the information they need here. But in so doing, we didn't want to limit coverage of the most popular hardware and software. Consequently, we had to set some limits for the range covered.

For the computers, we have covered the entire single-user microcomputer market up to and including the IBM PC/XT. This means, roughly, that we considered all computers with retail prices up to about $5,000. This includes all low-priced home computers, all portable microcomputers, all game computers, and all of the IBM compatibles and clones.

The peripherals that are covered include any peripheral that will work with the various types of computers just mentioned. In general, we stayed away from peripherals that only work with a single computer, unless they were an exceptional value.

The software falls into many different categories. There are programs for the IBM PC (PC–DOS and MS–DOS software), programs for CP/M computers, programs for Apple computers (including the Macintosh), programs for Radio Shack Computers (TRSDOS), and programs for the Atari and Commodore home computers. Also included are programs for some computers that are no longer being manufactured, such as the TI-99/4A. Even though these computers are no longer available, we didn't want to ignore the millions of people who still own and use them.

WHO CAN USE THIS BOOK?

Because of its simple, straightforward style, this book can be used by anyone, even the computer novice who has never touched a keyboard. If you fall into that category, you'll be glad to know that the section on home computers was written especially for you, the first-time buyer.

This doesn't mean that we have left out important technical details, however. Specifications and technical details are provided with all of the reviews and comparison charts, for those who understand them. The Utilities Software section in particular is geared toward experienced users and programmers who want to get the most out of their computer.

ORGANIZATION OF THE BOOK

The book is divided into three parts: Computers, Peripherals, and Software. Each of these parts is further divided into sections so that you can easily find the hardware or software you're looking for. If you're looking for a specific product, you can find it quickly by referring to the Product Index at the back of the book.

Because of the widespread popularity of the IBM PC, we have devoted an entire section to so-called IBM Compatibles, or computers that can run software written for the IBM PC. The other three computer sections are Portables, which covers portable computers from lap-size to 30-pound transportables, Home Computers, which covers low-priced systems intended primarily for games and educational use, and Others, which covers everything else. The Home Computers section also includes a preview of several MSX computers. (MSX computers are a new type of inexpensive home computer.)

Prices may vary; shop for discount prices.

The second part of the book covers peripherals, and is divided into seven sections: Floppy Disk Drives, Hard Disks and Tapes, Modems, Monitors, Plug-In Boards, Printers, and Miscellaneous. The Miscellaneous section includes many unique and useful products, such as uninterruptible power supplies, touch tablets, spoolers, and optional keyboards.

There are thousands of programs available for small computers, and the size and diversity of the software section attests to this. There is a section covering each and every type of software: communications, data management, education, finance, games, integrated, utilities, word processing, and others. Regardless of your software needs, you can find the program to help you in one of these sections.

THE RATINGS

At the end of each review, you'll find a set of ratings. On a scale of 1 (worst) through 10 (best), these ratings give you a quick appraisal of the product's overall value, performance, ease of use, and documentation. In the computer sections, there are also additional ratings for software selection (how much software is available for that particular computer) and expandability. For the portable computers, there is a portability rating rather than an expandability rating, because that is a more important consideration for portables.

The Overall Value rating is a measure of how well the product's performance, ease of use, and features compare to its price. Note that an over-priced product will not receive a very high Overall Value rating, even if it is a very good product, because this rating is a measure of value.

The Performance rating tells how well the product performs its various functions. It's important to remember that the Performance ratings for different products cannot be directly compared. The word processing program TI-Writer, for example, received a rating of 10 for performance, even though several word processing programs with more features received a lower rating. TI-Writer received a 10 because it pushes the TI-99/4A to its limits; it is the best-performing word processing program for that particular computer. A word processing program for the IBM PC, however, would be rated according to how much of the IBM PC's capability it uses, and not how well it compares to word processing programs in general.

The next rating is Ease of Use. This tells how easily you can use the product, assuming you have no prior experience with it. Almost any piece of computer hardware or software becomes easy to use after you have spent enough time with it to discover all of its quirks, so this rating is more a measure of how easy it is to learn to use the product. Unlike the Performance rating, the Ease of Use rating can be compared for different products within a section. The lower the rating, the harder the product will be to use.

The last rating is Documentation. This is a measure of how well the provided documentation (manuals and user's guides) explains the product's features, and how well the documentation is organized. If the documentation is informative and easy to use, the Documentation rating will be very high; if it is sloppy (or nonexistent, as in some cases), the rating will be very low.

HOW TO USE THIS BOOK

There are many ways to use this book, depending on your individual needs. If you're a first-time buyer, i.e., a person looking for their first computer, you'll want to start by looking at the comparison charts at the end of

Prices may vary; shop for discount prices.

the computer sections. Find the computers that are within your budget, and then read those reviews. Pay close attention to the ports and the operating system provided with each computer; these things tell you which peripherals and programs that particular computer can use. If, for example, the computer you're interested in has one RS–232C port, it can use any peripheral that has RS–232C listed for its interface. (If these terms are new to you, don't be intimidated by them—you don't need to understand their technical meaning to understand their function).

If you're shopping for peripherals or programs, you'll use this book a little differently. Chances are, you already know what type of peripheral or program you want—in that case, you can just turn to the appropriate section and browse. Or, you might want to look at the comparison chart first, to see which peripherals or programs will meet your requirements. In either case, you can narrow down your search immediately by turning to the right section.

Maybe you want to be able to perform a certain function on your computer, but you don't know exactly which type of program will allow you to do this. In that case, read the introductions to each section until you find a type of software that will help you. For example, if you want to keep your Christmas card list on your computer, you'll find the data management programs like dBASE II and PC–FILE will allow you to sort and organize your list. Look further, and you'll find mail merge programs, which allow you to send customized copies of a standard letter to many different people.

If you're looking for information on a specific product, turn to the Product Index to find it. Then, after reading the review for the product, check the comparison chart at the end of the section. You may find that there are other, less expensive options available.

HOW TO BUY

Personal computers have become so popular that there are now many different places where you can buy computers, peripherals, and software: national computer store chains, independent local dealers, discount department stores, and mail-order houses, to name a few. Since each of these options has its advantages and disadvantages, it is wise to consider all the possibilities before buying.

Because they buy in volume, retail department stores often sell computers and peripherals for less than the list price. When combined with special price incentives and manufacturer rebates, these prices become much better than the prices offered by computer stores. Though price and availability are advantages to buying from a mass merchandiser, there are some disadvantages that should be noted.

First is a lack of knowledge on the salesperson's part. An uninformed salesperson cannot provide the kind of individual technical advice that a more experienced computer user can. Salespeople in department stores are usually salespeople first and computer users second; at many computer stores it's the other way around. This is changing, however, as many department stores are setting up computer sales departments staffed with trained people.

Limited choice is another disadvantage. Retail stores cannot always carry a wide variety of computers or accessories, but this too is changing as home computers become more and more popular. However, you still have to visit several stores in order to have a variety of machines to consider.

Another potential problem is service. Department stores usually have to send a computer back to the

Prices may vary; shop for discount prices.

manufacturer if there are problems. Though factory service is the best service, it does take time. If you want to use your computer for business applications, you may not want to wait the weeks that factory service requires. Even if time is not a factor, this is still an inconvenience. This situation is also changing, however, as more computer manufacturers establish regional service centers or offer exchanges for non-working machines.

Despite these disadvantages, buying from a department store can give you both a low price and a dependable product. If you want to buy locally and you have a good idea of what you want, a department store may be your best bet.

Another option—perhaps the most obvious one—is to buy from a computer store. Whether you are buying or just looking, shopping at a computer store gives you several benefits. Because they specialize in selling computers and accessories, computer stores offer the widest selection of brands and models to choose from. Also, you will usually find knowledgable salespeople in computer stores. They can help you decide what you want a computer to do and offer advice on what you need to handle the applications you have in mind. Be wary, though, of salespeople who talk in computer jargon. If a salesperson really understands computers, peripherals, and software, he or she should be able to explain your options in plain old English.

Another advantage to shopping in a computer store is that they will usually let you try before you buy. Most computer stores have a wide variety of computer systems up and running for demonstrations. For any major purchase of hardware or software, you should ask for a hands-on evaluation before buying; computer stores are the most likely place to grant such a request.

The other big advantage to buying from a computer store is service. Many stores have their own service department, which means you don't have to wait for your computer or peripheral to be shipped to and from the factory if something goes wrong. Also, many computer stores will give you equipment to use while they service yours.

The main disadvantage to shopping in a computer store is price. You might be able to negotiate a 5 to 10 percent discount for a complete system, but if you're buying just one item you'll probably have to pay full list price. For this price, however, you're getting better selection and service than is available elsewhere. And if you aren't an expert yourself, it's good to know you bought your equipment from people who will be able to help you when something goes wrong.

Many people buy computers, peripherals, and software through another source: mail-order houses. These firms advertise in all of the major computer magazines, and they are sometimes a good way to go if you know exactly what you want and are simply looking for the best deal. The choice of products is extensive and the prices are often very low, but there are some hazards.

First, make sure you buy from an established, reputable firm. Some mail-order companies announce spectacular deals on new products months before they are available. In response, hundreds of people send thousands of dollars for products that are delayed or—in some cases—never released. There are now federal laws to protect you from this type of situation, but it's still an annoying and time-consuming problem. So, before you send your money in, be sure to find out about the reputation of the company. The best way to do this is to try to find someone who has actually purchased equipment through the company.

Prices may vary; shop for discount prices.

Second, make sure you know exactly what you're getting when you order. Misplacing a digit on your order form can result in the wrong product being shipped. Be sure to check your order carefully before you send it in and follow all ordering and shipping instructions exactly to be sure your order is processed correctly. Also, read the product description very carefully so that you know what you're really ordering.

Finally, note that you are responsible for checking out the equipment when it arrives. Most mail-order houses send out sealed boxes straight from the manufacturer, and because of the computer industry's well-deserved reputation for reliability, this usually means the equipment will work correctly. But what happens if it doesn't? A department store will usually take back defective equipment, but a mail-order firm may not. Be sure you know the mail-order company's policy on defective equipment; some firms will require you to send it back to the factory yourself for warranty service. This can be a time-consuming and annoying process.

As you can see, there are many options for buying your computer equipment. Consider all of them carefully before deciding which is best for you.

COMPUTERS

Because there are so many brands and models to choose from, shopping for a personal computer can be an overwhelming task. To make your job a little easier, we've broken the personal computer market into four major types: IBM compatibles, portable computers, low-priced home computers, and others. Each of these areas is covered in detail, with specific comparisons among the computers in each category.

First come the IBM compatibles. This section covers all of the single-user personal computers that use the PC–DOS or MS–DOS operating systems. To varying degrees, these computers can run the many programs that have been written for the IBM PC.

The second section covers portable computers. There are many definitions of "portable computer," so we've included a wide range of sizes and types.

The transportables are the largest and heaviest. These computers are suitcase-sized and weigh up to 35 pounds. The IBM Portable and the Kaypro computers are good examples of computers in this size range. Most of these computers require a wall outlet for power and include a built-in monitor and disk drives.

Another type of portable is the lap computer, or notebook computer. These computers get their name from the fact that they are small enough to be held on your lap while working, or about the size of a notebook. The HP–110 and Workslate fall into this category. Most of these models have LCD displays, microcassette or microfloppy drives, and battery packs that allow you to use them when you aren't near a wall outlet.

Prices may vary; shop for discount prices.

The low-priced home computers are next. This section covers computers that are designed primarily for games and education. Most of the computers in this category don't include a disk drive or monitor—optional cassette interfaces allow you to store programs and data on standard cassettes, and there is usually a video output that can use your television as a monitor.

The last section covers miscellaneous computers. These are the computers that don't fit into the other sections, but that doesn't mean they aren't worthwhile or significant. In fact, many popular computers are included in this section, such as the Apple Macintosh and the Epson QX–10.

You'll notice that a large portion of the computers in this section use the CP/M operating system, which was the most common microcomputer operating system before the IBM compatibles and MS–DOS. There are thousands of programs available for CP/M systems, and new software is still being developed. The biggest drawback to CP/M systems (when compared with MS–DOS systems) is that CP/M was designed for 8-bit processors like the 8080 and Z80, while MS–DOS was designed for 16-bit processors like the 8088 and 8086. Because of this, MS–DOS programs run faster than their CP/M counterparts.

IBM-COMPATIBLES

If you're considering the purchase of an IBM compatible personal computer, you're not alone. The IBM PC and its many imitators are the most popular type of personal computer. They all use versions of the same operating system (MS–DOS), and this standardization has resulted in the development of thousands of programs that will run under MS–DOS.

For the most part, this means that there is a wealth of software available for these machines. The exact selection of software for a given computer, however, depends on the degree of IBM compatibility built into that particular machine—the greater the compatibility, the greater the selection of software. A few manufacturers (Compaq, for example) have developed a reputation for their near 100 percent IBM compatibility, while other vendors use hardware or software that prevents many programs from running properly.

If you need to use a particular program in your work, ask to see it run on the computer you're considering. The two programs most commonly used to measure IBM compatibility are Microsoft's Flight Simulator and Lotus 1–2–3; if these programs run correctly, that machine will probably be able to run any other MS–DOS programs.

Another area where IBM compatible manufacturers strive for compatibility is in the expansion slots. These are the slots (usually inside the back of the machine) that accept add-on cards and multifunction boards. If the slots are IBM compatible, you can use multifunction boards designed for the IBM PC to increase the power and versatility of the machine. (For a look at the variety of options available in multifunction boards, refer to the peripherals section.

Prices may vary; shop for discount prices.

There are widely varying opinions within the computer industry about the merit of purchasing an IBM compatible personal computer. Some people believe that you should stick to the IBM name because of their readily available service and support around the country. Others point out that you can get more performance for less money from most of the IBM compatible machines, and many of the IBM compatible manufacturers now have service and support programs that can rival IBM's. Obviously, this is a matter of opinion that you'll have to decide for yourself.

Over the following 20 pages, you'll find reviews of the 20 most popular IBM compatibles, as well as the IBM PC and IBM PC/XT. Read the reviews carefully, keeping in mind your specific needs. At the end of the review section, a comparison chart clearly shows which machines offer the most memory, storage, expansion options, and other special features.

AT&T PC–6300
AT&T Information Services

Approx. Retail Price......................................$2795
RAM...128K
Operating System ....MS–DOS
Included Hardware: keyboard, graphics adapter,
360K floppy disk drive
Included Software: none

The PC–6300 is a joint venture between AT&T and
Olivetti. It uses the 8086-2 16-bit CPU and runs at an
8mhz clock speed. This makes the machine process
instructions 30 percent to 80 percent faster than the
IBM PC—the exact increase in performance depends
on which program you are running. There is a socket
on the PC–6300 for an 8087 math coprocessor, and the
computer is shipped with 128K bytes of RAM that can
be expanded to 640K bytes. There are eight expansion
slots available, and six or seven of them are available
for user expansion, depending upon the original configuration purchased. Three of the slots are designed
to take full advantage of the 8086-2 CPU's 16-bit bus,
and still work with older IBM-style expansion cards.
The standard PC–6300 comes with one 360K floppy
disk drive. A second drive is available as an option, as
is a 10 megabyte hard disk.

The keyboard is similar to IBM's except that LEDs are
mounted in the caps lock and num lock keys, making it
easy to tell when these features have been selected.
There is a connector at the rear of the system, designed
for a mouse interface. A monochrome green monitor
with built-in tilt stand comes as standard equipment.
An optional color monitor can be plugged in as well.
Both monochrome and color monitor electronics are
built into the system, so no additional plug-in boards
are required for either display. In the high resolution
color and monochrome modes the resolution is

Prices may vary; shop for discount prices.

640x400 if you use an optional graphics adapter. The standard resolution is 640x400 in the monochrome mode, and 320x200 (16 colors) in the color mode. The PC–6300 has a fairly small footprint. It measures 16½ inches deep, 6 inches high, and only 15 inches wide, making it one of the smaller systems on the market.

A number of operating systems are available, including MS–DOS, PC–DOS and concurrent CP/M–86. As you might suspect, a number of networking options are also available. These features will allow users to share information and peripherals in multi-user environments.

Some IBM software is directly compatible with this system. In other cases, software is being modified for the AT&T machine. Examples of existing software include Lotus 1–2–3, most software languages, dBase II, WordStar, and MultiPlan. Since these products are being sold through large, reliable dealers, you should have no problem seeing demonstrations of software prior to making a purchase.

The high speed and advanced design of the AT&T machine may mark the beginning of a real challenge for IBM. Certainly AT&T has the money to make a significant dent in IBM's market. Moreover, its alliance with large and important dealers and software manufacturers makes the PC–6300 an important product that you should consider.

RATINGS:

Overall Value	9	Performance	10
Ease of Use	9	Documentation	10
Software	8	Expandability	10

COLUMBIA MPC 1600–1
Columbia Data Products, Inc.

Approx. Retail Price $2495
RAM 128K
Operating System ....MS–DOS
Included Hardware: keyboard, two 360K disk drives
Included Software: MS–DOS 2.1, BASICA, Perfect Writer, Perfect Speller, Perfect Calc, Perfect Filer, TIM IV, Fast Graphs, Home Accountant Plus, Asynchronous Communications, Space Commanders, ATI tutorials

The Columbia MPC provides a high degree of IBM software compatibility, and it comes with an unusually large collection of software for the purchase price. The MPC is equipped with 128K of standard memory, which can be expanded (through the addition of accessory memory cards) to 1024K. The keyboard, similar in design to the IBM keyboard, is light in weight and attached to the system unit with a coiled cord. You can choose either a monochrome display (green on a black background) or a color display. The Columbia has the built-in circuitry necessary to handle graphics software with either type of display.

RATINGS:

Overall Value	8	Performance	8
Ease of Use	8	Documentation	8
Software	9	Expandability	9

Prices may vary; shop for discount prices.

DESKPRO PERSONAL COMPUTER
Compaq Computer Corp.

Approx. Retail Price.$2895
RAM........................128K
Operating System..............MS–DOS
Included Hardware:
keyboard, 12-inch monitor, one floppy disk drive
Included Software:
none

The Compaq Deskpro is an outstanding 8086–based desktop computer that is faster than the IBM PC. It is designed to support almost all of the software and add-on boards created for the PC. The keyboard, while similar to the Compaq portable keyboard, has tactile feedback and LED indicators on the caps lock and num lock keys. A 12-inch monochrome monitor, (25 lines by 80 characters), is available, and is available in either green or amber. It can be easily switched between text and graphics modes, like the display used in Compaq portable computers. An RGB color output is standard, as is a parallel printer port. There are eight IBM-style expansion slots, five of which are available to the user (four in hard disk models).

Deskpro's 8086 microprocessor can process data several times faster than IBM's 8088 processor. Because this speed produces problems with some entertainment and data communications packages, Deskpro has two operating speeds: common and fast. The common mode is equivalent to the speed at which the IBM PC and other 8088-based machines operate, while the fast mode runs at the full 8086 processing speed

(7.14 Mhz). Users can switch between the two modes using either software or keyboard commands. This is particularly useful for speed-sensitive communication and game programs.

The Deskpro is offered in four versions. Model 1 has one half-height floppy disk drive and 128K RAM. Memory can be expanded to 640K bytes in 64K increments. Model 2 has two half-height floppy disk drives and 256K RAM. Model 3 has a half-height single disk drive, a half-height 10 Mbyte shock-mounted hard disk, a serial/clock board and 256K RAM. Model 4 has a half-height floppy disk drive, a half-height 10 Mbyte hard disk, a serial/clock board, a 10 Mbyte hard disk (tape) backup and 640K RAM. All models include a 12-inch green or amber monochrome monitor. Twenty Mbyte and 40 Mbyte hard disk drives and high-resolution monitors may be made available in the future. Except for a diagnostic disk, there is no bundled software. MS–DOS 2.11 with Basic sells for $60.

The Deskpro continues Compaq's tradition of high IBM compatibility. You won't have any trouble running Lotus 1–2–3, Symphony, Flight Simulator, and many other popular programs. Compaq has done it again.

RATINGS:

Overall Value	10	Performance	10
Ease of Use	10	Documentation	8
Software	9	Expandability	10

Prices may vary; shop for discount prices.

EAGLE PC SPIRIT
Eagle Computer, Inc.

Approx. Retail Price . $2695
RAM 128K
**Operating
System** .... MS–DOS
Included Hardware:
keyboard, 9-inch monitor,
two 360K disk drives
Included Software:
MS–DOS 2.0, BASICA

The Eagle PC Spirit is an excellent transportable IBM PC compatible. Based on the 16-bit 8088 processor, the Spirit includes a 128K byte RAM memory that is expandable to 640K bytes in 64K increments. An optional 8087 coprocessor is available. Two double-sided, double-density 360K floppy disk drives are included in the Spirit. A more expensive model, the Spirit LX, contains one floppy disk drive and an internal 10 megabyte hard disk.

The PC Spirit has a self-contained 9-inch green monochrome monitor. This monitor can display 25 lines of 80 characters each. The Spirit also has a self-contained color graphics feature, capable of displaying monochrome graphics on the internal monitor (similar to the way Compaq does it), and 16 foreground and 16 background colors on external color monitors. One parallel and two serial ports are standard, as is an RGB monitor interface.

The standard keyboard contains 84 keys. Eagle offers an optional (deluxe) keyboard with 105 keys, including 24 function keys. The additional function keys on the optional, deluxe keyboard are specially labeled to support the bundled word processing software, and the cursor keys are independent of the numeric key pad. The standard keyboard is very much like those found on the Compaq and other IBM PC clones.

Eagle bundles MS–DOS, CP/M–86, and GW Basic. A wide variety of IBM compatible software works with this system as well. Moreover, Eagle offers networking software and word processing, electronic spreadsheet, and a windowing program. All of these are optional.

All Eagle computer products, including this one, have a fine reputation, and are distributed through ComputerLand and other dealers. You should have no trouble getting this product serviced. You will also find it to be one of the more compatible clones on the market.

As of this writing, Eagle was about to enter Chapter 11, due in part to the untimely death of its founder. Many industry watchers believe that Eagle will survive its reorganization and continue to grow.

RATINGS:

Overall Value	9	Performance	9
Ease of Use	9	Documentation	9
Software	9	Expandability	9

Prices may vary; shop for discount prices.

IBM PC
IBM Corporation

Approx. Retail Price ....
.............................$2945
RAM.......................256K
Operating System ....
.........................PC–DOS
Included Hardware:
keyboard, two 360K disk
drives
Included Software:
BASIC

The machine that set the standard, the IBM PC, is a computer that offers high performance and broad support. You'll generally pay more for these features when they have the IBM logo on them, but if these features are important to you, the IBM PC will deliver. The IBM PC follows a modular design philosophy; the basic unit consists of a system unit and a keyboard. You add other components, such as display, from a list of options. The system unit contains space for one or two standard height floppy disk drives. At one time, you could obtain a system unit with no disk drives, designed to use a cassette recorder for storage. But these units have been phased out of production, and the one-disk drive system unit is the "minimum system" that can be purchased in most stores. The cassette port is no longer provided. The disk drives use the common 5¼" floppy disks, and each disk can store up to 360K of information. The standard memory is 64K, upgradeable to 256K. Most business applications will require 128K or more. By using plug-in memory expansion cards, you can further expand the memory to 640K or more.

The system unit contains eight expansion slots (older versions have only five). These are used for the insertion of accessory cards that will add features and performance to the basic system. A key to the IBM PC's flexibility is this building-block design, using the expansion slots. By carefully choosing the proper cards, you can add the features that are right for you. Accessory cards are manufactured by IBM and a host of independent companies. Pay close attention to the accessory cards offered by reputable independent companies. They tend to offer more features at better prices than the comparable IBM versions.

The best word for the IBM PC's keyboard is controversial. Most people either love it or hate it. The keyboard has a solid, firm feel, as opposed to the soft, sometimes mushy feel of most of the PC-compatibles' keyboards. The keyboard also has what is called "tactile response"; you feel each key bottom out, and an audible click is heard as this happens. The keyboard is light, detached, and has a coiled connecting cord that lets you position it freely. There are rear "stilts" that can raise the back of the keyboard slightly. There are a few problems with the IBM keyboard. The key layout doesn't follow a standard typewriter. Instead, IBM chose to move the shift keys; for example, where you would expect to find the left shift key, you'll find a slash key instead. The return key is half the size of a normal return key, and it is slightly to the right of the normal return key placement. The caps lock and numeric lock keys don't lock into position or have lights to tell you when they are turned on, so it's easy to mistakenly leave these keys in the locked position.

On the matter of displays, you have a number of options. You must choose two items: a display adapter card of some sort, and a display. You can choose the IBM Monochrome Display, which offers excellent character sharpness. It provides green characters on a

Prices may vary; shop for discount prices.

12-inch screen. Along with it, you'll need the IBM Monochrome Adapter card, or a suitable replacement, like the Hercules Graphics Adapter. The IBM Monochrome Display does *not* handle much of the software that's designed to use graphics, unless it is connected to an accessory card that allows it to display graphics (such as the Hercules card). Another possible choice is the IBM RGB Color Monitor, which displays text and graphics in color with a medium range of sharpness. You'll need the IBM Color Graphics Adapter card (or an equivalent) to use the color monitor.

No software is included with the IBM PC; you must pay for the operating system (PC–DOS), and any applications software that you desire. The operating system costs $65, but you shouldn't think of it as an option; it's a necessity to use the computer.

Overall, the IBM Personal Computer is a computer that performs well on all fronts. Such an accomplishment does come at a price; a fully equipped IBM PC, with software, will cost much more than most PC-compatibles. But if you need a first-rate computer with a broad base of support and a reassuring level of software compatibility, then the IBM Personal Computer may be right for you.

RATINGS:

Overall Value	8	Performance	8
Ease of Use	8	Documentation	7
Software	10	Expandibility	8

IBM PC/XT
IBM Corporation

Approx. Retail Price ....
............................$4395
RAM 128K
Operating System ....
........................PC–DOS
Included Hardware:
keyboard, 360K floppy
disk drive, 10 mb hard
disk
Included Software:
BASIC, DOS 2.0, BASICA

If you need the features of an IBM PC with the built-in storage equivalent of over thirty floppy disks, then the PC/XT is your logical choice. The machine is visually similar to the IBM PC, but in the place of the right-hand floppy disk drive, there is a hard disk. The 10MB hard disk stores up to 10 million characters of information. The internal design of the IBM PC/XT also offers an improvement over that of the PC; the XT contains eight expansion slots for the addition of accessory cards, three more than the PC. A standard PC/XT, however, will have cards already installed in three of these slots, leaving five slots open for a display adapter card and other cards of your choice.

The PC/XT comes with an IBM Asynchronous Communications Adapter Card, and this card provides a connector that can be used with a modem.

RATINGS:

Overall Value	8	Performance	9
Ease of Use	8	Documentation	7
Software	10	Expandibility	8

Prices may vary; shop for discount prices.

MAD–1
Mad Computer Inc.

Approx. Retail Price. $4295
RAM 128K
Operating System .... MS–DOS
Included Hardware: keyboard, 12-inch monitor, two 360K floppy drives
Included Software: none

In 1982 a company called Mad Computer Inc. was founded in Santa Clara, California. Their first hardware product was the MAD-1 system. MAD is an acronym for Modular Advanced Design, and in fact the MAD-1 is modular.

The MAD-1 16-bit system consists of four basic modules: the display monitor, the computing module, the data module, and the keyboard. A fifth module called the expansion module provides up to four additional slots for expansion. The expansion module is required for serial and parallel ports. Two double-sided floppy disk drives (360K bytes each) can be internally mounted. Ten megabyte fixed or removable hard disks are also available options. The system is based on an INTEL 80186 cpu running at 7.2 Mhz.

The standard system comes with 128K of RAM, which can be expanded to 512K bytes. The included monitor is a 12-inch amber or green phosphore device with antiglare coating, and it is on an adjustable stand permitting up, down, and side-to-side adjustment. The system's video control board offers both standard IBM-style monochrome displays and 16 color graphics. MAD's detachable keyboard includes a comfortable palm rest and 10 special function keys arranged along the top of the keyboard. There is a 14 key numeric pad and separate cursor keys.

Software for the MAD-1 is sold separately. This is an MS–DOS compatible machine, and runs much of the available IBM PC software. Mad computer also sells MadPlan, an electronic spreadsheet created by Microsoft, and MadVision, their version of the Bruce & James WordVision software. An accounting package from Peachtree is also offered under the name of Mad Account software. Concurrent CP/M 86 operating systems are available as well. There are several versions of Basic, Cobol, Fortran, and Pascal that will work with the MAD-1, and four concurrent tasks are possible. The manuals provided with the MAD-1, including an MS–DOS MadPlan, MadVision, and GW Basic manuals, are adequate, but not outstanding.

This young company has attracted much attention in the press. Computer hobbiests and owners of small businesses have been the first to try this product. Their enthusiasm is wide-spread and genuine. While most of corporate America will be reluctant to tell their purchasing department to buy computers from a young company called Mad Computer Inc., less traditional and more adventuresome computer users are giving this computer a hard look and good marks.

RATINGS:

Overall Value	9	Performance	10
Ease of Use	9	Documentation	8
Software	9	Expandability	8

SANYO MBC 555
Sanyo Business Systems Corp.

Approx. Retail Price ....NA
RAM...128K
Operating System...................................MS–DOS
Included Hardware: keyboard, two double-sided floppy disk drives
Included Software: MS–DOS, BASIC, WordStar, Mail Merge, CalcStar, SpellStar, InfoStar, EasyWriter 1

Sanyo has long been known as a manufacturer of low-cost consumer electronic products like stereos and video recorders. Their entry into the personal computer market was no surprise. Like many of their consumer electronic counterparts, the Sanyo computer products closely mimic competitive products with emphasis on low-cost manufacturing and marketing techniques. The result, in the case of the MBC 555 is an extremely low-cost MS–DOS system well suited to simple home and business applications.

The MBC 555 is a 16-bit computer using the 8088 cpu. A detachable keyboard is standard, as are 128K bytes of RAM.

Expansion of the Sanyo system is slightly more difficult than with IBM and some of the other popular clones. Sanyo's design approach makes it impossible to plug in popular expansion boards from AST, Quadram, Hercules, and others. But for many users these add-on products are unnecessary. The Sanyo comes equipped with a Centronics parallel printer port, an RS–232C port (optional), a joystick port, a composite, high resolution monochrome monitor port, and an RGB color monitor port.

Sanyo also offers two monitors. These are optional devices and are not included in the list price of the machine. The monochrome green phosphore monitor measures 12 inches diagonally, and includes a high resolution graphics display of 560x240 dots. A 16 color, 13-inch monitor is also available from Sanyo. It uses the RGB interface.

Sanyo does bundle some software with this system, including Sanyo Graphics Basic, a Sanyo version of MS–DOS, EasyWriter I, WordStar, CalcStar, SpellStar, InfoStar, and MailMerge. Much has been written about Sanyo's compatibility with IBM PC software — this is one of the least compatible clones on the market. Most compatibility problems tend to be display oriented, and users intending to purchase the Sanyo for a specific software package not included in Sanyo's bundle should actually see the software run before purchasing the computer.

On-board memory expansion up to 256K bytes in 64K byte increments is provided, but expansion beyond this is difficult or impossible due to the lack of standard size expansion slots. The keyboard has a full typewriter-style device with ten function keys and a unique numeric/editing keypad.

The Sanyo 555 is certainly one of the lowest cost MS–DOS systems on the market today; careful shoppers might be able to put together a complete system for under $2,000. The only trade-off is IBM PC compatibility and future expansion. For users who don't need these things, the Sanyo 555 with double-sided drives is an excellent choice.

RATINGS:

Overall Value	9	Performance	8
Ease of Use	8	Documentation	7
Software	7	Expandibility	7

TANDY MODEL 2000
Tandy Corporation/Radio Shack

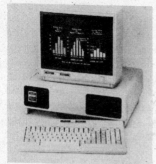

Approx. Retail Price ....
............................$2750
RAM 128K
Operating System ....
........................MS–DOS
Included Hardware:
keyboard, 12 inch mono-
chrome monitor, two 720K
disk drives
Included Software:
MS–DOS

The Tandy Model 2000, from the people who produce other computers under the familiar Radio Shack name, is a high-performance compatible with some attractive features. The computer consists of a monitor, keyboard, and system unit. The keyboard is comfortable and adjustable, with a layout that matches a standard typewriter. The keys have a firm feel, and twelve function keys are conveniently located across the top of the keyboard. The only odd feature of the keyboard is the layout of the cursor movement keys; they form an "inverted-T" design, sandwiched tightly between the numeric pad and the rest of the keyboard. We would prefer a diamond pattern with a little more room, but in all other respects, the keyboard rates above average.

The system unit contains the computer and two floppy disk drives. The disk drives are half height drives, which take up half the space of those in most computers, with no performance lost. The disk drives in the Model 2000 will store up to 760K per disk; that's twice the amount stored on the IBM PC and most other compatibles. The system unit also uses a microprocessor that operates at a higher speed than the one used in the IBM PC and other compatibles. As a result, the Model 2000 can process information faster than most IBM compatibles.

The Model 2000 contains 128K of standard memory; this can be upgraded to 256K without adding accessory cards, and up to 768K with the use of accessory cards. Four accessory slots are available for the installation of additional accessory cards. Both parallel and serial connectors are included with the system. One nice touch is the ability to place the system unit horizontally on a desk, or vertically on the floor, using an optional floor stand.

Two monitors are available with the Model 2000; a 12-inch green-character monitor, and a 14-inch color monitor. Both monitors provide good quality display of text and graphics. You can purchase optional accessory kits that increase the graphics resolution on either monitor.

Software for the Model 2000 is plentiful. Because the computer uses a higher-speed design, it is not totally software-compatible with the IBM PC. According to Radio Shack, the Model 2000 will run "approximately 50 percent" of the off-the-shelf software that's available for the IBM PC.

With the list price of a Model 2000 roughly $300 to $400 less than a comparably equipped IBM PC, the Model 2000 clearly provides more performance at less cost. Dealer support is extensive, due to the thousands of stores that Radio Shack maintains.

RATINGS:

Overall Value	9	Performance	9
Ease of Use	7	Documentation	8
Software	8	Expandibility	9

TAVA PC
Tava Corp.

Approx. Retail Price ....
................................$2395
RAM 64K
Operating System ....
........................MS–DOS
Included Hardware:
keyboard, monitor, two
320K disk drives
Included Software:
none

Glance quickly, and you'll probably mistake the Tava PC for an IBM. Bearing a strong physical resemblance, the Tava is a low-cost IBM-compatible that provides a high level of software compatibility at a very low price.

With the system, you get a main unit, keyboard, and monitor. The main unit gives you two floppy disk drives and 128K of memory that can be expanded to 256K. You also get standard parallel and serial connectors for printers or modems. A hard disk version is available. The Tava keyboard is nearly identical to that used on the IBM PC, but the keys have a soft, almost springy touch. The monitor displays reasonably sharp text and graphics, in green on a black background.

The Tava PC runs well over 90 percent of all software designed for the IBM PC. Word processing, mail merge, database, and telecommunications software is bundled with the computer.

RATINGS:
Overall Value	8	Performance	7
Ease of Use	8	Documentation	8
Software	8	Expandibility	7

Information accurate at time of printing; subject to manufacturer's change.

TI PROFESSIONAL
Texas Instruments

Approx. Retail Price ....
....$2195
RAM 64K
Operating System ....
...............................MS–DOS
Included Hardware:
keyboard, 12 inch hi-res
monochrome monitor,
320K disk drive
Included Software:
diagnostic disk

The Texas Instruments Professional Computer is a well-thought-out machine with the software and support necessary to meet most business needs. The TI Professional consists of a system unit, a monitor, the MS–DOS operating system, and a keyboard. The system unit houses the computer and one or two floppy disk drives, in an attractive beige case. As an option, you can add a 5MB or 10MB hard disk drive in place of the right-hand floppy disk drive. The system unit contains 64K of memory, which can be upgraded to 768K in 25K increments.

The keyboard on the TI Professional shows an encouraging change from the layout of most compatibles; TI elected to follow the design of the standard office typewriter. The shift keys are where they should be, the return key is large and correctly placed, and the cursor movement keys are laid out in a diamond pattern in a separate group, next to the numeric keypad. The keyboard also has a height adjustment that lets you control the angle of the keyboard.

TI offers two displays; a 12-inch green-character monitor, and a 13-inch color monitor. Both displays can

Prices may vary; shop for discount prices.

be used with software that makes use of graphics. Character sharpness and detail is a strong point of the TI Professional; the clarity of both displays is excellent, and an optional graphics adapter card can be added to further enhance the color display capabilities. Because of slight differences in the way the computer sends information to the display, you will not get correct results using a non-TI monitor. A parallel printer connector is standard, and serial connectors for modems are optional.

In the software department, you should first be aware that the TI Professional is not strictly software compatible with the IBM PC. While the TI Professional will read many disks that have been created on an IBM PC, its internal design doesn't closely mimic IBM's. What this means is that you can exchange files, such as letters written with a word processor, between an IBM PC and a TI Professional, but you cannot necessarily take the word processing software from the IBM PC and use it on the TI; many programs simply will not operate. This is only a problem if you must have software compatibility between the IBM PC and the computer of your choice. There's no shortage of business software for the TI Professional; Texas Instruments wisely convinced software companies to write TI versions of their IBM programs. As a result, hundreds of business applications are available.

The TI Professional can use standard printers or modems, and the dealer support and service network is fairly extensive. This is a well constructed business computer that you should consider as an alternative to the IBM PC.

RATINGS:

Overall Value	9	Performance	9
Ease of Use	8	Documentation	8
Software	6	Expandibility	8

ZENITH Z–161
Zenith Radio Corp.

Approx. Retail Price......................................$2399
RAM..128K
Operating System ....MS–DOS
Included Hardware: keyboard, 9-inch monitor, two floppy disk drives
Included Software: none

The Zenith Z–161 is an impressive IBM PC compatible portable. Based on the 8088 microprocessor, the Z–161 comes equipped with nearly everything one needs for computing. There is 128K of RAM standard, and it can be expanded to 640K bytes. Two half-height floppy disk drives are mounted horizontally, and flip out of the top of the system for use, then fold back down for transportation. Monochrome and RGB color ports are standard. There is one serial port and one parallel port as well. Most of the electronics can be found on plug-in boards, including the microprocessor. Even after the installation of everything necessary for operation, four IBM compatible slots remain available for the user (three in the hard disk model). The Z–161 measures 19.5 inches wide by 8.3 inches high by 19.3 inches deep and weighs just over 38 pounds for the single drive system.

The video section of this product is also worth noting. It is not as capable in the area of high resolution graphics as some of the other Zenith products, but this is because of Zenith's desire to remain IBM compatible. There is less flickering and much smoother scrolling on the Zenith than on many other IBM compatibles. It is possible to run dot-addressable, high resolution color graphics on a monochrome display; this is similar to the feature offered by Compaq, making it possible to display text and graphics on the same monitor. A sharp 9-inch amber screen is built into the Z–161.

The documentation with this product is very well illustrated, carefully organized, and useful for both experienced and first-time users. Zenith has designed an improved keyboard with LEDs to indicate the status of num lock and caps lock functions. In addition, the backslash key has been moved, and the return key is larger and L-shaped. Zenith is so proud of this keyboard that it hopes to sell it separately to owners of IBM computers. Another nice feature of the keyboard is auto-repeat on every key.

If you purchase a Zenith Z–161 you will be the owner of an excellent portable system with features not found on any of the other computers reviewed in this book.

RATINGS:

Overall Value	10	Performance	10
Ease of Use	10	Documentation	10
Software	9	Portability	9

	Apricot PC	Columbia MPC 1600–1
Manufacturer	ACT	Columbia Data Products
Operating System	MS–DOS	MS–DOS
RAM—Standard	256K	128K
RAM—Maximum	768K	1 megabyte
CPU	8086	8088
Ports	Centronics parallel and RS–232C serial	one parallel, two RS–232C seria
Expansion Slots	2	8
Disk Drives	two Sony 3.5 inch microfloppies	two 360K 5¼ inch floppies
Monitor	9 inch monochrome	none
Keyboard	96 keys	IBM PC standard
Approx. Price	$3100	$2495
Special Features	40 column LCD, high resolution monitor	8087 coprocessor

Columbia MPC–4	Compaq Desktop	Corona PC
Columbia Data Products	Compaq Computer Corporation	Corona Data Systems
MS–DOS	MS–DOS 2.11	MS–DOS
128K	128K	128K
1 megabyte	640K	512K
8088	8086	8088
one Centronics parallel, two RS–232C serial	parallel printer port	Centronics parallel and RS–232C serial
8	4 or 6 depending on configuration	4
one 360K 5¼ inch floppy, 10 MB hard disk	one 360K 5¼ inch floppy	One 360K 5¼ inch floppy
none	12 inch monochrome	12 inch monochrome
IBM PC standard	IBM PC standard	IBM PC standard
$4195	$2495	NA
8087 coprocessor	100% IBM compatible, can run faster than IBM	BASIC, Multimate, PC Tutor

	Eagle PC	IBM PC
Manufacturer	Eagle Computer, Inc.	IBM Corporation
Operating System	MS–DOS 2.0	PC–DOS
RAM—Standard	128K	64K
RAM-Maximum	640K	640K
CPU	8088	8088
Ports	one parallel, two RS–232C serial	none
Expansion Slots	4	5
Disk Drives	two 360K 5¼ inch floppies	one 360K 5¼ inch floppy
Monitor	9 inch monochrome	none
Keyboard	enhanced IBM PC	IBM PC standard
Approx. Price	$2995	$2100
Special Features	MS–DOS, BASIC A	BASIC

IBM PC/XT	Leading Edge PC	Mad–1
IBM Corporation	Leading Edge Products, Inc.	Mad Computer, Inc.
PC–DOS	MS–DOS	MS–DOS
128K	128K	128K
640K	640K	512K
8088	8088	80186
none	parallel printer, RS–232C serial	none
8	7	7
one 360K 5¼ inch floppy, 10 MB hard disk	two 360K 5¼ inch floppies	two 360K 5¼ inch floppies
none	12 inch monochrome	12 inch monochrome
IBM PC standard	83 keys	85 keys
$4395	$2695	$4295
BASIC, Asynch. Comm. Adapter	Leading Edge Word Processor	can run faster than IBM

	NEC APC–III	Sanyo 550
Manufacturer	NEC Information Systems	Sanyo Business Systems Corp.
Operating System	MS–DOS or CP/M–86	MS–DOS
RAM—Standard	128K	128K
RAM—Maximum	640K	256K
CPU	NEC proprietary	8088
Ports	Centronics parallel, RS–232C serial	parallel printer
Expansion Slots	none	none
Disk Drives	8 inch floppy	two 360K 5¼ inch floppies
Monitor	12 inch monochrome	none
Keyboard	86 keys	83 keys, five function keys
Approx. Price	$2750	$995
Special Features	sound chip, 22 function keys clock/calendar	sound generator, speaker, WordStar, CalcStar, EasyWriter 1

Prices may vary; shop for discount prices.

Seequa PC	Seequa PC/XT	Sperry PC Model 10
Seequa Computer Corporation	Seequa Computer Corporation	Sperry Corp.
MS–DOS	MS–DOS 2	MS–DOS 1.25
128K	256K	128K
640K	640K	640K
8088, Z80A	8088, Z80A	8088
Centronics parallel, RS–232C serial	Centronics parallel, RS–232C serial, RGB video output	NA
5	4	5
one 360K 5¼ inch floppy	one 360K 5¼ inch floppy, 10 MB hard disk	one 320K 5¼ inch floppy
9 inch monochrome	12 inch monochrome	12 inch
IBM PC standard	IBM PC standard	enhanced IBM PC
$1995	$3995	$2643
MBASIC, word processing, spreadsheet, communications software	Perfect Writer, Perfect Calc, Perfect Speller, Condor I, C-Term, GW–BASIC	switch selectable CPU speed

	TI Professional	Tandy Model 2000
Manufacturer	Texas Instruments	Tandy Corporation
Operating System	MS–DOS	MS–DOS
RAM—Standard	64K	128K
RAM—Maximum	256K	768K
CPU	8088	80186
Ports	one parallel	Centronics parallel, RS–232C serial
Expansion Slots	5	4
Disk Drives	one 320K 5¼ inch floppy	two 720K 5¼ inch floppies
Monitor	12 inch monochrome	12 inch monochrome
Keyboard	92 keys, adjustable	90 keys
Approx. Price	$2195	$2750
Special Features	high resolution monitor (720×300)	high speed processing

Tava PC	Zenith Z-161	Zenith Z-100
Tava Corporation	Zenith Data Systems	Zenith Data Systems
MS–DOS	MS–DOS	Z–DOS and CP/M
64K	128K	128K
640K	640K	768K
8088	NA	8088, 8085
one parallel one serial	one parallel one serial	Centronics parallel two RS–232C serial
5	4	5
two 360K 5¼ inch floppies	two 5¼ inch floppies	320K 5¼ inch floppy
monochrome	9 inch amber	none
83 keys	95 keys	95 keys
$2395	$2399	$2199

PORTABLES

Over the past five years, microcomputer technology has come a long way. Five years ago, programmable pocket calculators represented the state-of-the-art in portable microcomputers; today, there are many handheld machines available with large and sophisticated programs like Lotus 1–2–3 built right into them.

The Osborne portable computers were the first commercially successful portables. They did so well, in fact, that Osborne Computer Corporation became the fastest growing corporation in U.S. history, with over $100 million in sales their first year. Then other companies like Compaq and Kaypro came out with more powerful or less expensive portable computers, and Osborne Computer Corporation was soon filing for bankruptcy.

Although it hasn't been very good for Osborne, these developments are good news for the person who is shopping for a portable computer. Portable computer manufacturers have become very competitive, and you can choose from a variety of powerful, reasonably priced machines.

Many of the portable computers reviewed in this book are also IBM compatibles. In fact, many of the popular models are simply portable versions of IBM compatible desktop machines like the Corona, Columbia, and IBM computers. This means that you can use the wide range of MS–DOS software that is currently available.

Prices may vary; shop for discount prices.

Other portables, like the Kaypro and the Actrix, are CP/M machines. Although CP/M is not as high-performance as MS–DOS, there is enough good software available for CP/M machines that you can use these computers productively in all but the most demanding applications.

One type of portable that is becoming increasingly popular is the lap size computer, or notebook computer. These machines usually offer LCD (liquid crystal display) monitors, microfloppy or microcassette storage, and battery-operated portability. With a modem and telecommunications software, you can use one of these small computers to do work anywhere you may be, and then send the results back to your desktop computer at home or the office. At the rate they're catching on, these computers may soon become standard equipment for busy executives and travelling professionals in all fields.

Thirty popular portables are reviewed over the following pages. They range in size from handheld to over 30 pounds, and some cost under $1,000 while others cost nearly six times that much. The comparison charts at the end of the chapter give the size and weight of each machine, along with many other specifications. Read the reviews and charts carefully; with all this variety, there is sure to be a portable computer that can meet your needs.

ACTRIX
Actrix Computer Corporation

Approx. Retail Price .$2190
RAM..........................64K
Operating System....CP/M
Included Hardware:
keyboard, monitor, two
disk drives, printer,
modem
Included Software:
CP/M 2.2, MBASIC,
CBASIC, Perfect Software
Series, Personal Pearl,
Money Maestro

The Actrix is an 8-bit CP/M computer, and includes a seven-inch display screen that uses amber text and graphics. The amber display is easy on the eyes. Two floppy disk drives are provided, along with a detachable keyboard. The keyboard has a full set of keys that have a moderately firm touch, and a numeric keypad is included. The built-in printer provides dot matrix print of reasonable quality. There are two modems built into the Actrix; one is an acoustic modem that uses the handset of a standard phone, while the other is a direct-connect modem that uses the standard modular telephone jack.

Altogether, the Actrix provides a large number of features for the price. The dealer network is small, however, so you may want to make sure you can find support for this one before you buy.

RATINGS:

Overall Value	8	Performance	6
Ease of Use	7	Documentation	4
Software	8	Portability	7

Prices may vary; shop for discount prices.

APPLE IIC
Apple Computer, Inc.

Approx. Retail Price .$1295
RAM 128K
Operating System ....
...................Apple DOS
Included Hardware:
keyboard, disk drive
Included Software:
operating system

It usually takes about a year before a lot of software comes out for a new computer, but the new IIc is compatible with 90–95 percent of the thousands of excellent and innovative programs that run on the Apple IIe. The IIc is functionally equivalent to the IIe, yet it weighs just 7½ pounds and fits into any briefcase—perfect for the businessperson who needs to take a computer to and from the office. A 5¼" disk drive has been tucked right into the side of the unit.

Apple has spent a lot of money on market research to find out what people want in a home computer, and it shows on the IIc. The machine is sleek and good-looking (the exterior was designed by Hartmut Esslinger, who designed the Sony Walkman), and it includes friendly features such as a volume control, a headphone jack, an RF modulator for TV hookup, and a "drool cover" beneath the keys to protect the innards from spilled coffee. There is even a switch at the back of the keyboard that converts traditional QWERTY key placement to the increasingly popular Dvorak layout.

Like the Apple Macintosh, the IIc is designed with the novice user in mind. Simple icons on the back of the unit make it easy to hook up peripherals, and only a few cables are necessary. You don't need an interface card to attach a printer, a disk drive, or other peripherals.

The IIc comes with a few extras, such as an interactive computer literacy course, a 40–80 column switch, and "double hi-res" mode graphics capability. Good typists will appreciate the keyboard's tactile feel and the audible click when you press a key. Later this year, an optional flat panel display and battery pack will make the IIc a true portable. Since the computer is so little and it generates a lot of heat, Apple was forced to put air vents on top, so you can't rest a monitor there. The Apple monitor hangs over the computer pretty well but if you use another brand you'll have to raise it somehow or move it off to the side.

While the IIc is great for a first-time owner, the hardcore hackers who made Apple famous may not like it because it has a "closed architecture." This means you can't open the casing and add expansion cards or other hardware (such as a hard disk), as you could with previous Apples. The system is a self-contained box, which sacrifices some flexibility and limits expandability.

This closed architecture was intentional, however. Apple already has a computer for hackers—the IIe. The IIc is for beginners who don't want to open up their computers yet. Serious computerists would do better with the IIe, which has function keys and the optional ability to run CP/M software.

RATINGS:

Overall Value 9	Performance 8
Ease of Use 8	Documentation 8
Software 9	Portability 9

Prices may vary; shop for discount prices.

COMMODORE SX64
Commodore Business Machines, Inc.

Approx. Retail Price ..$995
RAM 64K
Operating System.........Commodore
Included Hardware: keyboard, monitor, one floppy disk drive
Included Software: BASIC, Commodore operating system

Here's the perfect portable computer for the executive on the go who likes to play games too. A business version of the Commodore 64 computer, the SX64 measures 14½"x5"x14½". It weighs less than 30 pounds, and contains a five inch color monitor with up to two half-height 5¼" floppy disk drives that can hold up to 170K bytes of information. The detached keyboard has 66 keys, including four function keys capable of being used for up to eight functions at a time. This 8-bit system uses a 6510A CMOS microprocessor.

Most of the popular Commodore disk, printer, display and joystick options can be used with the SX64. There is even a game cartridge slot on the SX64. In addition, many popular database management, accounting, inventory, word processing, home management, and other programs are available. Virtually all of the Commodore 64 software will run on the SX64.

RATINGS:

Overall Value	10	Performance	8
Ease of Use	9	Documentation	8
Software	8	Portability	10

COMPAQ PLUS
Compaq Computer, Inc.

Approx. Retail Price. $3995
RAM 128k
Operating System ....
........................MS–DOS
Included Hardware:
keyboard, monitor,
floppy disk drive,
10 mb hard disk
Included Software:
MS–DOS 2.02

The Compaq Plus is a powerful portable computer that is extremely IBM-compatible. It is about the size of a suitcase, and weighs just over 30 pounds. The Compaq computers have an established reputation for being solid, dependable, and more IBM-compatible than any of the competition. Another plus is that Compaq dealer support is first-rate.

The Compaq Plus comes with a 9-inch display, one 5¼" floppy disk drive, 128K of RAM (expandable to 640K), one parallel printer port, and a keyboard that is very similar to the IBM PC keyboard. Also included is a 10-megabyte hard disk; this is the feature that differentiates the Compaq Plus from the regular Compaq. Hard disk drives are very sensitive and portable computers tend to get treated roughly, so Compaq has taken this into consideration by mounting the hard disk drive in a shock-resistant aluminum frame.

Graphics features are a definite plus with the Compaq Plus. The machine can handle both monochrome and color graphics, even though the standard monitor only displays one color. (Connections are provided for a color monitor, if needed.) Another plus is that the machine is both software- and hardware-compatible with the IBM PC. Two expansion slots are provided, and these will accept any expansion card made for the IBM PC. If you need a serial port (which isn't provided with the basic system), you can add one with the appropriate expansion card.

No software is bundled with the Compaq Plus, other than the operating system (MS–DOS) and a BASIC interpreter. There is plenty of good software available, however, because the Compaq computers will run almost every program that has been written for the IBM PC.

Overall, the Compaq Plus is a good choice for serious computer owners and businesspersons. The dealer network is extensive, since most IBM dealers also carry the Compaq. If you need IBM-compatability, reliability, and mass storage in a portable computer, the Compaq Plus is one of the few machines built that can answer all of your needs.

RATINGS·

Overall Value	7	Performance	9
Ease of Use	7	Documentation	5
Software	9	Portability	6

EPSON HX–20
Epson America, Inc.

Approx. Retail Price ..$795
RAM 16K
Operating System...Epson
Included Hardware:
keyboard, monitor,
printer, cartridge slot
Included Software:
BASIC, operating system

Epson's HX–20 was one of the first notebook computers. This compact, battery-operated computer provides a full-size keyboard and a liquid-crystal display that shows four lines of 20 characters per line. It comes with 16K of memory, and can be expanded to 32K. The HX–20's screen is small in comparison to the other popular notebook machines like the NEC–PC8201 and the Radio Shack Model 100. However, the Epson provides two features that these machines do not; a built-in printer and a microcassette recorder for storage of programs and information. The computer has one serial connector for the connection of an external printer or a modem.

Software for the HX–20 is severely limited. The company does provide a built-in word processor, called SkiWriter, with the latest version of the HX–20. The BASIC programming language is also built into the computer.

RATINGS:

Overall Value	8	Performance	8
Ease of Use	9	Documentation	7
Software	6	Portability	9

60

IBM PORTABLE PERSONAL COMPUTER
IBM Corporation

Approx. Retail Price.$2795
RAM......................256K
Operating System ....
.........................PC–DOS
Included Hardware:
keyboard, monitor,
disk drive
Included Software:
none

The IBM Portable Personal Computer is a portable version of the IBM PC. For a full review of its features and capabilities, see the review of the IBM PC—the two computers are functionally the same. This review will only cover the differences between the Portable Personal Computer and the PC.

Like most other portables, the IBM Portable Personal Computer is a single unit, with a detachable keyboard that covers the monitor and disk drives when it is snapped into carrying position. The monitor has a 9-inch amber screen, and the two disk drives (which are mounted horizontally to the right of the screen) are standard 360K double-sided, double-density drives that handle 5¼ inch IBM format disks (360K capacity). The keyboard is similar to the IBM PC keyboard. The RAM size is 256K, and this can be expanded up to a maximum of 512K. There are five expansion slots available for adding multifunction boards.

RATINGS:

Overall Value	8	Performance	8
Ease of Use	8	Documentation	8
Software	9	Portability	5

Information accurate at time of printing; subject to manufacturer's change.

KAYPRO II
Kaypro Corporation

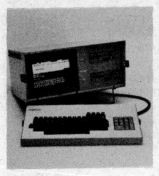

Approx. Retail Price .$1295
RAM........................64K
Operating System....CP/M
Included Hardware:
keyboard, monitor, two
single-sided disk drives
Included Software:
CP/M 2.2, BASIC,
WordStar, MailMerge,
CalcStar, DataStar,
SuperSort, Profit Plan,
The Word Plus

The Kaypro II is one of the best microcomputer bargains available. For only $1,295, you get a fully functional 8-bit CP/M computer with 64K of memory, a 9-inch monitor with full 80 column capability, and two disk drives (single-sided, single-density, 190K capacity each). But the best part is the other half of the deal—over $2,000 (retail) worth of software, which comes bundled with the computer.

Up until this year, the Kaypro computers came with Perfect Software's series of programs, such as Perfect Writer and Perfect Calc. But recently Kaypro made a deal with Micropro International (the makers of WordStar), and now every Kaypro computer comes with Micropro software, in addition to the CP/M operating system and BASIC. The complete list of software that comes with the Kaypro II includes the operating system (CP/M 2.2), word processing (WordStar, with MailMerge and The Word Plus, a spelling checker), data management (DataStar and SuperSort), two spreadsheets (CalcStar and Profit Plan), and Microsoft BASIC with 13 games. This is enough software for you to get started using your

Prices may vary; shop for discount prices.

Kaypro right away, and if your use is limited to the more common computer chores, you may never need any additional software.

The Kaypro computers all come with a full size keyboard that includes a numeric keypad. A program (included with the system) allows you to reconfigure the keypad in any way you like. The cursor keys have an odd layout (in a horizontal row at the upper right side of the keyboard), but in all other respects we found the Kaypro keyboard to be comfortable and easy to use. Like most portables, the Kaypro uses the keyboard to form the base of the system while it is being transported; two plastic latches attach it to the main unit.

The disk drives can read a wide variety of formats, including Osborne, Xerox, Radio Shack, and Zenith. One Centronics parallel printer port and two RS–232 serial ports (for a printer and a modem) are provided. The entire system weighs 26 pounds, which is a little heavy but not as bad as some other portables.

The Kaypro II's faults are few. Games and educational software are limited, as with all CP/M machines. A color monitor cannot be used, and the system's metal case has all the styling of an army jeep. The 64K memory cannot be expanded, but this is also true of most CP/M machines. Altogether, the Kaypro II is an outstanding value for home and small business use.

RATINGS:

Overall Value	9	Performance	8
Ease of Use	8	Documentation	8
Software	8	Portability	8

SENIOR PARTNER
Panasonic Company

Approx. Retail Price. $2495
RAM......................128K
**Operating
System**..............MS–DOS
Included Hardware:
keyboard, 9-inch monitor,
360K floppy disk drive,
printer
Included Software:
MS–DOS 2.0, GW-BASIC

When it became evident that the IBM PC was going to be the "standard" personal business computer, a number of vendors rushed PC clones to the market. Some were more carefully thought out than others. The Panasonic Senior Partner is an example of an excellent IBM compatible portable computer with some unique features.

The Senior Partner has a green 9-inch display and up to two two-sided (360K) disk drives. Like so many other IBM clones, it also has a detachable keyboard. There is an 8088 16-bit microprocessor and 128K bytes of RAM, expandable to 512K in 128K byte increments. The display is a pleasure to look at, with sharp, bright, well-focused characters and graphics. An RGB color monitor output is provided, making it easy to interface top quality color monitors.

Centronics-style parallel and RS–232C serial ports are both standard, and there is an optional expansion slot that can use many IBM PC compatible boards. Not all boards will work in this slot, so you should contact Panasonic or the manufacturer of the expansion board you are planning to use prior to purchase. The Senior

Prices may vary; shop for discount prices.

Partner weighs less than 29 pounds and is roughly the same size as the Compaq, one of its primary competitors.

A major feature of the Senior Partner is its built-in, roll-fed printer. The printer accepts 8½-inch wide roll paper with 11-inch perforations, and prints either 132 or 80 characters per line. The quality is excellent.

GW-Basic is provided at no extra cost with the system, as is MS–DOS 2.0. Many of the popular IBM software packages will run on the Senior Partner, including a wide range of bundled packages: PFS:FILE; PFS:REPORT; VisiCalc; PFS:GRAPH and WordStar. Moreover, users can purchase most IBM compatible software and run it with no problems, including software that challenges the graphic capabilities of PC clones.

Like the Compaq computers, the Senior Partner is very nearly 100 percent compatible. Because of the bundled software and standard built-in printer, the Panasonic Senior Partner is an exceptional value. Users should be certain that they do not need more than one expansion board slot. Also, as of this writing there was no internal hard disk available for the Senior Partner. Users needing an internal hard disk should look at the Compaq Plus, the Texas Instruments Portable Professional, and the IBM Portable.

RATINGS:

Overall Value	10	Performance	10
Ease of Use	10	Documentation	9
Software	9	Portability	10

TI PORTABLE PROFESSIONAL COMPUTER
Texas Instruments Data Systems Group

Approx. Retail Price.$2400
RAM 64K
**Operating
System** ....MS–DOS
Included Hardware:
keyboad, 9-inch monitor,
floppy disk drive
Included Software: none

The Texas Instruments Portable Professional may be the most powerful transportable computer available, particularly when fully loaded with all of the available options. Unfortunately, due to marketing decisions made at Texas Instruments and a somewhat smaller than necessary dealer network, the TI Portable Professional has not received the widespread acceptance it deserves. Moreover, a few design decisions made by TI prevent this from being a truly IBM compatible portable. Nonetheless, it deserves your close scrutiny, particularly if you already have a Texas Instruments desktop computer.

Based on the INTEL 8088 16-bit microprocessor, the TI Portable Professional comes with a minimum of 64K bytes of memory, which can be expanded to 680K bytes. Five expansion slots are offered, but not all IBM compatible expansion boards will work with them. Check with your dealer or expansion board manufacturer before making purchases. You can choose from either TI's 9-inch green monochrome display, or a stunning full color monitor, also available as a built-in. Either one or two floppy disk drives can be ordered, and a 10 megabyte internal hard disk is available. A

Prices may vary; shop for discount prices.

parallel printer port is standard. The RS–232C serial port is available on an optional plug-in card. TI also offers a plug-in modem and related communications software.

The detached keyboard contains a total of 97 keys, including 12 special function keys, a unique cursor cluster, and a 10 key numeric pad. It is connected to the system via a coiled cord. Like the Compaq and IBM portables, the keyboard folds up for transit, protecting the disk drives and monitor.

The TI portable can be used in networks using the Texas Instrument Ether series local area network hardware and software. Another unusual option is TI's Speech Command System, which provides both voice recognition and speech synthesis features.

While the TI Portable Professional is an MS–DOS compatible machine, not all IBM PC compatible software will work on the TI Portable. In many cases, software vendors have created special versions of their software for the TI family. Examples include Lotus 1–2–3, SuperCalc, and many of the PFS software packages.

The documentation, while adequate, is less informative than similar packages from some competitive vendors. The base price of the Texas Instruments Portable Professional is about $2,400, and it is possible to spend more than $10,000 for a fully configured system. The power and flexibility offered by such a fully featured portable make it worth considering, particularly if you do not need 100 percent IBM compatibility, and if there is a strong, knowledgeable TI dealer in your area.

RATINGS:

Overall Value	10	Performance	10
Ease of Use	10	Documentation	10
Software	9	Portability	9

Information accurate at time of printing; subject to manufacturer's change.   **67**

WORKSLATE
Convergent Technologies

Approx. Retail Price $895
RAM 16K
Operating System.................................proprietary
Included Hardware: keyboard, LCD display micro-cassette recorder
Included Software: tutorial program

Recent advances in micro-electronics have made powerful, battery operated computers a reality. It is now possible to carry around more computing power in a briefcase then could be found in most of the large, air conditioned computer centers of the sixties and early seventies. The Convergent Technologies WorkSlate is an example of this phenomenon.

Weighing in at a little under four pounds, this 8¼"x11"x1" business tool combines a number of unique features to make it a complete desk away from the office. The WorkSlate consists of a 46 character by 16 line display, full keyboard, voice and data cassette recorder, an internal built-in modem and impressive ROM-based software. The WorkSlate can even be used as a speaker telephone. Up to five spreadsheets can be processed at the same time, making complex financial modeling possible. In addition, the WorkSlate can be used as a calculator, alarm clock, short memo writer, and scheduling tool.

The calculator-style keyboard includes 60 keys, five special function keys, and five soft keys, which work in conjunction with variable menus displayed above the keys on the LCD display. The micro-cassette recorder has two tracks, one used for storing computer data, while the other is used for voice information, making it possible to verbally describe computer information as it is being saved to tape.

Prices may vary; shop for discount prices.

Four standard A-size batteries or an optional rechargeable battery pack can be used to power the WorkSlate. In addition, two smaller batteries are used to backup the memory, in case the main batteries fail. The WorkSlate has 16K bytes of low power RAM and an additional 64K bytes of read-only-memory (ROM), containing most of the system's software. Both serial and parallel ports are offered. Worksheets can be 128 columns wide and up to 128 rows deep.

Convergent Technologies is also offering optional software packages they call Taskware. Ranging in price from $30 to $50 or more, these template packages help with personal finance tax planning, estate planning, loan analysis, property management, and other specific tasks. An optional 4½-inch wide roll paper printer is available. It is battery operated, can create four-color alphanumerics, and prints at approximately 8 characters per second.

The nicely written and organized owner's manual is supplemented by two 30 minute instructional audio tapes, which can be used in the micro-cassette recorder. A leather carrying case and blank tape round out this fine offering.

This is an excellent portable computer for business people and students with a need to take computing power with them. Unfortunately, journalists and others requiring serious word processing capabilities need to look elsewhere–this is not a strong point in the current WorkSlate offering. People with big word processing jobs might be better served with the Radio Shack Model 100 or NEC portables.

RATINGS:

Overall Value	9	Performance	10
Ease of Use	10	Documentation	10
Software	9	Portability	10

	Actrix	Apple IIc
Manufacturer	Actrix	Apple Computer, Inc.
Size	33 lbs.	12×11×2.75 inches, 7 lbs.
Operating System	CP/M 2.2	Apple DOS
RAM—Standard	64K	128K
RAM—Maximum	64K	128K
CPU	Z80A	65C02
Ports	one Centronics parallel, one IEE-488, two RS–232C serial	one parallel, one serial
Disk Drives	two 5¼ inch floppies	one single sided 5¼ inch floppy
Monitor	7 inch monochrome	none
Keyboard	76 keys	63 keys
Approx. Price	$2190	$1295
Special Features	Epson printer, acoustic modem, direct-connect modem	utility and tutorial software

Prices may vary; shop for discount prices.

Bytec Hyperion	Columbia VP Portable	Commodore SX–64
Bytec-Comterm	Columbia Data Products	Commodore
18 lbs.	32 lbs.	14½ × 5 × 14½ inches, 30 lbs.
MS–DOS	MS–DOS or CP/M-86	Commodore
256K	128K	64K
256K	256K	64K
8088	8088	6510A
one serial	one Centronics printer port, RS–232C serial port	cartridge port, VICModem port, joystick port
one 5¼ inch floppy	two 5¼ inch floppy	one 5¼ inch floppy
7 inch monochrome	9 inch monochrome	5 inch color
84 keys	81 keys	66 keys
$3195	$2995	$995
on-line help provided	Perfect Writer, Perfect Speller, Perfect Calc, Perfect Graph	game cartridge slot, BASIC 2.0, Commodore operating system

	Compaq Plus	Corona Portable PC
Manufacturer	Compaq Computer Corporation	Corona Data Systems
Size	31 lbs.	28 lbs.
Operating System	MS–DOS 2.02	MS–DOS
RAM—Standard	128K	128K
RAM—Maximum	256K	512K
CPU	8088	8088
Ports	Centronics parallel	one parallel, one RS–232C serial
Disk Drives	one 320K 5¼ inch floppy, 10 MB hard disk	two 5¼ inch floppies
Monitor	9 inch monochrome	9 inch monochrome
Keyboard	IBM PC standard	IBM PC standard
Approx. Price	$4995	$2545
Special Features	shock-mounted hard disk	GW BASIC, Multimate, PC Tutor, 4 expansion slots

Prices may vary; shop for discount prices.

Eagle PC Spirit 2	Epson HX–20	Gavilan Mobile Computer
Eagle Computer	Epson	Gavilan Computer Corporation
19.5×16×8.5 inches, 28 lbs.	11.4×8.5×1.75 inches, 4 lbs.	11.4×11.4×2.7 inches, 9 lbs.
MS–DOS 2.0	ROM residence monitor	MS–DOS 2.0
128K	16K	64K
640K	32K	288K
8088	8-bit 6301	8088
two RS–232C serial, one parallel	RS–232C serial	one RS–232C serial, telephone jack
two 360K 5¼ inch floppies	microcassette	360K 3½ inch microfloppy
9 inch monochrome	4 line, 24 column LCD	16 line, 80 column flat panel
84 keys	68 keys	60 keys
$2995	$795	$3995
BASICA	printer, clock, tone generator	modem, battery pack

	GRiD Compass	HP–110
Manufacturer	GRiD Systems Corporation	Hewlett-Packard
Size	11×15×2 inches, 10 lbs.	13 × 10 × 2⅞ inches, 9 lbs.
Operating System	GRiD, MS–DOS	MS–DOS
RAM—Standard	256K	272K
RAM—Maximum	512K	272K
CPU	8086	8088
Ports	RS–232C, RS422 serial, IEEE–488	two RS–232C serial, one HP–IL
Disk Drives	384K bubble memory	none
Monitor	25 line, 80 column flat panel	16 line, 80 column LCD
Keyboard	57 keys	76 keys
Approx. Price	$5955	$2995
Special Features	8087 coprocessor, clock/calendar	Lotus 1–2–3, Memo Maker, Terminal, and HP PAM in ROM

IBM Portable PC	Kaypro II	Kaypro II+
IBM	Kaypro Corporation	Kaypro Corporation
30 lbs.	18×8×15.5 inches, 26 lbs.	18×8×15.5 inches, 26 lbs.
DOS 2.1	CP/M 2.2	CP/M 2.2
256K	64K	64K
512K	64K	64K
8088	Z80A	Z80A
none	one Centronics parallel, two RS–232C serial	one Centronics parallel, two RS–232C serial
one 5¼ inch floppy	two 191K 5¼ inch floppies	two 400K 5¼ inch floppies
9 inch monochrome	9 inch monochrome	9 inch monochrome
IBM PC standard	72 keys	72 keys
$2795	$1295	$1595
5 expansion slots	MicroPro software including WordStar, MBASIC	MicroPro software including WordStar, MBASIC

	Kaypro 4	Kaypro 10
Manufacturer	Kaypro Corporation	Kaypro Corporation
Size	18×8×15.5 inches, 26 lbs.	18×8×15.5 inches, 31 lbs.
Operating System	CP/M	CP/M
RAM—Standard	64K	64K
RAM—Maximum	64K	64K
CPU	Z80A	Z80A
Ports	one Centronics parallel, two RS–232C serial, one telephone jack	one Centronics parallel, two RS–232C serial
Disk Drives	two 5¼ inch floppies	one 5¼ inch floppy, 10 MB hard disk
Monitor	9 inch monochrome	9 inch monochrome
Keyboard	72 keys	72 keys
Approx. Price	$1995	$2795
Special Features	clock/calendar, modem, MicroPro software including WordStar, SBASIC, CBASIC, and MBASIC	MicroPro software including WordStar, SBASIC, CBASIC, and MBASIC

		Panasonic
Morrow MD3–P	NEC PC–8201	Sr. Partner
Morrow Designs	Nippon Electric Corporation	Panasonic
18.5×7.25×15.3 inches, 30 lbs.	12×8.5×2.5 inches	18.5×13×8 inches, 29 lbs.
CP/M 2.2	NEC proprietary	MS–DOS 2.11
64K	16K	128K
64K	64K	512K
Z80A	CMOS 8085	8088
one Centronics parallel, two RS–232C serial	one parallel, one serial, one cassette	one Centronics parallel, one RS–232C serial
two 384K 5¼ inch floppies	none	one 5¼ inch floppy
5×9 inch monochrome	8 line, 40 column LCD	9 inch monochrome
91 keys	77keys	IBM PC standard
$1995	$799	$2495
New Word, Personal Pearl, SuperCalc, BASIC–80, Pilot	BASIC, text editor, telecommunications	thermal printer, WordStar, VisiCalc, PFS Series, GW–BASIC

	Pivot	Seequa Chameleon Plus
Manufacturer	Morrow Designs	Seequa Computer Corporation
Size	13×5.6×9.5 inches, 10 lbs.	18×8×15.5 inches, 28 lbs.
Operating System	MS–DOS 2.X	MS–DOS
RAM—Standard	128K	128K
RAM—Maximum	512K	640K
CPU	80C86	8088, Z80A
Ports	parallel printer, RS-232C serial, telephone jack	one serial, one parallel
Disk Drives	two 360K 5¼ inch floppies	360K 5¼ inch floppy
Monitor	16 line, 80 column LCD	9 inch monochrome
Keyboard	63 keys	IBM PC standard
Approx. Price	NA	$1595
Special Features	modem, calculator, clock/calendar	word processing, spreadsheet, BASIC

Prices may vary; shop for discount prices.

Sharp PC–5000	Sord IS–11	STM PC
Sharp Corporation	Sord Computer Corporation	Semi-Tech Microelectronics
13×12×3.5 inches, 9 lbs.	11.8×8.5×1.5 inches, 4.4 lbs.	4×10.5×20 inches, 17 lbs.
MS–DOS 2.0	proprietary	MS–DOS
128K	32K	256K
256K	64K	512K
8088	CMOS Z80A	80186
RS–232C serial, cassette interface	one RS–232C serial, one Centronics parallel	one parallel, two serial
none	microcassette	two 720K 5¼ inch quad density floppies
8 line, 80 column LCD	8 line, 40 column LCD	25 line, 80 column LCD
72 keys	72 keys	83 keys
$1995	NA	$3495
two expansion slots, optional bubble memory	integrated software	internal modem, hard disk controller

	TI Professional Portable	TRS–80 Model 100
Manufacturer	Texas Instruments	Radio Shack
Size	32 lbs.	3.5 lbs.
Operating System	MS–DOS, CP/M-80 Concurrent CP/M-86	ROM resident monitor
RAM—Standard	64K	8K
RAM—Maximum	768K	32K
CPU	8088	80C85
Ports	one parallel	RS–232C serial, Centronics parallel, cassette interface
Disk Drives	two 720K 5¼ inch floppies	none
Monitor	9 inch monochrome	8 line, 40 column LCD
Keyboard	92 keys	72 keys
Approx. Price	$2395	$799
Special Features	5 expansion slots, modem, high resolution graphics	text processor scheduler, BASIC, telecommunications

Prices may vary; shop for discount prices.

TRS–80 Model 4P	Workslate	Zorba 2000 HD
Radio Shack	Convergent Technologies	Modular Micros, Inc.
16.5×13.25×9.75 inches, 26 lbs.	8×10 inches	18×16×9 inches, approx. 25 lbs.
L-DOS	proprietary	CP/M 2.2
64K	16K	64K
128K	16K	256K
Z80	8-bit CMOS	Z80A
one RS–422 serial, one Centronics parallel, cassette	300 baud communications, printer port	one parallel, one RS–232C serial, one IEEE-488
two 5¼ inch floppies	microcassette	one 800K 5¼ inch floppy, 10 MB hard disk
9 inch B&W	16 line, 46 column LCD	NA
70 keys	60 chiclet keys	95 keys
$1799	$895	$2995
TRS–DOS 6.0, emulation software for TRS-80 Model III	built-in telephone and modem, executive software	CP/M, WordStar MailMerge, InfoStar

HOME COMPUTERS

There are many inexpensive home computers available today, and they offer a wide range of capabilities. Some are only useful for playing games, while others can be used to learn programming or run educational software. In this chapter, we review some of the most popular systems.

The basic starter systems include the Commodore 64, the Atari 800XL, the Coleco Adam, and the Radio Shack Color Computer. These computers can be used for a variety of things, but they are most valuable to the novice who wants to learn about computers without being overwhelmed. They are also good systems for children to learn on.

Another type of home computer, one that you'll be hearing a lot more about in the future, is the MSX machines. MSX is the name of a standard for home computers that was developed by a group of Japanese and American firms, including Microsoft. All MSX machines have certain things in common: a Z80 processor, a Texas Instruments Graphics Processor, the MSX operating system, MSX BASIC, 10 function keys, and a game cartridge port.

This standardized approach has many advantages. The first is that you can mix and match peripherals and software from any MSX machines—this should make hooking up your home computer as easy as hooking up your home stereo. You could, for example, use a Sony disk drive, Toshiba printer, and Hitachi word processing program on your Panasonic MSX computer. All of this would be accomplished without any special connectors or software.

Prices may vary; shop for discount prices.

MSX–DOS, the MSX operating system, was developed by Microsoft, the company that developed MS–DOS for the IBM compatibles. The similarity in the names of these operating systems is more than coincidence; MSX–DOS was designed with the ability to read disks created under MS–DOS, so that MSX computer owners could take their MS–DOS disks home from the office to work on them. The MSX computer will not run MS–DOS software, but MSX software can be used to read and modify files created with MS–DOS software.

The following reviews include several new MSX machines. These machines were not yet available in the U.S. when this book went to press, but they should be out by the time you read this. Certain specifications may have changed, however—check with your computer dealer or a salesperson for current information.

ADAM
Coleco, Inc.

Approx. Retail Price ..$599
RAM........................80K
Operating System ..Coleco
Included Hardware:
keyboard, printer,
wafertape storage,
game paddles
Included Software:
BASIC, Smart Writer,
Buck Rogers game,
operating system

When you turn Adam on, it's an instant word processor. This is a very friendly word processor—it even draws a picture of a typewriter roller so you'll feel right at home. The keyboard detaches and has a smooth feel, as well as ten command keys, six function keys, and five cursor control keys. You can also use the joystick to move the cursor around if you like.

Adam stores 18 double-spaced pages in its memory, and you can store another 250 pages on a "digital data pack," which is a high-speed cassette storage system. The letter-quality printer that comes with Adam will gladly number your pages for you automatically, and even print subscripts and superscripts. Adam also features strong three-voice sound, covering five octaves.

Adam is a good game machine, and plays all Colecovision cartridges as well as games on tape. It also plays all Atari VCS cartridges with an optional expansion module. Owners of Colecovision can turn their game machines into full-function Adams for less than $500.

The printer is the weakest part of the system. Since most good letter-quality printers cost $600 by themselves, Coleco had to make a lot of sacrifices to sell their printer, tape drive, and keyboard for just $700. The printer is very noisy and prints very slowly—it will take a half an hour to print out a ten-page term paper. Strangely, Coleco put Adam's power supply within the printer, so you have to turn the printer on even if you only want to work on the screen. That also means that if the printer breaks down, your entire Adam is out of commission until it is repaired. Also, the printer won't work with any other computer and Adam won't accept any other printer.

Adam's word processor is easy to use, but it has some drawbacks. It can't underline, justify type, or print in boldface. Scrolling is very slow, and the screen can only hold 36 characters per line.

While the data packs are better than audio cassette recorders, they still use tape, which is fragile, unwieldy, and slow. The Buck Rogers game that comes with the Adam, for example, takes a good three minutes to load. Regular cassette tapes won't work with Adam, and Coleco's blanks cost $10 each.

Adam is a good computer for a beginner, but more experienced users may want to look elsewhere.

RATINGS:

Overall Value	8	Performance	6
Ease of Use	8	Documentation	7
Software	6	Portability	5

COMMODORE 64
Commodore Business Machines, Inc.

Approx. Retail Price ..$189
RAM......................64K
Operating System ....
....................Commodore
Included Hardware:
keyboard
Included Software:
BASIC, operating system

For just $189, the Commodore 64 offers as much RAM as either the $900 Apple IIe or the $1,000 PC*jr*. In fact, the 64 gives you more "bytes per buck" than any other computer. It's no wonder Commodore has sold three million of them.

The 64 supports smooth-scrolling text and fine graphics, but the system really shines when it comes to sound. The famous SID (Sound Interface Device) chip can simulate just about any sound imaginable, including crying babies and gunshots. SID gives you complete control over the pitch, tone, and volume of three musical voices, all of them playing at the same time. When you use a program like Waveforms's Musicalc with the 64, you've got a professional-sounding synthesizer for less than $500.

For the million or so people who own the low-powered Commodore VIC–20, the 64 is a good step up. While VIC–20 cartridges are not compatible with the 64, the joysticks, cassette recorders, and modems can be used with either system. Inexpensive printers, speech synthesizers, and other peripherals are also available. The Commodore 1541 disk drive is about

Prices may vary; shop for discount prices.

$100 cheaper than Atari's drive, and it stores twice the data. The Commodore Automodem can be purchased for less than $90, including software.

The Commodore 1541 disk drive is very slow loading, and they're also quite hard to find. Unfortunately, you can't do much with the 64 unless you've got a drive, so 80 percent of all owners end up buying one. The 64 itself is cheap, but once you add a drive, a printer, a modem, and some software, you're hitting $1,000 for the whole system.

The 64 keyboard is slightly unusual. There is no audible feedback, and for some reason they put the apostrophe and quote marks in the top row, which is out of the way. The INST/DELETE key is right next to the CLR/HOME key, so it's not unusual to send the cursor up to the top of the screen when you're just trying to backspace. Also, you have to hit two keys to move the cursor left or up.

The Commodore 64 is the most inexpensive 64K computer on the market. If price is your most important consideration, buy it.

RATINGS:

Overall Value	10	Performance	8
Ease of Use	8	Documentation	8
Software	9	Portability	7

IBM PC*JR*
IBM Corporation

Approx. Retail Price ..$999
RAM 128K
Operating System ....
........................DOS 2.10
Included Hardware:
cordless keyboard, one
360K disk drive
Included Software:
BASIC, Keyboard
Adventure

The PC*jr* is an expensive home machine that you can really count on. IBM has a solid reputation, and their thousands of product centers provide service and backup that no other company can match. (The PC*jr* comes with a full-year warranty—most others are three months.) The PC*jr* uses the same CPU chip as the IBM PC, so some (but not all) PC software runs on PC*jr*. The system is partially intended for businesspeople who use a PC at the office and want to bring work home.

Though it has less memory than the PC, PC*jr* has twice as many colors (16), three times as many voices (3), and it accepts cartridges. *Junior* has a good sound chip made by Texas Instruments, and the graphics are remarkable (take a look at the Sierra On-Line game King's Quest, for example). It is also simple to set up, with clear and easy documentation, and it supports a wide variety of monitors, light pens, modems, and other peripherals.

The most innovative feature of PC*jr* is the cordless keyboard, which can be used up to 20 feet from the

Prices may vary; shop for discount prices.

computer. This is a nice idea, but it doesn't work very well. TV remote control can interfere with the signal, and you can't use two PC*jr*s at the same time in the same room. (The keyboard can be used with a cord, however.) In addition, the keyboard requires batteries, which can leak.

Junior is trying to hit two markets—the family and the businessperson—but misses both of them. First, it's overpriced for a family computer, and IBM charges $20 or $30 extra for every little cable and adapter you need to hook the thing up. Second, the entry model doesn't do much more than play games, and it only displays 40 columns of text.

In designing PC*jr* for the business market, IBM got caught in a Catch-22. They had to make the *Junior* compatible with their PC, but if it was too good, there would be no reason to buy the PC anymore. So PC*jr* is deliberately "crippled." It has a much slower video update and features just one disk drive.

The PC*jr* has not sold well initially, which has served to reduce the amount of new software coming out for it. But if IBM replaces the keyboard and makes the price competitive with other computers in its class, it could still take over the home market the same way the PC took over the business market. IBM will do whatever is necessary to make PC*jr* a success.

RATINGS:

Overall Value	9	Performance	8
Ease of Use	8	Documentation	8
Software	8	Expandibility	7

MSX COMPUTERS

This review covers four of the first MSX computers, manufactured by Pioneer, Yamaha, JVC, and Spectravideo.

The Pioneer MSX computer is cosmetically one of the best computer designs of all times. It doesn't even look like a computer. Unlike most other MSX devices, it is made up of two parts—the computer/memory unit, and the keyboard. The keyboard is relatively standard MSX, although it has special function keys for its laser disk player.

The memory unit looks more like a low profile video recorder than it does a computer. In the front is a slot for inserting MSX program cartridges. There are also controls for I/O interfaces, a stereo balance selector, and a volume control. The unit also has a built-in speaker, which plays one of two stereo sound channels. The other channel can be played through your TV set, giving you true stereo video.

The laserdisk interface is the most exciting feature of this computer. The computer can display any frame of a laser disk, in any order, forward or backward, and at selectable speeds. The MSX computer issues the control commands to the laser disk controller. It also can superimpose graphics made by the computer over the laser disk images.

Although the Pioneer computer is probably more expensive than the other MSX computers, it is the most attractive, and does provide a video processing capability. You should keep in mind, however, that the laser disk machines, which can also play movies, will probably add an additional $800 to the cost of the computer. The list price of the Pioneer is about $500.

Prices may vary; shop for discount prices.

Yamaha also has an interesting computer. It consists of a keyboard with all of the electronics built-in, and costs about $450.

Where the Pioneer excelled at video processing, the Yamaha is very strong as a music processor. An optional adapter provides an 8-voice synthesizer. Using this adapter you can create some exceptional music and sound. Unfortunately, this is only available for the Yamaha MSX machine.

The JVC is more of a basic MSX machine than the first two. It features a typical MSX keyboard configuration and sells for about $400.

The JVC computer is designed to interface with JVC's VHD video disk player, which provides faster response time than the Pioneer laser disk. Although JVC claims that they plan to introduce the VHD player in the U.S. at about the same time as the MSX, this may not happen due to commercial failure of the machine in the Orient and Europe.

The Spectravideo SV-728 is another garden-variety MSX machine. It has a standard keyboard, and a single cartridge slot. Unlike the other MSX machines, the 728 will reportedly be CP/M compatible. This will provide access to a large library of existing software.

RADIO SHACK TRS–80
EXTENDED BASIC COLOR COMPUTER
Tandy Corp.

Approx. Retail Price ..$260
RAM 64K
Operating System ....
.......Extended Color Basic
Included Hardware:
keyboard, game cartridge
Included Software:
none

The Radio Shack 64K extended BASIC color computer is a natural outgrowth of its predecessors. Radio Shack was one of the first manufacturers to realize that people wanted to program their own games in addition to playing them and this graphics and sound-oriented computer family from Radio Shack caught on quickly. Soon there were several computer magazines dedicated to the Radio Shack Color Computer and a whole after-market industry providing cartridges, accessories, and other items of interest to the owners of the early machines. Radio Shack has greatly expanded its line of color computers as a result of this interest. The 64K extended BASIC machine is now their top-of-the-line unit.

As the name implies, the system contains 64K bytes of memory. In addition, it has a full size keyboard, cassette interface, and printer interface. Music and sound effects can be generated quite simply with the system, and there are powerful graphics routines available, making spectacular high resolution color graphics possible. Serious programmers can use PEEK, POKE, and USR commands.

Prices may vary; shop for discount prices.

It is now possible to expand the color computer to include one or more floppy disk drives, a multi-pack interface (which makes it possible to switch from one game cartridge to another without unplugging them), and even a color mouse for improved cursor control. The mouse can be used with many games and also facilitates creation of color graphics.

It is even possible to do word processing on the color computer using Radio Shack's inexpensive color Scripsit package. An editor/assembler is available, along with disk graphics packages and a number of games, both from Radio Shack and from other vendors.

While many of these features can be added to the earlier, less expensive versions of the Color Computer, readers are encouraged to purchase this more expensive 64K extended BASIC computer, rather than spending extra money to upgrade the less capable units. This strategy will save you money in the long run.

RATINGS:

Overall Value	10	Performance	10
Ease of Use	9	Documentation	10
Software	9	Expandibility	10

RADIO SHACK TRS 80 MODEL 4
Tandy Corp.

Approx. Retail Price .. $999
RAM 64K
Operating System ....
.... TRS–DOS
Included Hardware:
keyboard, 12 inch monitor
Included Software:
M–BASIC, TRS–DOS

For many reasons, the Radio Shack Model 4 is not given the consideration it deserves when people shop for small business and home computers. True, it is an 8-bit machine. There are no color capabilities built-in. Diskettes hold a maximum of 180K bytes. There are no expansion slots, although accessories and options can be added to the Model 4. There are, however, several real justifications for purchasing the Model 4.

First of all, it works with all of the Model III and most of the Model I software. Second, it is extremely competitively priced, particularly when you consider that it includes everything you need for small business computing, except possibly specific applications software and a printer. One of the things in the Radio Shack Model 4's favor is its wide availability. Accessories and repairs can be obtained in virtually every neighborhood across the United States, and this is one of the few computers for which you can find printer ribbons on Sunday.

The Radio Shack Model 4's internal black and white monitor measures 12 inches diagonally. Upper and lower case letters can be displayed on the screen in

94

standard with a high resolution option available. The keyboard is permanently fastened to the system. It contains seventy keys including three programmable function keys and a 12 key numeric pad. Up to 4 floppy disk drives can be supported by this system. Two of them can be mounted internally. Up to four Radio Shack 5 Mbyte hard disks can also be interfaced. Other vendors have designed larger Model 4 compatible hard disks. The Radio Shack Model 4 is designed to work with a wide variety of dot matrix and letter quality printers, and external modems can be used with either the TRS 80's special serial port or an optional RS–232C interface.

M–Basic and the TRS–DOS operating system are included with the Model 4. Compatible versions of PFS:FILE, PFS:REPORT, Scripsit (a word processing program), Superscript, dictionary software, VisiCalc, MultiPlan, and many other packages are available through Radio Shack.

The manuals provided with the Radio Shack Model 4 are better than average. They are carefully designed and contain many useful examples.

For those times when local stores do not have answers to your questions, a factory hotline is available.

The Model 4's plastic case and its nickname ("Trash 80") prevent many people from taking a good, close look at this product. This is unfortunate; the Model 4 is an excellent system, manufactured and supported by a reliable manufacturer.

RATINGS:

Overall Value	10	Performance	9
Ease of Use	9	Documentation	10
Software	8	Expandibility	7

	Atari 800XL	Coleco Adam
Manufacturer	Atari, Inc.	Coleco Industries, Inc.
Operating System	ROM-resident	Personal CP/M
RAM	64K	80K
CPU	6502C	Z80, MC 6801
Ports	two joysticks, one serial I/O	none
Storage	none	256K cassette
Monitor	none	none
Keyboard	62 keys	75 keys, includes two joysticks
Approx. Price	$1099	$595
Special Features	Atari BASIC, color graphics, 4 channel sound	printer, BASIC, word processor Buck Rogers game

Prices may vary; shop for discount prices.

Commodore 64	Commodore Plus 4	IBM PCjr
Commodore	Commodore	IBM Corporation
ROM-resident	ROM-resident	DOS 2.10
64K	64K	64K
6510A	7501	8088
serial bus, game cartridge port	NA	none
none	none	one 360K 5¼ inch floppy
none	none	none
66 keys	67 keys	62 keys
$189	NA	$999
built-in music synthesizer		cordless keyboard

	Radio Shack Extended Color Computer 2	**Radio Shack Model 4**
Manufacturer	Radio Shack	Radio Shack
Operating System	ROM-resident	TRSDOS
RAM	64K	16K
CPU	6809E	Z80A
Ports	RS–232C serial, two joysticks, cassette	RS–232C serial, cassette, parallel, keyboard
Storage	none	16K cassette
Monitor	none	monochrome
Keyboard	53 keys	70 keys
Approx. Price	$260	$999
Special Features	extended BASIC	BASIC, M BASIC

Spectravideo SV–328	VIC 20
Spectravideo, Inc.	Commodore
ROM-resident	ROM-resident
80K	5K
Z80A	6502A
composite video, audio, cassette	audio/video, serial I/O, cassette, communications
none	none
none	none
87 keys	66 keys
NA	$99
BASIC, CP/M compatibility, graphics and sound capability	PET BASIC 2.0, graphics and sound, expansion to 32K RAM

OTHER COMPUTERS

Although the IBM compatibles have become the most popular type of personal computer system, they aren't your only choice. For many users, other systems can provide all of the necessary features for less money. Also, some users need multitasking or other special capabilities that cannot be provided by MS–DOS machines. If you are in one of these groups, you may find the computer you need in this section.

The computers in this section vary widely, but there are a few common types. First, you'll notice that many of these computers are CP/M machines. As we said earlier, CP/M machines provide enough capability for many applications in business and word processing. The performance is not as high as MS–DOS, but this is partially made up for by the huge library of CP/M software that is available.

Another popular type of computer included in this section is the Apple series. The Apple II family of computers has a great amount of software available for it, especially in the areas of games and education. Another Apple computer, the Macintosh, provides strong graphics and ease of use in a simple and straightforward package. And if the Macintosh isn't everything you thought it would be, check out the review of the Lisa 2, which is a very powerful system that uses much of the same technology as the Macintosh.

Another computer that provides advanced graphics capabilities is the Mindset. It uses two specially developed graphics processors to control the generation of high-resolution images on the screen, and the results are spectacular. Actual animation is possible with this computer, a feat that had not yet been accomplished on a standard personal computer.

Prices may vary; shop for discount prices.

The HP–150 is another interesting machine in this section that uses advanced technology. The HP–150 has a touch-sensitive screen that allows you to make selections by simply pointing at them on the screen.

Altogether, there are many unique and useful computers reviewed on the following pages. Read through the reviews, check the comparison charts, and you may find a system that provides the features you need.

ALPHA MICRO AM–1000
Alpha Microsystems

Approx. Retail Price ....
............................$5850
RAM 128K
Operating System ....
........................AMOS/L
Included Hardware:
keyboard, two 800K floppy
disk drives
Included Software:
none

The Alpha Micro AM–1000 and AM–1000E systems are multi-user, multitasking desktop computers. Alpha Micro has designed these systems to be low-cost, high performance alternatives to higher priced minicomputer systems.

The AM–1000 and 1000E systems are built around the 16-bit Motorola MC68000 microprocessor, and all models include 128K bytes of RAM, three serial I/O ports, and a real time clock/calendar. The AM–1000 is offered in four configurations. The 1000FF has the base configuration plus two 800K disk drives. The 1000VW comes with a 10 megabyte hard disk and a VCR interface. The 1000WF provides one 800K byte disk drive and a 10 megabyte hard disk, and the 1000VWF has an 800K drive, a 10 megabyte hard disk and a VCR interface. The AM–1000E is offered in two configurations. The 1000EVW has a 30 megabyte hard disk and a VCR interface, and the 1000VWF has the same plus one 800K disk drive.

Alpha Micro offers an optional smart terminal for $1,000. This includes a monochrome display and a typewriter-style, detachable keyboard. The AM–60 is a

Prices may vary; shop for discount prices.

12 inch green phosphor monitor with 24 lines of 80 upper and lowercase characters, plus 2 status lines. It has a resolution of 640×240 pixels and can be tilted and rotated. The keyboard has 105 keys including function keys and eight programmable keys, and a six foot coiled cable.

The AM–1000 family can be expanded to 384K bytes of RAM, while the AM–1000E can be increased to 512K bytes. All models can expand the storage via three external disk subsystems. The AM–1000 can expand to 70 Mbytes and the AM–1000E to 120 Mbytes. Another available option is a four-port serial board that also provides a Z80 microprocessor for using CP/M. Alpha RJE communications software is available with this option. When this software or CP/M is in use, only two of the additional four serial ports are available for terminal or printer connection.

The systems run under AMOS/L, the multi-user, multitasking, time sharing Alpha Micro Operating System. The use of AMOS/L allows the desktop computer to utilize more than 100 business applications programs that have been developed, and makes the AM–1000 software-compatible with the other members of the Alpha Micro 68000-based products.

Alpha Micro has an excellent reputation, but receives less attention in the press than it deserves. If you are considering a micro-based multi-user system for business, you should explore the AM–1000 family. If you are interested in high resolution graphics and game playing, there are better choices.

RATINGS:

Overall Value	10	Performance	9
Ease of Use	9	Documentation	9
Software	9	Expandibility	10

APPLE LISA 2 SERIES
Apple Computer Inc.

Approx. Retail Price $3495
RAM 512K
Operating System ....proprietary
Included Hardware: keyboard, 12 inch monitor, 400K microfloppy disk drive, mouse controller
Included Software: Mac Work, Mac Write, Mac Paint

There are three Lisa 2 products. In addition to the standard Lisa 2 there is the Lisa 2/5 and Lisa 2/10. The lowest cost family member, the Lisa 2, includes 512K of RAM, one 400K byte diskette drive, a built-in CRT, a detached keyboard with 10 key numeric pad cluster, the now famous mouse, one parallel and two serial ports. The Macintosh operating system is also provided. Lisa 2/5 and Lisa 2/10 machines have the same features as the Lisa 2, plus either a 5 or 10 megabyte hard disk. All of the Lisa 2 products support dot matrix and letter quality printers. There are communications accessories available as well.

All of the Lisa computers can be expanded from their original 512K RAM to slightly over one million bytes of memory, and they are all based on the 32-bit 68000 microprocessor. All three models offer the Sony 3½ inch micro-diskette drive.

A wide range of software is both offered and under development for the Lisa 2 family, including UNIX-based software which will make Lisa networks possible. The Lisa 2/5 and 2/10 systems are large enough to permit operation of the Lisa Office System Operating System, which contains an integrated office automation package, that allows users to manipulate text, numbers and graphics, and to pass the information from one application to another by using cut and paste techniques. This integrated software includes LisaWrite, LisaCalc, LisaDraw, LisaGraph, LisaProject, LisaList and LisaTerminal. Each of these packages can be purchased separately.

The 12 inch black and white display provides very pleasing images. Up to 130 characters and up to 40 lines of type can be displayed at the same time. There are eleven type faces and styles available. In the graphics mode, 720×364 pixels are displayed.

The Lisa 2 family is one of the few systems that make it easy for users to display and print non-English characters. The 76-key ASCII keyboard has the ability to generate alternate characters for foreign languages and math symbols. Most of the software (word processing, database, etc.) can handle these characters, something that can not be said for many competitive computer systems. This makes the Lisa 2 an excellent choice for those doing scientific or international work.

RATINGS:

Overall Value	9	Performance	10
Ease of Use	10	Documentation	8
Software	7	Expandibility	7

APPLE IIe
Apple Computer, Inc.

Approx. Retail Price ....
.............................$1395
RAM 64K
Operating System ....
.....................Apple DOS
Included Hardware:
keyboard
Included Software:
Applesoft BASIC

The Apple IIe is an improved version of the Apple II Plus. It only needs two integrated circuits to do the work of 79 in the II Plus, so it runs cooler and is more reliable. All Apple II printers, modems, disk drives, and joysticks are compatible with the IIe, and almost all of the thousands of Apple II programs will run on the IIe. Most new Apple software is made specifically for the IIe.

The IIe is very flexible. It has seven expansion slots, and accepts a wide variety of plug-in boards, including 80 columns and CP/M. It also features upper and lower case keys, auto repeat on all keys, program-mable function keys, and cursor control keys. It is expandable to 128K.

Although the IIe is easier to use than the II Plus, it is a little bit over the heads of beginning computer users. It will take you at least a few hours to set up the IIe and begin using it. Some add-on cards are required to use the external ports, and the IIe lacks a numeric keypad (even Franklin's Apple clones have them), the disk drive loads very slowly, and letters on a color screen are sometimes fuzzy. And $900 is still a lot to pay for a

Prices may vary; shop for discount prices.

64K computer when you can get a Commodore or Atari machine for $200.

Altogether, though, the Apple IIe—like the Apple II and II Plus before it—is a good choice for a home computer, mainly because there is so much software available for it. If you want a reliable 64K computer for games and education, the Apple IIe is a good choice.

RATINGS:

Overall Value	9	Performance	8
Ease of Use	8	Documentation	9
Software	10	Expandibility	9

HP–150
Hewlett Packard

Approx. Retail Price ....
.............................$3995
RAM......................256K
Operating System ....
.........................MS–DOS
Included Hardware:
keyboard, 9 inch mono-
chrome monitor, two
264K microfloppy disk
drives
Included Software:
MS–DOS 2.0, Personal
Applications Manager

The HP–150 is an interesting machine. It uses a microprocessor from the same family of chips as the IBM PC
and can run many MS–DOS programs, but it doesn't
accept any standard IBM expansion cards. Rather than
imitating the other PC clones, the designers at
Hewlett-Packard developed a computer that was very
different.

Looking at the unit shows many of the obvious differences right away—the keyboard is different. It in-
corporates a somewhat better letter arrangement than
the PC, has a numeric keypad, only 8 function keys
(compared to the PC's 10), and special keys for editing
and other commands.

Beyond the keyboard, you'll notice that the disk drives
are also different from the IBM PC. The 264K disks and
drives have less capacity than those on the PC, and
they are the 3½ inch Sony drives (as used in the
Macintosh). This new format allowed the designers to
build a more compact computer. Beyond that, however, the microfloppy drives use sealed disks. Instead

Prices may vary; shop for discount price

of a flat black package, the Sony disk is a hard plastic case, looking like something used in an instant camera. The 3½ inch square package can easily fit into a shirt pocket. The only visible feature on the disk case is a metal shutter that slides over the enclosed magnetic disk when it isn't actually inserted into the drive. This makes it rather difficult to damage a disk—unless you really want to.

The disk is bonded to a center metal hub, which allows the Sony drive mechanism to more accurately grab and spin the disk, and gives it the ability to store more data. Unfortunately, although the Sony disk mechanism will probably be tomorrow's standard, it's currently nonstandard—this means there isn't a lot of software available on the 3.5 inch disks. The most impressive feature of the HP–150 is the monitor, which also comes with the computer. Along the edges of the bezel just in front of the screen is a series of dots. These make up what H–P appropriately calls the "touch screen." These holes are actually an array of infrared light emitting diodes and receivers. When an item appears on the menu, touching the appropriate selection with your finger breaks the beams and enters your choice into the computer.

Because of the disk drives, there is a basic problem you may encounter—unless a program is already developed in an H–P format, on those 3½" disks, you won't be able to use it on your HP–150.

RATINGS:

Overall Value	8	Performance	8
Ease of Use	9	Documentation	8
Software	7	Expandibility	8

MACINTOSH
Apple Computer, Inc.

Approx. Retail Price ....
................................$2495
RAM 128K
Operating System ....
.....................proprietary
Included Hardware:
keyboard, 9 inch hi-res
monochrome monitor,
400K microfloppy disk
drive
Included Software:
Notepad, Calculator,
Puzzle, Calendar,
Scratch Pad

The Apple Macintosh is a very powerful, easy to use desktop computer. It is significantly different from most other personal computers, which has earned it much praise as well as much criticism. The praise is usually for Macintosh's ease of use, and high-resolution graphics; the criticism is usually aimed at its lack of IBM compatibility, lack of expansion options, slow disk access, and lack of serious business software.

The Macintosh comes with a built-in Sony 3½ inch microfloppy disk drive (400K capacity), a separate keyboard, and a mouse controller. The main unit, which stands 13.5 inches tall, houses a 9 inch black and white monitor. The keyboard is attached to the unit by a short coiled cord, and the entire system takes up about as much desk space as a standard legal notepad.

Macintosh uses the Motorola 68000 processor, which makes it much faster than the IBM PC and compatibles (which use the Intel 8088 or 8086 processor). It also

110

includes many other technological advances, such as the microfloppy disk drive, which uses sealed disks that are much sturdier and more reliable than standard 5¼ inch floppies. There are two serial ports: a standard RS–232 port, and a high-speed RS–422 (Applebus) port. Other hardware features include an internal clock and a bit-mapped display that allows any combination of text and high-resolution graphics.

When you look at the Macintosh screen for the first time, you won't see the things you normally expect to see on a computer screen. There is no cursor (instead, a small arrow indicates your position), and there are no commands to memorize or enter. Rather than choosing from a menu of words and phrases, you give instructions to the computer by selecting small, detailed symbols called *icons*. If you want to delete something, for example, you would point to the item and then point to the garbage can icon.

"Pointing" is accomplished by moving the mouse controller over your desktop, which moves the arrow on the screen. After moving the arrow to your selection, you push the button on the mouse to indicate your choice. After a few minutes of selecting icons and moving items, the mouse controller becomes a very intuitive way of working with a computer; you may not want to go back to a keyboard-controlled system.

Programmers enjoy writing software for the Macintosh (because of its many fancy programming tools stored in ROM), so new software is coming out daily. In many cases, the Macintosh versions of popular software packages provide more capability than the original, because programmers have taken advantage of the Macintosh's capabilities.

In spite of all of this, there are a few problems with the Macintosh. The system comes with only one disk drive and a port for hooking up a second drive. At the time of this writing, additional disk drives were not available, because they were all being used in new Macintoshes and other computers. Another problem is the lack of a parallel printer port. This prevents you from using Macintosh with a letter-quality printer. Some companies have announced hardware and software products that allow the Macintosh to use specific letter-quality printers through the serial port, however. The other problem is that the RAM is not expandable beyond 128K.

Overall, the Macintosh is a unique and powerful machine that can be used by anyone. If you absolutely must have color graphics, IBM compatibility, a letter-quality printer, or more than 128K of RAM, Macintosh is not the computer you need. For everyone else, however, Macintosh is the most sophisticated, easy to use computer in its price range.

RATINGS:

Overall Value	9	Performance	10
Ease of Use	10	Documentation	8
Software	6	Expandibility	6

MINDSET
Mindset Corporation

Approx. Retail Price ....
................................$2400
RAM.......................256K
Operating System ....
.........................MS–DOS
Included Hardware:
keyboard, two floppy
disk drives
Included Software:
GW–BASIC, Lumena

Like the HP–150, the Mindset is a PC-compatible computer with some major differences. It also looks quite a bit different than most PCs or PC clones, and these differences are more than cosmetic.

The keyboard has the standard arrangement, with 10 function keys and no keypad. It is detachable from the main unit. The main unit is a compact module roughly the width of the keyboard. In this main module, you get the processor, an Intel 80186 chip, two specially developed graphics processors, 64K of RAM (only 32K is available to the user), and two cartridge slots.

The main unit itself won't do much for you, however. To configure the computer to compare with most others, you'll need to add a couple of 360K single-sided, double-density drives, RS–232 or Centronics ports, and extra memory. You can also add a stereo output module for generating stereo sound. A system with this configuration will cost around $2,398. The extra drives and expansion components fit into a structure that stacks on top of the Mindset.

The Mindset, in the configuration described above, is something of a bargain when compared to the rest of the PC market. It will run most, but not all, MS–DOS programs, but has capabilities that none of the others even approach.

The most important capability of the Mindset is its very strong graphics processing. The Mindset has 11 graphics resolution modes. These range from, at the low end, a PC graphics emulator, all the way up to a very high resolution of 640×400 pixels in four colors. As the resolution drops, the choice of colors increases.

Available software allows you to draw pictures, then rotate and otherwise manipulate them. A program soon to be released will be designed to assist in Computer Aided design work—instead of drafting with paper and pencil, actual engineering drawings can be made with the Mindset. As a CAD tool, the Mindset may prove to be of great value.

Beyond the exceptional graphics, however, is another excellent feature—speed. The Mindset performs much faster than the PC and probably faster than any other IBM-compatible computer. This extra speed is evident in the high speed generation of images, which allow actual animation to run on-screen without the blinking and delays common to most computers.

RATINGS:

Overall Value	9	Performance	9
Ease of Use	8	Documentation	7
Software	8	Expandibility	8

NORTH STAR ADVANTAGE
North Star Computers Inc.

Approx. Retail Price ....
.............................$2999
RAM 64K
Operating System....CP/M
Included Hardware:
keyboard, monitor, two
floppy disk drives
Included Software:
CP/M

North Star was one of the early pioneers in micro-processor-based personal computers. The company continues to thrive and grow, albeit at a slower rate than many of its younger, more aggressive competitors. North Star products, when supported by a strong local dealer, represent an excellent value in reliable, sophisticated systems.

Because of the many options offered by North Star, their pricing and configuration list is rather confusing. Basically, there are two models in the family, the Advantage and the Advantage 8-16. The basic 8-bit Advantage system offers 64K RAM which can be expanded to 256K bytes, with an additional 20K bytes of RAM dedicated to the bit map display. The Advantage 8-16 system adds an 8088-2 16-bit microprocessor to the basic system. It is possible to upgrade an Advantage to an Advantage 8-16, if you so desire.

Similar to the Radio Shack TRS 80 Model 4 in shape and size, the North Star Advantage computers have a built-in 12 inch diagonal monochrome monitor and an attached 87 key selectric-style keyboard. Dual floppy diskette drives, or a combination of diskette and hard disk drive can be installed inside the main housing. There are 5, 15, and 30 megabyte internal hard disk drives available. Five additional expansion slots are available for serial, parallel, and other expansion options. These expansion slots are not compatible with IBM-style expansion boards; they are instead S-100 slots.

Up to 24 lines of 80 characters can be displayed. The green phosphor display with its nonglare glass provides sharp, clear, easy to read text and graphics. In the graphics mode, 240×640 pixels are displayed. North Star does not offer its own printer, although most of today's popular dot matrix and letter quality printers will work with these systems. If your applications call for frequent printing of high resolution graphics, you may need the help of an informed North Star dealer to select the proper printer for your system.

As many as 64 Advantage systems can be linked together to form a local area network. NorthNet expansion boards are required in each workstation. In addition, a hard disk is required for networking. MS–DOS and CP/M 80 operating systems are offered, but not all MS–DOS software will work properly with this system.

If you are looking for a system that was designed to be used in local area networking, and if you have access to a knowledgable North Star dealer, and if you don't need IBM compatible plug-in boards and software, the Advantage family is an excellent value.

RATINGS:

Overall Value	9	Performance	9
Ease of Use	9	Documentation	9
Software	9	Expandibility	9

Prices may vary; shop for discount prices.

QX–10
Epson Computer

Approx. Retail Price ....
.............................$2995
RAM 64K
Operating System ....
..........................Valdocs
Included Hardware:
keyboard, 12 inch mono-
chrome monitor, two 380K
disk drives
Included Software:
Valdocs, calculator,
scheduler, electronic
mail, graphics

The QX–10 represents Epson's attempt to develop a uniquely friendly computer with full capabilities. In some ways they've succeeded brilliantly.

The QX–10 is an attractive-looking computer. The keyboard includes a full set of alphanumerics, although some keys are oddly located in nonstandard locations. The keyboard has a numeric keypad, arrow keys, and special function keys for accessing functions that work exclusively on the Epson system.

The QX–10 is, surprisingly, a 64K machine, built around the Z–80 chip. The Z–80 is the same 8-bit processor that's used in most smaller capacity office machines, like Kaypro, Osborne, and Morrow. As such, the QX–10 comes with CP/M, providing access to a large library of software titles.

However, when you use the CP/M titles, you lose the simplicity that is designed into the system, because the major component providing that elusive ease of use is QX–10's unique operating system—Valdocs. Valdocs is supposed to make computer operating easy, and almost intuitive. However, other than Epson, there are few, if any firms developing software that make use of Valdocs. Further, Valdocs was not well documented by Epson, and, as a result, many authors stepped in to try to explain how to use the computer—with mixed results. Although many people may, at first, like the QX–10, so far it's been relatively unsupported.

Epson hasn't taken this poor acceptance lightly, however. They've licensed and modified some excellent programs. As an option, they've added MS–DOS compatibility, as well as additional available memory. Just *how* compatible this addition is remains to be seen—without function keys, the MS–DOS software may not be very useful. Our recommendation is to check this one out closely before you buy—it may give you all you need, or it may fall far short.

RATINGS:

Overall Value	8	Performance	8
Ease of Use	8	Documentation	8
Software	7	Expandibility	8

RAINBOW 100 PLUS
Digital Equipment Corporation

Approx. Retail Price ....
................................$5475
RAM 128K
Operating System ....
...........................CP/M-86
Included Hardware:
keyboard, 12 inch monochrome monitor, two 400K floppy disk drives, 10 mb hard disk
Included Software:
none

The computer is a product of one of the largest computer mainframe manufacturers, Digital Equipment, and is built to function as a serious business computer. The 100 Plus uses a Z80A microprocessor (which makes it CP/M compatible), plus an 8088 microprocessor (which makes it MS–DOS and CP/M–86 compatible). With the addition of an optional hard disk operating system, the 100 Plus can be compatible with the three most popular operating systems (CP/M, MS–DOS, and CP/M–86).

The keyboard is well designed, and features a full sized, full stroke ASCII key arrangement in addition to a numeric keypad, separate cursor control keys, and numerous function keys.

RATINGS:
Overall Value 7	Performance 8
Ease of Use 8	Documentation 7
Software 9	Expandibility 9

WANG PROFESSIONAL COMPUTER
Wang Laboratories, Inc.

Approx. Retail Price.$2595
RAM 128K
Operating System ...Wang
Included Hardware:
keyboard, 12-inch monitor,
360K floppy disk drive
Included Software:
none

The Wang PC–001 is the entry-level personal computer from Wang. Others in this family build on the basic PC–001 design, adding additional features like extra memory and larger disk storage.

The PC–001 is equipped with an 8086 microprocessor, 128K bytes of RAM (expandable to 640K bytes), and a single 5¼ inch double-sided 360K byte disk drive. A very nice detached keyboard is also standard. Since Wang has been in the office automation industry for many years, its products are aimed primarily at business users.

A standard 12 inch monochrome monitor features an adjustable stand and sharp green characters on a black background. Graphics capabilities (800×200 black and white or 640×250 color) require an optional interface card.

Users have a choice of purchasing specially modified software packages that run on the Wang or an optional personality card that makes the Wang nearly 100 percent IBM PC compatible. Since Wang offers a wide

Prices may vary; shop for discount prices.

variety of its own modified software, you may not need the IBM option. For example, Wang offers a number of word processing programs and its own versions of MultiPlan, VisiCalc, and Lotus 1–2–3. Business graphics and accounting packages are also available in the Wang format. These include offerings from Peachtree and other major software publishers. Communications software is available from Wang, making it possible to emulate IBM, DEC, and other communications protocols. It is possible to create local area networks using Wang's interconnect option, which can use remote devices as far away as four miles.

New users with heavy business computer requirements should consider the Wang PC–001. Since it is expandable and compatible with a wide family of other Wang office automation products, and since it comes from a reliable, well-known vendor, the Wang Professional Computer deserves serious consideration. When receiving price quotes on Wang systems, insure that fully configured systems are quoted, since many items that are standard equipment in other computer families are options from Wang.

RATINGS:

Overall Value	9	Performance	9
Ease of Use	9	Documentation	9
Software	8	Portability	8

ZENITH Z–100 FAMILY
Zenith Radio Corp.

Approx. Retail Price......................................$3295
RAM..128K
Operating System.....................................Z–DOS
Included Hardware: keyboard, 320K floppy disk drive
Included Software: Z–DOS 2.1, Lotus 1–2–3

Knowledgeable users have long admired Heathkit's early entries in the microcomputer race. When Zenith purchased Heath recently, the tradition of Heath quality was continued as new products were added to their computer line. The Zenith Z–100 series is an example of that continued commitment to quality and features.

The Z–100 family contains three products: the Z–100, the Z–110, and the Z–120. These are all marketed through the HeathKit Electronic Centers, mail order houses, and some local independent dealers. The Z–100 family computers contain two microprocessors: the Intel 8088 16-bit microprocessor and an 8085 8-bit chip as well. Like the North Star Horizon, this product family is built around the S–100 bus, which means that expansion boards designed for IBM-style products will not work in these systems. Zenith and other manufacturers, however, offer a wide range of S–100 expansion boards, making this less of a problem than it seems.

All of the Z–100 computers have five expansion slots and are equipped with 128K bytes of memory. Two RS–232C ports and a Centronics-style parallel printer port are also offered as standard equipment.

Prices may vary; shop for discount prices.

The Z–100 contains one 320K byte disk drive and no monitor. The Z–110 consists of two 320K byte disk drives and an RGB monitor. The Z–120 system is shipped with two 320K byte disk drives and no display. An 11 megabyte hard disk is available as a built-in option. Like Radio Shack, North Star, and others, the Zenith Z–100 family has a built-in attached keyboard. There are 108 keys, including an 18 key numeric keypad with cursor controls, and 13 special function keys. You can add 64K bytes of RAM to the main board, and additional memory can be added by installing S–100-style memory cards available from vendors other than Zenith. The maximum memory permitted in the Z–100 family is 768K bytes. While it's possible to purchase a printer from Zenith, most other popular dot matrix and letter-quality printers will also work with the Zenith computers.

Z–DOS 2.1 and Lotus 1–2–3 are supplied with the system. Z–DOS (the Zenith version of MS–DOS) and CP/M 85 are the two operating system options. Microsoft Basic and Z–Basic Color Extension are available along with Microsoft Cobol and Microsoft Fortran. All of these are extra cost options. While the Zenith is not sold as a 100 percent compatible MS–DOS machine, many programs designed for IBM systems will run on it, including MultiPlan, WordStar, MailMerge, dBase and many other popular packages. This is particularly true if the programs do not use graphics. Examples of available software include most of the Peachtree accounting packages, MultiPlan, WordStar, MailMerge, Magic Wand, and Magic Spell.

RATINGS:

Overall Value	8	Performance	10
Ease of Use	8	Documentation	10
Software	8	Expandibility	9

	Acorn Model B	Advantage
Manufacturer	British Broadcasting Corporation	North Star Computers
Operating System	proprietary	G–DOS
RAM— Standard	32K	64K
RAM— Maximum	32K	64K
CPU	6502	Z80
Ports	one RS 423 serial, one serial I/O, one Centronics Parallel	none
Storage	none	two 320K 5¼ inch floppies
Monitor	none	12 inch monochrome
Keyboard	77 keys	87 keys
Approx. Price	$995	$2999
Special Features	high speed serial link for second processor	G–BASIC, six expansion slots, auxillary micro-processor for keyboard and disk

Prices may vary; shop for discount prices.

Alpha Micro AM-1000	Apple IIe	Attache
Alpha Microsystems	Apple Computer	Otrona Advanced Systems Corporation
AMOS/L	Apple DOS	CP/M
128K	64K	64K
512K	128K	64K
68000	6502	Z80A
none	none	two serial ports
two 800K floppy disk drives	none	two 360K 5¼ inch floppies
none	none	5.5 inch monochrome
105 keys	63 keys	63 keys
NA	$1395	$3795
	7 expansion slots	clock/calendar

	Attache 8:16	**Bondwell 12**
Manufacturer	Otrona Advanced Systems Corporation	Bondwell Industrial Co., Inc.
Operating System	MS–DOS, CP/M	CP/M
RAM— Standard	64K	64K
RAM— Maximum	256K	64K
CPU	8086, Z80A	Z80A
Ports	RS–232C serial, parallel printer	two serial, Centronics parallel
Storage	two 320K 5¼ inch floppies	two 180K 5¼ inch floppies
Monitor	5.5 inch monochrome	9 inch amber
Keyboard	63 keys	63 keys
Approx. Price	$3795	$995
Special Features	8087 math coprocessor, WordStar, MultiPlan, disk manager, Valet, Charton	speech synthesizer, BASIC, CP/M, MicroPro software

Prices may vary; shop for discount prices.

DecMate II	Dimension 68000	Epson QX–10
Digital Equipment Corporation	MicroCraft Corporation	Epson America, Inc.
WPS-8, COS-310	CP/M–68K	Valdocs
64K	128K	64K
96K	512K	256K
CMOS 6120	68000	Z80A
one serial port	Centronics parallel, RS–232C serial	programmable parallel, Multi-Protocol serial
two 400K 5¼ inch floppies	two 400K 5¼ inch floppies	two 380K 5¼ inch floppies
12 inch monochrome	none	12 inch monochrome
105 keys	83 keys	78 keys
$3245	$3995	$2995
optional CP/M–80 processor	coprocessor options can run almost any software available. CP/M, PC–DOS, TRSDOS, Apple DOS, UNIX	clock calendar, CPM 2.2

	Franklin Ace 1200	HP–150
Manufacturer	Franklin Computer	Hewlett-Packard
Operating System	Apple DOS	MS–DOS 2.1
RAM— Standard	128K	256K
RAM— Maximum	128K	640K
CPU	6502, Z80A	8088
Ports	one serial, one parallel	two RS–232C serial, one HP–IB IEEE–488
Storage	one 143K 5 ¼ inch floppy	two 264K 3½ inch microfloppies
Monitor	none	9 inch monochrome
Keyboard	72 keys	107 keys
Approx. Price	$1995	$3995
Special Features	runs Apple and CP/M software	touch sensitive screen, P.A.M. clock/calendar

Lisa 2	Macintosh	Mindset
Apple Computer, Inc.	Apple Computer, Inc.	Mindset Corporation
proprietary	proprietary	MS–DOS
512K	128K	64K
1 megabyte	128K (512K expansion will be available soon	256K
68000	68000	80186
two serial, one parallel	two serial, one external drive	none
400K 3½ inch microfloppy	400K 3½ inch microfloppy	360K per 5¼ inch floppy disk
12 inch monochrome	9 inch monochrome	none
76 keys	58 keys	84 keys
$3495	$2495	$2400
high resolution graphics, mouse controller, pulldown menus	high resolution graphics, mouse controller, pulldown menus	two custom VLSI graphics processors for high resolution graphics and animation

	Morrow MD3-e	**Rainbow 100 Plus**
Manufacturer	Morrow Designs	Digital Equipment Corp.
Operating System	CP/M 2.2	CP/M-86 MS–DOS
RAM— Standard	64K	128K
RAM— Maximum	128K	896K
CPU	Z80A	Z80, 8088
Ports	one Centronics parallel, two RS–232C serial	2 serial ports
Storage	two 384K 5¼ inch floppies	two 400K disk, one 10Mb hard disk
Monitor	12 inch monochrome	12 inch monochrome
Keyboard	91 keys	105 keys
Approx. Price	$1499	$5475
Special Features	NewWord, Co-Pilot, Correct-It	built-in VT100 terminal emulation

Sony SMC–70	TRS–80 Model 16B	Wang PC
Sony Micro-computer Products	Radio Shack	Wang Laboratories, Inc.
CP/M 2.2	TRSDOS	MS–DOS
64K	256K	128K
768K	768K	640K
Z80A	68000	8086
one parallel, one serial	two RS–232C serial, parallel printer	Centronics parallel, RS–232C serial
280K, 500K optional	1.5 Mb per drive	one 360K 5¼ inch floppy
none	12 inch monochrome	none
72 keys	82 keys	101 keys
$995	$3999	$2595
outstanding high resolution color graphics, un-usual expansion approach	expansion slots, multi-user option	five expansion slots, sound generator

PERIPHERALS

With the exception of bundled systems (computers that include peripherals and software in the basic purchase price), most of the computers reviewed in this book need peripherals in order to be really useful. Most computers will require a printer, and some computers don't come even with essentials like a monitor or keyboard. Even if you buy a complete system that includes everything you need right now, eventually you're going to want a faster printer, a better keyboard, or some other option.

Peripherals come in many types. There are common peripherals that can be found in almost every personal computer system, like floppy disk drives, monitors, and keyboards. Other popular peripherals include hard disks, modems, and multifunction boards. All of these are reviewed on the following pages, along with a host of specialized devices such as power supplies, print spoolers, and graphics tablets.

Because of the wide variety of products that are available, there is usually more than one type of peripheral that can answer your needs. If you're looking for increased storage, for example, don't just consider hard disks; there are several high-capacity floppy disk drives out on the market now, and one of them might be just right for your requirements. If you aren't sure of what your options are, you should look through computer magazines, contact a user's group, or even enlist the help of a consultant.

After you've decided on the peripheral or peripherals you need, make sure that you know what will be required to make the peripheral work with your particular computer. If you're considering a hard disk,

Prices may vary; shop for discount prices.

for example, make sure that you know whether or not you'll need to buy a separate hard disk controller. When you buy a modem, don't expect to be able to go on-line with The Source or CompuServe as soon as you get it home—you may need to buy additional software first.

For external peripherals (those that work outside your computer, as opposed to circuit boards that plug into it), you'll need to purchase the right cable or cables. Sometimes the cable will be included with the peripheral, but even then it may not be the right cable for your particular computer. If you aren't technically inclined, you should be aware that connections between computers and peripherals are not as simple as the cords and cables on your television or stereo; the fact that two computer devices have the same type of connector on them doesn't tell you very much about whether they will work together. Once again, it's a good idea to contact an expert if you aren't sure how things will go together.

Internal peripherals can also present special problems and considerations. Perhaps the most important of these is the added load on your computer's power supply. The fact that your computer has eight empty expansion slots doesn't necessarily mean that it can provide enough power to operate eight add-on boards. If you look through your computer's documentation, you should be able to find ratings for the power supply; keep this information in mind when you consider buying an internal modem or multi-function card. If you overload the power supply, the system may not work, or you could even do damage to the hardware.

FLOPPY DISK DRIVES

Many users purchase computers with only one floppy disk drive and later wish to add a second drive. For some, the answer is a quick trip to a dealer, where the service department will install the extra drive. Users who are slightly more technically inclined may wish to add one or more drives themselves.

Adding a drive is a fairly simple process. The steps usually include opening up the computer itself, removing a plastic or metal slot cover, screwing the drive into place, and snapping two connectors (one for power and one for the data) onto the new disk drive itself. In some cases, it may be necessary to set one or more switches inside the computer itself. Occasionally, jumpers or switches must be modified on the new disk drive as well.

If you intend to add a drive for the first time, it is advisable to purchase the add-on drive from a dealer who will give you assistance. Some dealers will provide a printed instruction sheet. Other dealers may give an actual demonstration of how to install the drive when you get back to your home or office.

There are a number of factors to consider when purchasing add-on drives. First, the drives must be compatible with your system. If the other floppy drive or drives in your system are single-sided double-density, you will probably want to purchase an additional single-sided drive, rather than a double-sided drive. This will assure compatibility and make it possible for you to use the same diskettes in either drive. Some people with single-sided drives may decide to convert to double-sided drives. This will

Prices may vary; shop for discount prices.

require removing the single-sided drive and replacing it with one or two of the higher capacity double-sided drives.

The most common double-sided drives in use today have 48 tracks per inch. Depending upon the system in which they are used, double-sided drives typically store between 340K and 360K or more per diskette. It is possible to purchase disk drives capable of storing a megabyte or more of data per diskette. This is advisable only if your system can format and access drives with this capacity. In some cases, a special drive controller card and software modifications may be required to take full advantage of these features. You should consult with a technically competent dealer if you are interested in these additional features.

The physical size of the drives themselves is also a consideration. Originally, floppy disk drives were about 3½ inches high. Recent technological advances have made it possible to shrink the size of these drives to half that size, so that two floppy disk drives can fit in the space once occupied by only one. These new smaller drives are frequently referred to as "half-height" drives. It is possible, for example, to put four half-height drives in the space originally designed to hold two drives on the IBM PC, Compaq, and other units. In some cases, it may be necessary to purchase brackets and/or cables designed for this task. You may need to ask a dealer about using half-height drives with your system.

In our survey of repair technicians, we could find no reliable evidence that there are significant differences in the quality or reliability of disk drives from various manufacturers. In many cases, drive manufacturers sell their drives to more than one company. It is possible, therefore, that you might purchase a Panasonic drive that was manufactured by someone other than Panasonic. In fact, many computer vendors, including IBM, have more than one source for their floppy drives. Computer vendors may ship Tandon drives at one time, Panasonic drives another, and TEAC drives at a different time. This is possible because manufacturers have standardized the physical shape and functioning of 5¼ inch drives. The reviews that follow show examples of these standards.

MPI 102
Micro Peripherals, Inc.

Approx. Retail Price	$475
Size	full
Density	double
Sides	double

This 5¼-inch full-size, double-sided disk drive is capable of recording up to one megabyte of information per diskette. It is possible to create 100 tracks per inch, or a maximum of 168 tracks on a diskette. The track-to-track access time is 5ms minimum, with an average of 150ms. The drive's speed is precisely controlled at 300 rpms. A unique head-mounting technology makes these drives more accurate than many others, permitting the high-density storage.

Two versions of the drive are available with different doors. One is similar to the Tandon door with a relatively small flip-open access handle. The other design uses a wider, less familiar drive door approach. We prefer the smaller, Tandon-style door, although this is a matter of personal taste. The physical dimensions of this drive are 3.2 inches high, 5.7 inches wide, and 7.75 inches deep. MPI also makes a line of half-height drives, with specifications similar to those offered by Tandon and TEAC. If you decide to purchase this MPI one-megabyte floppy disk drive, be certain that your computer hardware and software can use the added capability.

RATINGS:

Overall Value	10	Performance	10
Ease of Use	9	Documentation	NA

Tandon TM–100–1
Tandon Corporation

Approx. Retail Price $250
Size ....full
Density..double
Sides.. single

A popular drive found in many computers, the Tandon TM–100–1 is a full-size, single-sided, double-density drive. It has 48 tracks per inch and places 40 tracks on a floppy diskette. Only one side of the diskette is used. Therefore, less expensive single-sided, double-density floppy diskettes can be used in the TM–100–1. This drive rotates diskettes at 300 rpm.

The unformatted capacity of this drive is 256K maximum. Actual information density will depend upon the computer and disk operating system used. Typically, these are advertised as 160K drives. Track-to-track access time is 5ms minimum with an average of 75ms. The physical dimensions are 5¾ inches wide, 3¼ inches high, and 8 inches deep. The drive requires 900 milli-amps of 12 volts DC along with 600 milli-amps of 5 volts. These drives are frequently used in IBM, TAVA, and many other computers.

RATINGS:
Overall Value.................8 Performance.. 8
Ease of Use....................10 Documentation .... NA

Tandon TM–100–2
Tandon Corporation

Approx. Retail Price $340
Size ....full
Density..double
Sides ....double

The TM–100–2 is the double-sided, double-density, full-size version of the TM–100–1. This is perhaps the most popular drive style in use in personal computers today. You may see these advertised as 320K or 360K drives. In fact, it is possible to record more than 360K of information on diskettes with this drive. The 320K and 360K specifications is a shorthand way of indicating to shoppers that these drives work well in IBM and IBM compatible systems using MS–DOS version 1 or 2. The TM–100–2 records 48 tracks per inch on both sides of a disk; thus 80 tracks can be recorded on one floppy diskette.

With this type of drive, it is safest to use diskettes that have been certified on both sides. Some people use diskettes that have been certified for one side only and find that they work quite well. Since most systems check (certify) diskettes when they are formatted, it is sometimes possible to save money by using diskettes advertised as single-sided in double-sided drives. The minimum and average access times for the TM–100–2 are 5ms and 75ms respectively. They are 5¾ inches wide, 3¼ inches high, and 8 inches deep. Like its single-sided cousin, the TM–100–2 requires 900 milli-amps at 12 volts DC and 600 milli-amps at 5 volts DC maximum.

RATINGS:
Overall Value .... 9 Performance 9
Ease of Use ....10 Documentation .... NA

TEAC 55A
TEAC Corporation of America

Approx. Retail Price $299
Size...half
Density...double
Sides ....single

The TEAC 55A is a half-height, single-sided, double-density drive. Instead of the flip-open door found on many disk drives, the TEAC 55A drive has a little handle that is rotated to the open position when disk-ettes are being loaded and unloaded, and to the closed position for actual disk drive operation. Unlike the larger full-size drives, the TEAC 55A uses a direct drive approach. Full-size drives frequently use a belt drive mechanism which takes up considerably more room.

Like the Tandon TM–100–1, the TEAC 55A can record 48 tracks per inch, 40 tracks per diskette. The drive operates at 300 rpm. Its unformatted storage capacity, when used a a double-density drive, is 256K. Access times are similar to those of the full-size Tandon drive. Since the 55A is physically half as high as a full-size drive, two of them can be placed in the same space as one full-size drive. Normally, special brackets will be required to mount drives this way. The TEAC 55A is a very popular drive, now being used by a number of computer manufacturers as standard equipment.

RATINGS:
Overall Value ....8 Performance................8
Ease of Use...................9 Documentation ..... NA

TEAC 55B
TEAC Corporation of America

Approx. Retail Price	$360
Size	half height
Density	double
Sides	double

The TEAC 55B is the double-sided, double-density version of TEAC's half-height drive. It is capable of 48 tracks per inch, for a total of 80 tracks per diskette. It rotates diskettes at 300 rpm. It is possible to store a maximum of 500K on this drive, although you will normally see it advertised as a 360K or possibly 320K drive. The TEAC 55B has become a very popular drive since, with many computers, it is possible to put two of these drives in one drive position and a hard disk in the next, offering the best of both worlds.

RATINGS:

Overall Value	9	Performance	9
Ease of Use	9	Documentation	NA

	Tandon TM–100–1	TEAC 55A
Manufacturer	Tandon Corporation	TEAC Corporation of America
Size	full size	half-height
Single/Double Sided	single	single
Single/Double Density	double	double
Approx. Price	$250	$298
Comments	48 tracks/inch	48 tracks/inch

Prices may vary; shop for discount prices.

Tandon TM–100–2	TEAC 55B	MPI 102
Tandon Corporation	TEAC Corporation of America	Micro Peripherals, Inc.
full size	half-height	full size
double	double	double
double	double	double
$340	$360	$475
48 tracks/inch	48 tracks/inch	100 tracks/inch

HARD DISKS AND TAPES

If you find that your files are getting too big for your floppy disks, you may want to consider purchasing a hard disk drive. These drives offer many advantages over floppy disk drives. Most use a fixed disk, meaning that the disk cannot be easily removed or replaced.

The most important advantage to a hard disk is the great amount of storage they offer. Common hard disk sizes for personal computers range from 5 megabytes up to 30 megabytes or more. Compare this to floppy disk drives, which usually hold 360K or less—a 30 megabyte hard disk can store more information than eighty 360K floppies. With a hard disk, most users can store all of their software on the same disk, eliminating the hassle of finding and swapping disks each time a different program is needed.

The second advantage to using a hard disk is that they are much faster than floppy disks when it comes to reading and writing information on them. Floppies can be very slow when you are loading large programs or creating large data files, but these operations will take a fraction of the time if you have a hard disk.

Another advantage to using a hard disk is that you usually have more software options. Many large, sophisticated programs and operating systems can only run on a hard disk system. If you have a hard disk, you can use these programs in addition to all of the programs that work with floppy disks.

Prices may vary; shop for discount prices.

The one inconvenience caused by a hard disk is the need to back it up regularly. Backing up a disk means to make an extra copy of the information on the disk so that you can retrieve your files if something disastrous happens to the disk. With floppies, you can simply copy the disk to a blank floppy. But since hard disks hold much more information than you can put on a floppy, it would be a very tedious process to copy the information on your hard disk to the many floppies required. Instead, most hard disk users buy some type of tape backup system. These devices are designed specifically for backing up hard disks, and most of them can copy an entire hard disk to tape very quickly. Some tape backup units are reviewed along with the hard disks in this section.

Because a hard disk is such a big investment, you should be careful when shopping for one. Make sure that you know any limitations before you buy. The most common limitation that can cause headaches for users is the requirement that a single operating system be used on the entire disk. This means that you can't use MS–DOS programs and UCSD p-System programs on the same disk, for example. If you need that capability, ask specifically whether it is supported by the hard disk you're considering.

BANK TAPE–BASED HARD DISK BACKUP
Corvus Systems Corp.

Approx. Retail Price $2195
Type ....external
Available for ....most systems

The Corvus Bank Mass Storage System is a cartridge tape backup device. If you own a hard disk, it is important to establish and adhere to strict backup policies. You need a way to recover important files if a hard disk fails or if on-line disk data is otherwise damaged or destroyed.

The Bank works only on the Corvus Omninet network. It is designed to be used by the system supervisor and ties up the supervisor's computer while it is working. The special tape cartridges look like small video cassettes and are available in 100 MB and 200 MB tape cartridges.

Corvus Software (included in the purchase price) helps supervisors format and test new cartridges, backup all or portions of a hard disk, and restore all or portions of a damaged disk's data. Any hard disk in the network can be backed up. Even floppy disk data can be stored on the Bank. There is password protection as well as other features to assure that only the supervisor has access to the tapes.

Multiple Banks can be installed in your network making it possible to transfer tape-to-tape without using a disk as an intermediary.

Depending on the backup task to be performed, it can take from a few minutes to up to six hours or more. For this reason a timer feature is built into the software that will accomplish backup and format tasks after everyone has gone home.

Prices may vary; shop for discount prices.

Hardware installation consists of setting some address switches on the Bank, plugging in a power cord, and adding a tap to the Omninet wire already installed in the office. Then, the supervisor's Omninet software diskette needs to be modified. This all takes less than an hour and no special tools are required.

It takes a long time to format, verify, and fill a tape; and tapes wear out after about 200 hours of motion. None the less, this is a much better (and faster) approach to hard disk backup than using floppies.

The Bank is not a product designed for casual users, nor is it likely to be used by them. Experienced supervisors will have no problem adding the needed operating skills to their bag of tricks. We have seen easier to use operating approaches, but there are no serious problems here.

It is possible to cause some errors. For example, if a user tries to use a file being backed up, unpredictable results can occur. The supervisor can deny user access to files during the backup process to avoid these problems.

The manuals are complete and professionally done. They match the rest of the Omninet manuals and contain an index, helpful diagrams, and charts. They are written for experienced system supervisors.

All-in-all the Bank is a fine backup tool. With the cost of hard disk drives falling, however, you should consider a second drive as a way to backup instead of the Bank. In some cases it may be a simpler, faster way to accomplish the same thing .

RATINGS:

Overall Value	8	Performance	9
Ease of Use	9	Documentation	8

DAVONG HARD DISK FAMILY
Davong Systems, Inc.

Approx. Retail Price $1995
Type ....external
Available for ....IBM PC, Apple II

Davong was one of the early leaders in providing hard disk systems for personal computers. They continue to be active leaders in the industry, and continually improve and update their hardware and software.

The Davong hard disk family consists of a series of hard disks with 5, 10, 15, 21, and 32 megabyte capacities. These products are compatible with many operating systems, including PC–DOS, the UCSD p-System, CP/M and others. It is possible to mix operating systems on the same disk. A networking feature called MultiLink makes it possible for as many as 255 computers to share the same disk drive. Multiple disks can be placed in the network, and it is even possible to mix competitive products (i.e.: Apple and IBM).

Excellent software is provided with these hard disks, speeding the installation and backup process. Other special features of MultiLink include passwords that permit access to be limited, read only or read and write, and locks that prevent one user from changing data while another user is working with that file. Pipes, which allow different applications being used on separate workstations to communicate and trade data are also part of the MultiLink package. A streaming tape backup option is available. One adapter board and some software is included in the basic price of the drives. Networking software and interface boards for additional workstations are priced separately, adding to the cost of each workstation you plan to add to your network.

Prices may vary; shop for discount prices.

The Davong family offers many options, and it is important to understand these options prior to committing a lot of information to the disk. There is a quick installation software program that will make some decisions for you, but this will not create the best configuration for your needs.

The unit we reviewed performed flawlessly. We found the ability to mix operating systems on the same hard disk a real plus. We were unable to test a configuration using competitive computers (i.e.: Apple and IBM).

Most of the information needed to install and operate the hard disk is available in the documentation. The organization of the information, however, is not very good. There is no overview, and the documents assume more knowledge than many novice users will have.

If you're looking for a hard disk system, you should look into these Davong products. You will find that they are very fully featured and quite competitive in terms of cost and performance.

RATINGS:

Overall Value 9	Performance 9
Ease of Use 8	Documentation 8

PC–BACKUP CARTRIDGE TAPE STORAGE UNIT
Alloy Computer Products

Approx. Retail Price $2195
Type ....external
Available for ....IBM PC and compatibles

There are many ways to lose the data on a hard disk. It is possible to accidentally format the entire disk, power outages can occur during directory track updates, causing all of the information to be lost, even faulty application software can damage all or some of the information on a disk. Unfortunately, most people don't create adequate backup procedures until this has happened to them. This is frequently an expensive and time-consuming lesson to be learned.

The PC–Backup Cartridge Tape subsystem provides low-cost, high-performance data storage/retrieval and Winchester hard disk backup for personal computers. This system includes an IDS–PC tape controller, 6400 BPI ¼-inch 4-track cartridge tape drive, a tabletop cabinet with integral power supply, TIP–SIX software, and data cables.

This is a file-oriented hard disk backup and restore system. It transfers data at 0.7 mb per minute, and up to 16.5 megabytes of data can be stored on 555 feet of tape. It measures 8.5×16×5 inches, and weighs 18 pounds. The entire PC–Backup subsystem is FCC compliant and meets all Class B electromagnetic radiation specifications.

The IDS–PC controller is an intelligent interface that utilizes a Z–80 microprocessor and proprietary firmware to provide a high-speed data link between a computer and the PC–Backup system. It occupies a single slot in the PC bus and is interfaced directly to the backup hardware via a 37 pin shielded data cable.

Prices may vary; shop for discount prices.

The 6400 BPI 4-track serial tape drive is compact and accepts easy to handle 4"×6" ANSI standard ¼-inch tape cartridges.

TIP–SIX (Tape Interchange Program) is customized for the computer. It allows the user to freely transfer data to and from the cartridge tape. It is a comprehensive disk-to-tape backup package under either DOS 1.1/ 2.0 or CP/M 86 allowing single or multiple file save and restore commands. The menu prompts the operator for the various commands to be executed, and the file names to be stored or restored. Optionally, TIP may be executed from a batch file. The software contains two utility files, allowing the user to create customized cartridge tape control programs if desired.

A plug-in board must be inserted in any empty slot on your computer. A cable interconnects this board with the external tape backup system. Altogether, installation should take less than 15 minutes in most cases.

It takes between 6 and 7 minutes to backup an entire 10 megabyte disk. A variety of choices make this a flexible, easy to use backup system.

The documentation is rather straightforward and well organized. Parts of it are slightly more technical than necessary. Some first-time users may want to get some training from their dealers.

This is an excellent addition to any hard disk owner's system. The best time to buy one is before you need it.

RATINGS:

Overall Value 8	Performance 7
Ease of Use 9	Documentation 8

ZOBEX ADD–ON HARD DISK KIT FOR THE IBM PC
Zobex

Approx. Retail Price $1295
Type ....external
Available for ....IBM PC and compatibles

The Zobex kits include a MiniScribe hard disk drive, a Zobex controller card (printed circuit board), and software. On the model we tested, only the controller card resides in the computer. The rest sits nearby.

The Zobex 3.00 software we reviewed is designed for only MS–DOS files. It does not permit partitioning for MS–DOS, Pascal, and CP/M. As is the case with most add-on hard disks for the IBM PC, you cannot "boot" directly from the Zobex-supplied hard disk. You must boot using the Zobex software on a floppy disk in drive A.

The Zobex software modifies and complements PC–DOS versions 2.00 or 2.10. It contains a hard disk installation program, a disk format program (used in place of IBM's), and some other necessary files. It is possible to use the software with drives other than the MiniScribe. A power down program moves the drive head(s) into a safe position for transport.

The controller card can control up to four hard disk drives—you can write-protect each drive individually. There is a built-in power-on diagnostic feature. Many of the controller card's features are not needed by the MiniScribe. For example, the controller supports cartridge change signals for systems using removable platters.

Prices may vary; shop for discount prices.

Installation is very simple. The controller board is shipped from the factory with jumpers and switches pre-set. We found the cable running from the controller to the drive a little short. It makes it difficult to put the MiniScribe drive out of the way. The Zobex software installation process is simple and painless.

We have had no problems reading or writing data. The speed of this system seems comparable with other similar systems tested. We did find our MiniScribe drive motor noticeably noisy. If noise in the office bothers you, it might be worthwhile to listen before you purchase.

Two books arrived with the kit. The first is a manual for the controller card and software. It fits in an IBM manual binder and even has the printed edge stripe for quick reference. This booklet is a cross between an installation tutorial and an engineering specification. The second manual is for the MiniScribe drive. It is larger than the other booklet, won't fit in an IBM binder, and is best described as an engineering and service manual. Fortunately, most users will not need to read this (excellent) technical document. A quick, start-up booklet for end-users would be a nice addition to this otherwise complete set of documents.

This is a fine group of products from a company that has been in the micro business for more than six years. You can count on support and competitive pricing from this friendly firm. By the time you read this, Zobex will probably be offering new, improved versions of their hardware and software.

RATINGS:

Overall Value	10	Performance	9
Ease of Use	10	Documentation	8

	Add-On Hard Disk Kit	Backup Cartridge Tape Storage System
Manufacturer	Zobex	Alloy Computer Products
Formatted Capacity	10 mb (higher capacities also available)	16.5 mb
Size	5¼ inch	¼ inch tape
Type	external	external
Computers Supported	IBM PC and compatibles	IBM PC and compatibles
Operating Systems	PC–DOS, MS–DOS	PC–DOS, CP/M-86
Approx. Price	$1295	$2195
Comments	includes controller card	

Prices may vary; shop for discount prices.

Bank Tape Hard Disk Backup	Corvus Omninet System	Davong 10012 Series
Corvus Systems Corporation	Corvus Systems Corporation	Davong Systems, Inc.
100 mb or 200 mb cartridges	5.5 mb (higher capacities also available)	5 mb–32 mb
See Corvus Omninet	5¼ inch	5¼ inch
external	external	external
See Corvus Omninet	Apple, IBM, DEC, TI, Zenith, and others	IBM PC and compatibles, Apple II, IIe, and III, and Osborne
See Corvus Omninet	MS–DOS, CP/M, USCD p-System, and others	PC–DOS, CP/M, USCD p-System, and others
$2195	$1995	$1995–$3995
backup system for Corvus Omninet	multi-user capability and ability to mix Apple and IBM	can mix operating systems

	Dynaframe Hard Disk System	Superior Hard Disk System
Manufacturer	Vista Computer Company	Great Lakes
Formatted Capacity	5 mb (higher capacities also available)	10 mb (higher capacities also available)
Size	5¼ inch	5¼ inch
Type	external	external
Computers Supported	IBM PC and compatibles	IBM PC and compatibles
Operating Systems	PC–DOS, MS–DOS	MS–DOS, PC–DOS, CP/M-86
Approx. Price	$2695	$1295
Comments	available with up to eight additional IBM expansion slots	

Prices may vary; shop for discount prices.

Tallgrass
TG3012

Tallgrass
Technologies
Corporation

12.5 mb

5¼ inch

external

IBM PC and
compatibles, TI
Professional

PC–DOS 1.1,
PC–DOS 2.2, TI
MS–DOS, CP/M-86

$2995

includes cartridge
tape backup system

MODEMS

Modems are fast becoming the most popular peripheral of all. Due to the rapidly increasing number of on-line information services, many persons and businesses purchase personal computers simply to gain access to all of the information that can now be obtained over phone lines.

When shopping for a modem, there are many things to consider. Modems have a variety of technical specifications, and these specifications must match your computer, your communications software, and the information services you intend to use or the computer and modem you intend to connect with. (Although the emphasis here is on information services, modems are also used to communicate between personal computers. This gives you the ability to transfer messages, files, and programs from one computer to another via the telephone line.)

One modem specification that you've probably heard before is the baud rate. This is a measure of the rate at which the modem sends and receives information. (Actually, it is technically correct to use bits per second rather than baud rate, but baud rate has become the more common term.) Common baud rates are 300 and 1200. Almost every information service provides 300 baud communication, and many provide 1200 baud. If you need to use a specific service, check which baud rates are supported before buying your modem. Multispeed modems, which can use a variety of baud rates, are also available. For most uses, the best combination is a modem that can use either 300 baud or 1200 baud.

Prices may vary; shop for discount prices.

Two other specifications that are important when buying a modem are the protocol used and the type of transmission. Protocol refers to the way that the information is interpreted, and there are two common protocols: Bell 103 and Bell 212. The type of transmission can either be synchronous or asynchronous, but asynchronous is the most common. Once again, you don't need to understand the technical definitions of these terms, just make sure you know which type you will need for your intended uses.

Another consideration in modems is whether to buy an internal modem or an external one. Internal modems mount inside the computer's case, and external modems come in their own separate enclosure. An internal modem is more convenient because of the lack of connecting cords, but an external modem is easier to switch from one computer to another, if that is one of your requirements.

One final consideration in your purchase of a modem is the communications software you will be using with it. It is very important that your communications software supports all of the features offered by your modem; otherwise, you may not be able to use those features. For example, if you buy a modem that supports auto-dialing and auto-answer, your communications software should also have auto-dialing and auto-answering capability.

PC:INTELLIMODEM
Bizcomp Computer Corp.

Approx. Retail Price $499
Type..internal
Available for ....IBM PC and compatibles

One unique feature of this modem separates it from the rest in a very crowded market. The IntelliModem lets users quickly switch between voice and data during the same phone call.

PC:IntelliModem is an internal modem designed for IBM and compatible computers. It connects directly to the phone line and provides 110, 300, and 1200 BAUD (bps) communications using the Bell 103/212A standards. Three modular phone jacks on the rear of the modem make it possible to plug in a regular phone line, a standard telephone, or just the handset from a telephone. If just the handset is used, your computer can control dialing, off-hook conditions, etc. A small speaker on the IntelliModem provides ringing and line monitoring capabilities. A diskette containing communications software written in BASIC is standard, and the software permits storage of up to 99 names, phone numbers, and automatic logon sequences. Unlike some communications software, this software does not monitor responses from the host during the logon process; users must estimate the time delay between logon functions. Bizcomp claims the modem will work with Crosstalk communications software as well, but we did not test this combination.

It is possible to toggle between voice and data communications using function keys on the computer. This feature works best when both parties are using IntelliModem hardware and software. Only ASCII files can be transferred using the supplied software. A

Prices may vary; shop for discount prices.

nice automatic file capturing and naming feature makes unattended reception of files possible.

Installation is quite simple. A jumper plug can be rotated to switch between COM 1 and COM 2 settings. This is slightly less convenient than the switches used on competitive products, but causes no great difficulty. Installation should take 10 minutes or less.

Bizcomp provides excellent documentation for the most part. There is a nice overview, a number of diagrams, and other helpful aids. The book fits the IBM-style half-size binders. The instructions do not include the procedures required to transfer communications software from the supplied floppy disk to an IBM PC XT hard disk, even though Bizcomp claims the modem is XT-compatible.

The only drawbacks to the PC:IntelliModem are the fact that the supplied software does not transfer non-basic files, and the fact that it does not monitor host systems during the logon process.

If you frequently need to exchange data and voice in the same telephone conversations, and if other users you telecommunicate with have IntelliModems, this Bizcomp product is an excellent choice.

RATINGS:

Overall Value	8	Performance	9
Ease of Use	9	Documentation	9

R212A INTELLIGENT MODEM
Rixon, Inc.

Approx. Retail Price $499
Type ....external
Available for ....RS-232 port

This R212A external modem looks deceivingly simple from the outside, with no external controls or lights, but it is one of the most fully featured modems we have tested. It contains considerable memory with a battery backup, has the ability to dial numbers from the keyboard using the R212s built-in dialing feature, and up to 10 phone numbers can be stored in the modem itself and displayed on your computer's display, along with the text describing the numbers and providing other information desired by the operator. It can also emulate the Hayes command set, making it possible to use communications software designed for the Hayes modem.

There are several types of re-dial features, including a command to dial different phone numbers in sequence until one of them answers. Stored logon sequences are possible. Originate and answer modes are standard. Speeds supported include 110, 300, and 1200 BAUD (bps).

This modem provides both pulse and tone dialing. First, it tries to dial a number using the tone dialing mode. If this is unsuccessful, it switches to the pulse mode, assuming that your phone line cannot support tone dialing. It is also possible to mix pulse and tone dialing in situations where that is appropriate.

Considering the wide array of features offered on this modem, installation is very easy. Users must provide their own RS–232C cable, but much of the rest of the installation process has been automated by the mod-

Prices may vary; shop for discount prices.

em's internal microprocessor. At power-up, the user simply presses the carriage return on his or her terminal twice, and the speed, parity, and other operating characteristics of the terminal are determined automatically by the modem.

Once we got over the lack of an internal speaker and status lights, we found this modem to be more capable than the Hayes competitor, a standard most people use for comparison these days. One area where it falls short of the Hayes, however, is that it can get confused if you accidentally send commands from the keyboard when you mean to send data. There are other small quirks as well. The parentheses characters, used so frequently when typing long distance phone numbers, are interpreted by the Rixon to mean that information enclosed within the parentheses should not be displayed. This is a security feature that may add confusion to your telephone directory. Our version of the modem had the data terminal ready (DTR) feature disabled, which meant that the modem automatically answered the phone even if the terminal or computer power was turned off. We understand that this has been (or will be) corrected on future versions of the product. The documentation is very nice, with plenty of helpful charts and diagrams. Unfortunately, there is no index.

This product has an incredible array of features. It has been very carefully engineered, and we think it is an exceptional value. Simple communications software may be required to make your personal computer run this modem, but you will not need anything fancy, since auto-dialing and other features are built into the modem itself.

RATINGS:
Overall Value	10	Performance	10
Ease of Use	10	Documentation	9

300/1200 EXTERNAL MODEM FOR IBM PC
Hayes Microcomputer Products

Approx. Retail Price $699
Type ....external
Available for......................................RS–232 port

Two versions of this Hayes external modem are available. One version operates only at 300 BAUD and is Bell type 103 compatible. The second version is actually two modems in one box—it offers 103 and 212A compatibility, at BAUD rates of 110, 300, and 1200 bps. These are both direct connect modems, meaning that the modems themselves plug directly into your telephone jack.

Hayes modems offer a variety of automatic phone dialing features that can be controlled by software or from the terminal keyboard itself. Both tone and pulse dialing are available. There is a built-in audio monitor (with a volume control), making it possible for you to listen to the automatic dialing procedures and to determine whether or not a connection has been successfully made.

The modem itself contains its own microprocessor, which receives commands from the user (or user's software) over the RS–232C link between the computer and the modem. Both operational and configuration commands can be sent. Speed, number of parity bits, dialing characteristics, and many other details of modem operation can be selected in this manner. The front panel of the Hayes external modem contains a number of indicator lights making it possible for the user to determine the status of the modem, the phone line, and other items at a glance.

The Hayes external modems require an RS–232C cable, which is not provided. Moreover, your computer

Prices may vary; shop for discount prices.

will need to have an RS–232C serial port. The Hayes external modems also require communications software, which is not provided. Because of the popularity of the external Hayes modems, most commonly used software can be used.

Performance of these Hayes products is outstanding. The modems are much better than many of the imitators that have come out since the introduction of the Hayes offerings. Unfortunately, when sending commands to the Hayes modem from your computer, you must use uppercase letters. This can be confusing to first-time users, and annoying to experienced users as well.

With several years of experience with both the 300 and 1200 BAUD versions of this product, we have never experienced any serious operational problems. It is no wonder that these modems have become the standards by which others are judged.

Depending on your experience level, the documentation for the Hayes external modem is either fair or excellent. Not enough attention is directed to first-time modem users in the organization of this book. All of the necessary information is available; it is simply presented in a somewhat confusing order.

There are less expensive copies of this modem available, and there are more expensive modems that emulate many of the Hayes features. Chances are you will find everything you need on the Hayes product, and will never be disappointed by its performance. This is not necessarily true of many of the Hayes imitators.

RATINGS:

Overall Value	9	Performance	10
Ease of Use	8	Documentation	 8

1200B INTERNAL MODEM FOR IBM PC
Hayes Microcomputer Products

Approx. Retail Price $599
Type...internal
Available for ....IBM PC and compatibles

The Hayes 1200B can be configured to work with COM 1 or COM 2 ports on your computer. This modem comes with the necessary cable to connect the 1200B directly to your phone line. There is also a jack on the modem into which your telephone can be plugged. A relay disconnects this phone from the telephone line when in the telecommunications mode to avoid accidental errors created by picking up the phone during data communications. (The feature does not prevent problems from other phones on the same line.) The internal modem does not have operator status lights. Power for the modem is obtained from the computer itself.

There are only three configuration switches on the Hayes 1200B internal modem. They are set at the factory to the most common settings. Installation is as simple as opening your computer, plugging the board into an empty slot, and connecting the telephone line from the modem to the wall. Installation should take no more than ten or fifteen minutes at the most.

The 1200B internal modem is an outstanding product. We have found even the high-speed (1200 BAUD) data communications to be quite reliable under difficult conditions where other modems have failed. The Hayes Smartcom software provided with the modem offers a wide variety of features including the ability to automatically dial remote computers and accomplish the entire logon process without human intervention. You can create files containing all necessary phone numbers, passwords, and other logon parameters.

Prices may vary; shop for discount prices.

The software and modem work together to monitor the remote computer's activities. The system can wait for correct responses before taking the next sequential step in the logon process. For example, Smartcom software can be "taught" to wait for prompt characters from a host computer before sending passwords and other logon data automatically. Other software features permit establishment of special function keys for different communications tasks.

One problem exists when using the 1200B with a color monitor and the IBM graphics monitor board. Annoying "snow flakes" appear on the display when text scrolls on the screen. Because of this, Hayes recommends using the package only with the monochrome monitor and monochrome display driver board. We don't think the problem is all that serious, and know of people that regularly use the 1200B with color monitors. It takes a while to learn how to use all of the Hayes software features, but it is time well spent.

Like other Hayes documents, the 1200B and Smartcom manuals are complete but organized in a curious fashion. First-time users will need to do some hunting to find the information they need to make the whole process make sense. There are many excellent diagrams and charts along with photos and detailed technical specifications. Quick reference cards are provided that you will also find very helpful.

If you have an IBM or IBM-compatible computer with an empty expansion slot and you're looking for a fine 103–212A modem, this is it. You may want to watch the system perform with a color monitor and graphics card if that is how your system is configured.

RATINGS:

Overall Value	9	Performance	10
Ease of Use	8	Documentation	8

	1200B Internal Modem	300/1200 External Modem
Manufacturer	Hayes Microcomputer Products	Hayes Microcomputer Products
Type	internal	direct-connect external
Baud Rate	110/300/1200 baud	300/1200 baud
Interface	IBM expansion slot	RS–232
Approx. Price	$599	$699
Other Features	Smartcom II included	uses "AT" command set

Prices may vary; shop for discount prices.

Code-A-Phone Tele-Modem	PC–1200B Modem	PC:IntelliModum
Code-A-Phone	Novation	Bizcomp Computer Corporation
direct-connect external (includes phone)	internal	internal
300/1200 baud	110–300/1200 baud	110/300/1200 baud
RS–232	IBM expansion slot	IBM expansion slot
$695	$595	$499
Hayes compatible, 103/212A, pulse and touch tone dialing		103/212A

	R212A Intelligent Modem	Signalman Mark VI Modem
Manufacturer	Rixon, Inc.	Anchor Automation, Inc.
Type	direct-connect external	internal
Baud Rate	110/300/1200 baud	110/300 baud
Interface	RS–232	IBM expansion slot
Approx. Price	$499	$279
Other Features	Hayes compatible, pulse and touch tone dialing	optional RS–232C port

Prices may vary; shop for discount prices.

Room Networker	
Room Telephonics	
Internal	
10–300 baud	
Apple bus	
129	

MONITORS

While buying a modem is a complicated process involving many decisions, buying a monitor is fairly simple and straightforward. The most important decision you will need to make is whether you need color and how much you want to spend. You can purchase a monitor for less than $200, or you can spend over a thousand dollars, and with the exception of a few special features that can be provided, the price is simply a reflection of the quality of the display.

Monochrome (single-color) monitors usually have one of three types of display: white, green, or amber characters on a black background. Many studies have been done to measure the effects of these different colors on eye-strain and productivity, and the results of these studies have often been contradictory. In general, though, most people believe that a green or amber display is easier to work with for long periods of time than a simple black and white display. Try to get a look at all three types yourself before you make a decision.

If you decide to purchase a color monitor, there are two common types: RGB and composite. RGB monitors usually provide clearer, sharper colors and images, but there are high-quality composite video monitors available also.

If you need graphics capability on your monitor, pay careful attention to the resolution specifications. Resolution is usually defined in terms of how many individual points of light (*pixels*, for picture elements) can be displayed in one row or one column. A monitor that has 640x400 resolution can display 640 pixels in each row and 400 pixels in each column.

Prices may vary; shop for discount prices.

When comparing the cost of graphics monitors, be sure to include the cost of any necessary graphics adapters or graphics cards. Many computers do not come with the hardware necessary to take advantage of a high resolution graphics monitor, so you must add hardware options to provide this capability. Usually this comes in the form of expansion cards. Graphics expansion cards are reviewed in the chapter on multifunction boards.

The final consideration in purchasing a monitor is size. Monitors are usually measured by a diagonal line across the screen, like television sets. The two most common sizes are 9 inch diagonal and 12 inch diagonal, but there are also a few other sizes available. A 12 inch monitor is usually best for prolonged use, because the characters are larger and easier to read.

AMDEK COLOR II AND II+
Amdek Corp.

Approx. Retail Price $559
Type ....RGB
Available for ....most systems

Amdek Color II and II+ monitors are very pleasing RGB color monitors with 13IM diagonal tubes. The power switch, contrast control, and brightness control are located on the front panel. There are no tint or color controls. The monitors come with an IBM PC cable, but Apple computers can be interfaced using Amdek's optional DVM board.

While parts of the documentation are corny and excessive, three of four pages contain useful technical information including pinouts and cables construction information.

These are very quiet monitors. The principle difference between the II and the II+ is that the II+ displays rich color. We feel the extra money for the II+ is warranted for most applications.

These are both good displays, thus their popularity. In the competitive monitor field you may be able to find slightly better values from other vendors, although none we know of offer a warranty as long as Amdek's.

RATINGS:
Overall Value 9   Performance 8
Ease of Use...............NA   Documentation ....NA

HX12 COLOR MONITOR
Princeton Graphics Systems

Approx. Retail Price $695
Type...RGB
Available for ....most systems

The Princeton Graphics PGS–HX12 RGB monitor works with the IBM PC or compatible clones (e.g.: Compaq). It can also be used with the Apple IIe if you purchase an optional ($185) RGB80 card. Apple III owners can also use this display with the correct cable. It has a recessed picture tube, a power switch, brightness control, and power indicator lamp. The rear panel has horizontal and vertical hold controls and a nine-pin signal connector. A 60-inch connecting cable is supplied.

The sharpness and focus of the HX12 is quite nice, even in the corners. The color is pleasing, providing a subtle, easy-to-look-at image.

The small booklet contains nearly everything you need to know in a well-organized fashion. The book even gives pinout information for the monitor. You are on your own when it comes to the "computer end" of the non-IBM-style cable making projects.

This monitor is worth the price.

RATINGS:
Overall Value 10   Performance 10
Ease of Use...............NA   Documentation ....NA

QUADCHROME MONITOR
Quadram Corp.

Approx. Retail Price ..$695
Type ....RGB
Available for ....
..................most systems

This is a 12IM diagonal RGB monitor supplied with an IBM cable. It displays eight colors with two intensity levels. The resolution is 690 H×240 V. We found the color to be exceptionally warm and pleasing. There are on/off, brightness, vertical hold, horizontal hold, horizontal width/centering, and vertical height/centering controls. The monitor itself is 11×15.1×16.5 inches.

Installation is quite simple, particularly if you are using this with an IBM or compatible computer. Everything you need is included.

The documentation is straightforward and to the point. Again, everything you need is at hand.

This is one of the nicest looking color monitors we have seen. Its performance rivals that of displays costing $100 to $200 more. Ours had excellent focus, even at the edges.

RATINGS:

Overall Value 10	Performance 10
Ease of Use...............NA	Documentation ....NA

TAXAN KG–12N AND KG–12NUY
PSK Electronics Corp.

Approx. Retail Price $189
Type...amber
Available for ....most systems

The Taxan KG–12N and KG–12NUY 12-inch diagonal monitors provide a 25 line by 80 character screen format. Green on black and amber on black characters are possible, depending on the model selected. These Taxan monitors have an 18 Mhz band width, higher than many of the others we've tested. Controls include power, brightness, horizontal hold, vertical hold, and contrast.

As with most monochrome monitors, installation is quite simple. The power cord and a composite video cable need to be connected. And like other monitors, users will require a composite video output from their computers.

This is a very nice display with exceptional brightness, sharpness, and overall appearance. It is one of the best that we have tested.

This series of monitors has slightly higher list prices than those of its competitors, so it may be worth your time to shop around to find these monitors at discounted prices.

RATINGS:

Overall Value 9	Performance 9
Ease of Use...............NA	Documentation ....NA

TAXAN RGB 420 COLOR MONITOR
PSK Electronics Corp.

Approx. Retail Price $700
Type ....RGB
Available for ....most systems

The RGB 420 12IM color monitor has 640×262 resolution, a brightness level knob, power switch, and LED power light. The rear panel contains a mode switch, two interface connectors, power cord, and controls for horizontal position, vertical position, hold, size, and focus. A chart above the mode switch shows the proper setting for each system.

The 420 provides a crisp and well-defined picture with exceptional color. However, when using a program called Energraphics, yellow appears red-brown. This monitor model has been fine-tuned to improve the color brown, affecting yellow on some, but not all programs. The 15 KHz noise seems slightly louder than many other monitors tested.

The accompanying manual is well done and uses charts and pictures throughout. Mode settings are discussed in detail.

The Taxan RGB 420 deserves your careful consideration. Its clear, crisp images and color richness rival many higher resolution units. Just be sure the yellow works to your satisfaction and listen to the high pitched noise before you purchase.

RATINGS:

Overall Value 9	Performance 9
Ease of Use 9	Documentation 8

ZENITH ZVM 122/123
Zenith Data Systems

Approx. Retail Price $169
Type ....amber/green
Available for......................................most systems

Most low-cost monitors are comparable. The Zeniths ZVM 122 and 123 12" diagonal monitors have a slight edge on the competition. The ZVM 122 displays amber characters, the 123, a pleasing shade of green.

There are front panel brightness and contrast controls. Vertical and horizontal hold controls can be found in the back. There is a 40/80 character switch that shortens the sweep in the 80 character mode to assure full display of all characters.

We have seen some slight linearity problems on some Zenith monitors. Generally, there is good sharpness and fair to excellent brightness. The 40/80 switch is a very nice feature not normally found on low-cost monitors. We found the Zenith monitor to be quieter than many others we have tested as well.

These two Zenith monitors may be the best we have seen in their price category.

RATINGS:
Overall Value 10   Performance 10
Ease of Use...............NA   Documentation ....NA

	Amdek Color II	**Amdek Color II+**
Manufacturer	Amdek Corporation	Amdek Corporation
Size	13 inch diagonal	13 inch diagonal
Color Type	RGB	RGB
Character Display	24 lines, 80 columns	24 lines, 80 columns
Resolution	560×240	560×240
Bandwidth	NA	NA
Approx. Price	$529	$559

Amdek Video 300	HX-12 Color Monitor	Quadchrome Monitor
Amdek Corporation	Princeton Graphics Systems	Quadram Corporation
12 inch diagonal	12 inch diagonal	12 inch diagonal
monochrome green	RGB	RGB
24 lines, 80 columns	25 lines, 80 columns	25 lines, 80 columns
900×800	690×240	690×480
18 mhz	15 mhz	NA
$179	$695	$695

	Taxan KG-12N	Taxan RGB 420
Manufacturer	Taxan	Taxan
Size	12 inch diagonal	12 inch diagonal
Color	monochrome amber	RGB
Character Display	25 lines, 80 columns	25 lines, 80 columns
Resolution	640×262	640×262
Bandwidth	18 mhz	NA
Approx. Price	$189	$699

Prices may vary; shop for discount prices.

Zenith VM122

Zenith Data Systems	
12 inch diagonal	
monochrome amber	
25 lines, 80 columns	
800×510	
NA	
$169	

MULTIFUNCTION BOARDS

It is not coincidence that the Apple IIe and the IBM PC, the two most imitated personal computers, have what is known as open architecture. Open architecture means that the computer allows future expansion and the addition of capabilities that didn't even exist when it was designed. This is accomplished in the Apple IIe and IBM PC by providing expansion slots. Expansion slots are sockets inside the computer that can accept specially designed circuit boards. Expansion slots can accept and use any circuit board that conforms to their specifications; this can include boards that provide many different capabilities.

The most common types of expansion boards offer added memory, 80 columns of text (for the Apple II), or interfaces for printers, monitors, and disk drives. Because many people choose the same set of options, there are multifunction boards available that combine many capabilities on one expansion board.

There are several important considerations when shopping for expansion boards. First is whether or not you have room for it. Careful planning is important; if you have one slot available on your computer, don't fill it with a fancy option before you have all of the basics, like a printer and disk drive interface. If you fill all of your expansion slots, you have to give up boards in order to add new ones.

Prices may vary; shop for discount prices.

Another consideration is whether or not the rest of your system can take advantage of the new capability provided by an expansion board. A fancy graphics board won't do you any good if your monitor or software don't have the ability to create high resolution graphics. Likewise, additional RAM memory won't help you if your software can only use the memory you now have.

Since expansion boards get their electrical power from the computer's power supply, you must be careful not to overload the power supply by adding too many power-hungry boards. Each expansion board you buy will have a specified power requirement, and the sum of these power requirements should never be more than your computer's power supply is rated to handle. Another closely related problem is the heat generated by some boards; you may need to install a fan to keep them cool so they don't affect the computer's circuitry.

The following pages review many of the most popular and most powerful expansion boards. Try to find the multifunction board that combines the most features that you can use with your system.

QUADBOARD 512+
Quadram Corp.

Approx. Retail Price $895
Type..memory/serial port
Available for ....IBM PC and compatibles

The variety of combinations of functions available on multifunction boards is mind boggling. The Quad 512+ should be considered by those who need up to a half megabyte of expansion memory and a serial (RS–232C) port. Those needing clock/calendar features, parallel printer ports, game ports, and other options should look at other Quadram products or those offered by competitors.

This board is designed for those wanting to add up to 512K of expansion memory to their IBM PC and compatibles. There is a serial port that can be configured as COM 1 or COM 2. There isn't a 20 milli-amp current loop feature on the RS–232C port. Unless you plan to interface an old teletype machine, the 20 ma. RS–232C feature is not needed. Most contemporary PC products do not offer current loop circuitry. The Quad 512+ comes with software, making it possible to use all or part of the expansion memory for RAM disk or printer spooling functions.

As with all Quadram board products, the installation of the 512+ is simple, thanks in large measure to the quality of Quadram's documentation. Installation of this board should take less than ten minutes, unless you decide to add your own memory, in which case the process might take an additional ten or fifteen minutes.

Prices may vary; shop for discount prices.

We had no problems getting this product to perform as advertised. Unlike AST and some of its competitors, the software provided with this product did not include a way to clear (reset) memory above 544K. It is necessary to do this on IBM and IBM-compatible products that do not clear memory above that point. If you have an older IBM computer or a compatible that assumes no more than 544K of RAM, this may be a problem, unless you write or obtain your own memory clearing software.

Quadram's excellent 25-page manual is designed to fit in the IBM "Guide to Operations" binder. But there were some pages of addenda provided with this manual; we prefer manuals with the information where it belongs.

If you are looking for a simple way to add 512K of memory and an RS-232C port to your computer, you should consider the 512+. If you need other features such as a clock/calendar or game port, you should consider the Quadboard by Quadram instead, or one of the many competitive products available.

RATINGS:
Overall Value 8   Performance 9
Ease of Use 9   Documentation 9

QUADLINK
Quadram Corp.

Approx. Retail Price $680
Type ....Apple emulator
Available for ....IBM PC and compatibles

Quadlink lets you run Apple software on IBM computers. It is a "single board computer" that plugs into an expansion slot on the IBM PC and several of its clones. The PC's existing monitor, keyboard, speaker, disk drives, and power supply are used, making two computers out of one. You can switch back and forth between the Apple mode and the IBM mode using simple keyboard commands.

In the Apple mode your system simulates a 64K Apple II+ with 25 lines of 40 character, UPPERCASE only display. It does not simulate the newer IIe or IIc. Software for 80 character text is said to be in the works, but at this writing, we were not able to obtain a copy to test. Low and high resolution Apple graphics are provided. There is a game port just like the one on the Apple. Software is provided for converting Apple text files to IBM text files and back. There is also a disk speed test program. The "freeze" function makes it possible to stop Apple processing, then start later where you left off.

A graphics board is required in your IBM PC for Apple-like displays. Compaq owners need an *external* monitor and hard-to-find cables to use the Quadlink at all. Columbia users also need special cables.

Quadram publishes a list of Apple programs that work and won't work with the Quadlink. Consult the list or your dealer before purchasing a Quadlink for use with a particular Apple software package.

Prices may vary; shop for discount prices.

It took us 30 minutes to install the Quadlink in our IBM PC the first time, 5 minutes the second. Every board in the system must be removed. The cables make some tight turns. If you install a Quadlink in a Compaq, you need special cables and must take extra care. The Compaq speaker connection procedure is difficult. There are no instructions with the Compaq cables, and it is possible to install one of the connectors backward. For these reasons, you should consider having the Quadlink installed by someone with a technical background. This is particularly true if you own a Compaq.

Games may be the best excuse for adding a Quadlink to your PC. With the exception of half track copy protected disks, the games ran flawlessly. They sure look great on an RGB color monitor. You need an IBM graphics card and color monitor to take full advantage of the Apple graphics.

The freeze feature makes it possible to stop mid-game and start up again later. You could also stop a business program this way too, but this has less application.

The system flips into and out of the IBM mode easily. Because the Quadlink has its own memory on board, it is possible to have undisturbed IBM programs resident in the PC's memory while you use the Apple mode. The reverse is also true.

The Quadlink manual contains tutorial materials for new users and reference materials for techies. It contains complete, well-illustrated installation and operation tutorials, a section on Apple DOS, and several nice reference sections including specifications, problem solutions, memory maps, and a glossary of terms. There is even a list of suggested magazines and books.

RATINGS:

Overall Value	9	Performance	9
Ease of Use	9	Documentation	9

Information accurate at time of printing; subject to manufacturer's change.

SIXPAKPLUS
AST Research

Approx. Retail Price $395
Type ....memory/printer/communications/clock
Available for ....IBM PC and compatibles

Most IBM PC owners want to add additional memory, parallel printer ports, serial device ports, and a clock/calendar option to their computers. Expansion slots inside the PC make this possible. A number of vendors offer multifunction boards enabling you to add a variety of features to the PC while only using one expansion slot. AST Research is one of the most successful manufacturers of these products. The SixPakPlus is an excellent example of the reason for their success.

With this one board it is possible to add up to 384K of RAM, a parallel printer port, an RS–232C serial port, a clock/calendar, and an optional game port. Depending upon the age of your IBM PC it may be possible to use one of these boards to expand the system to 640K or more of RAM, although in many cases application's software can only use up to 512K of this RAM.

In addition to the hardware, AST Research provided a diskette containing software to run and set the clock, and to permit the use of some or all of the memory on the SixPakPlus board as a RAM disk and/or as a print spooling system. In RAM disk and print spooling applications, this software makes it possible to use more than 640K of system RAM. There is also software to reset memory above 544K so that false parity errors do not occur when using memory not reset by IBM's power-up routines. Few other vendors take the trouble to explain this problem let alone provide a simple, automatic solution.

Prices may vary; shop for discount prices.

The RS–232C port is very flexible. It is possible to force CTS, DSR, and DCD lines if necessary. The RS–232C port can also be disabled if you wish. There is no current loop feature on this serial port. The serial port can be configured as COM 1 or COM 2.

The parallel printer port can be configured as port LPT 1, 2, or 3. It is automatically configured as 1 or 2 based on the presence or absence of IBM's monochrome card with its own self-contained parallel port. This automatic assignment can be overridden. The parallel port feature and the other features on the AST system are compatible with IBM's diagnostic software.

The software used to set the clock/calendar is very easy to use. Additional software is provided that can be used to set the PC's internal clock at power-up. This eliminates the need to answer the "Time" and "Date" prompts when DOS is booted. This software can be run automatically from a batch file—AST shows you how.

The clock/calendar contains its own battery backup, making it possible for the system to keep time when the computer is turned off; the battery is only used when the computer's power is turned off. The clock runs with MS–DOS, CP/M 86, and CCP/M 86 software.

The RAM disk and print spooling software are very flexible and provide a number of options, all designed to speed the overall productivity of your computer system.

RATINGS:

Overall Value	10	Performance	10
Ease of Use	10	Documentation	10

ULTRATERM
Videx

Approx. Retail Price $379
Type ....80 column display
Available for ....Apple bus

A number of companies have made a nice living overcoming the Apple II family's 40 column display limitation. The Ultraterm card may just be the "ultimate" answer.

This plug in board provides Apple II, II+, and IIe users with a variety of screen formats. It offers 7×9 and 9×16 character sets. Characters can be displayed in standard or inverse video and it is possible to vary the brightness of characters displayed. Block graphics and line drawing utilities are also provided on this card.

A wide variety of characters per line and lines per screen are offered. In addition to the standard 24 lines of 40 characters, 8 other options are provided, including a maximum of 160 characters on 24 lines. This mode is extremely useful for displaying spreadsheets and other wide documents.

There are optional character sets offered in ROMs. They are most frequently used for the display of foreign characters. UK, German, French, Italian, Swedish, and Spanish fonts are offered.

Installation of Ultraterm is quite easy and should take less than two minutes. The board is inserted into an empty slot inside the Apple and one other simple connection is made using a cable that is provided with the Ultraterm board.

Prices may vary; shop for discount prices.

It is very important to use a good, wide band width monitor with reasonable character persistence. In order to faithfully display 132 characters per line, a 15 Mhz band width is necessary. In order to display 160 characters per line (the maximum) a 20 Mhz band width monitor will probably be required.

As with most monitor boards that increase the capability of the Apple display system, the Ultraterm may not be compatible with all existing Apple software. For this reason, a number of pre-boot disks are available from Videx for many software packages. These pre-boot packages may simply improve the performance of the software itself (making it possible to display more columns, for example), or they can be used to make the software function with the Ultraterm card. If you are in doubt about the compatibility of the Ultraterm with your hardware or monitor, you may want to contact the helpful people at Videx, prior to purchasing the board.

The documentation is well done. There is an overview, a table of contents, an index, a glossary, and even schematics for technical people. There is a chapter on customizing the board and software for unusual applications. This manual is full of helpful hints for both novices and serious computerists.

The name fits the board. This may be the ultimate video control board for the Apple II family.

RATINGS:

Overall Value 10	Performance 10
Ease of Use................ 9	Documentation 10

PRINTERS

The choice of the right printer for your system can be very important, especially if you use your computer for business correspondence, reports, or presentations. Thirty popular printers and plotters are reviewed in this chapter.

There are many types of printers and plotters to choose from. In the past, printers have been described as being either letter-quality or dot matrix models. Letter-quality printers produce characters that look very much like those produced by a typewriter; this type is usually suitable for any use. Dot matrix printers produce characters that are made up of patterns of small dots. These characters are not as clear and sharp as letter-quality characters, so dot matrix print is unsuitable for some types of work. The advantage to dot matrix printers is that they are usually cheaper and can print graphics.

The distinction between dot matrix and letter-quality printers is not as clear as it once was, however. There are now several dot matrix printers available that can produce letter-quality type, and some letter-quality printers now have graphics capability. A better way to categorize printers is by the print mechanism, or the way that the printer puts the characters on paper. The most common print mechanisms are daisywheel, dot matrix impact, ink jet, and thermal dot matrix.

Daisywheel printers use a spoked wheel (the daisy wheel) that has a character on the end of each spoke. The wheel rotates to bring the proper character into position, and then the character strikes a ribbon against the paper. This process produces crisp, clear letter-quality type.

By far the most popular printers on the market today are dot matrix impact printers. These printers use a vertical row of needle-like pins that individually strike against the ribbon to produce characters. This approach produces poorer quality type than the daisy wheel, but it can be used to draw graphics.

Another type of printer is the ink jet. These printers produce characters and graphics that are made up of dots, but they do it without touching the paper; a small nozzle sprays tiny drops of ink onto the paper to create the dots. Because nothing hits the paper, these printers are extremely quiet and fast.

Thermal dot matrix printers are an inexpensive alternative to dot matrix impact printers. They use a technique that scorches the dots onto specially treated paper. These printers often sell for under $200.

Regardless of which type of printer you choose, it's a good idea to get a look at the output before you buy. There are varying degrees of print quality among each of the printer types just mentioned.

ALPHACOM 81
Alphacom, Inc.

Approx. Retail Price ..$170
Print Type......................
.........Thermal Dot Matrix
Interface ..serial or parallel
Speed ....80 cps

Thermal printers are generally looked down upon by computer users, and for no good reason. It's true that thermal printers can't produce the same crisp characters that dot matrix or daisy wheel units can, but they provide a low-cost alternative for text and graphics printing. One good thermal printer is the Alphacom 81, an 80-column thermal printer that costs just $170.

The Alphacom 81 is very quiet in operation; in fact, you can hardly hear it as its printhead skims the specially coated paper from side to side. Like all other thermal printers, the 81 uses specially treated roll paper. The paper the 81 uses, however, is off-white, not silver as in some other thermal printers. This provides for good contrast and more pleasing printouts.

The 81 prints at 80 characters per second, or about the same speed as a moderate-cost dot matrix printer. And like a dot matrix printer, characters are formed by a series of dots. Graphics are produced one dot-line at a time, which is very slow, but the graphics resolution is much better than you'd expect in such an inexpensive package.

196

Alphacom has taken a unique approach in packaging the 81. The printer comes with an interface cable adapter for a specific computer. The cable not only serves to connect the 81 to the computer, but allows special print functions as well. Alphacom also makes all-purpose cables/adapters for standard RS–232C serial, Centronics-type parallel, and IEEE-488 parallel ports.

The main disadvantage of the Alphacom 81 is common to many thermal printers: The 81 requires the use of specially coated paper. This paper is quite expensive; if you do a lot of printing, you should stay away from a thermal printer.

For its price, though, the Alphacom 81 thermal printer can't be beat. When moderate quality print is acceptable, the 81 is a perfect choice. The unit is available with adapters for specific popular computers.

RATINGS:
Overall Value 9   Performance 6
Ease of Use 8   Documentation 7

CGP–220 COLOR INK JET PRINTER
Tandy Corporation

Approx. Retail Price ..$699
Type..............color ink jet
Interface......serial/parallel

More and more computer users are turning to color printers. Ink jet printing technology has made low-cost color printing practical. The Radio Shack CGP–220 is an excellent, low-cost, color ink jet printer.

In the text mode, this printer creates 5×7 dot matrix characters on paper up to 8½ inches wide. In the color graphics mode, it prints up to 640 dots per line. By combining magenta, cyan, and yellow ink, it produces seven colors (red, yellow, green, cyan, blue, magenta, and violet). Color ink cartridges are easy to load and slip into the printer. Up to four million characters can be printed using one cartridge. Color cartridges cost about $15.00. Lower-cost, black ink cartridges are available for less than $10.00.

Special roll and sheet-fed ink jet paper is available. Radio Shack recommends the use of these products with the use of their printer. Regular paper may cause blurring and other quality problems. The roll paper is sold in three packs. Each package costs $9.95. The 8½×11-inch paper is sold in 250 sheet packages for $6.95, a little less than three cents per sheet. Both Centronics and Radio Shack color computer interfaces are provided. There is also a screen print utility used with the TRS 80 color computer to create multi-color print-outs of color screens produced from any graphics program run on the color computer. It is also possible to send color commands from most other computers using print statements.

Installation is very straightforward. Buyers are cautioned that they will need to purchase a separate cable for the ink jet printer—they range in price from less than $5 to nearly $40 depending on which Radio Shack computer you plan to interface.

We found the requirement to use roll and sheet paper slightly annoying. The printer is very quiet and provides color that is quite pleasing. We could find no way to disable the automatic line feed feature of this printer, but that may be a problem with software that always supplies its own line feeds. The cartridges were easy to load and use. This printer behaved quite well even after sitting for extended periods of time. We also noticed that the standard characters are higher than they are wide. There is a control code that can change these to characters that are more like those people are used to seeing on ink jet printers.

The documentation contains no index but is otherwise a good collection of instructions, containing everything needed to install, operate, maintain, and interface the printer. There are a number of technical appendixes with very complete and helpful information.

This is a fine, low-cost, color ink jet printer. Owners of non-Radio Shack computers should look at non-Radio Shack color ink jet printers as well.

RATINGS:

Overall Value	8	Performance	9
Ease of Use	8	Documentation	9

DAISYWRITER 2000
Computers International Inc.

Approx. Retail Price $1495
Type ....daisy wheel
Interface...serial/parallel

A number of printer manufacturers offer printers using the Brothers Daisywheel print mechanism and their own electronics. The Daisywriter 2000 is one of the best examples of this type of product.

This is a letter-quality, daisywheel printer that uses IBM selectric ribbons in easy-to-load cartridges. Twenty fonts are offered and in twenty-five languages. Both RS–232C and Centronics-style interfaces are standard. All that is needed to switch from RS–232C to Centronics is a different cable and some changes to front panel switch settings. The Daisywriter 2000 comes with a 16K internal buffer that can be expanded to 48K. One of the most unique features of the Daisywriter 2000 is its ability to emulate many different kinds of printers. Examples of printers emulated include NEC, Diablo, Qume, Epson, etc. It is possible to use the internal memory of the Daisywriter to repeat printing jobs. Pitches offered include 10, 12, 15, and proportional spacing. It is even possible to software select a 20 character per inch printing mode. The maximum characters per line varies with the pitch selection from a minimum of 132 characters to a maximum of 256 characters per line.

Installation is fairly complex due to the flexibility of this product. It is important to purchase the correct cable for the Daisywriter.

Ads for the Daisywriter 2000 lead users to believe that this is an extremely fast, productive printer. It is not. This printer is in the slow to medium speed, letter-quality printer range. It is not remarkably faster than any of the other Brothers-based products. There are some productivity advantages obtained through the use of unique logic on-board the printer, which speeds placement of the print head and movement of the paper in cases where white space is encountered, but overall, the printer is not remarkably faster than others. The type quality, however, is excellent. The emulation modes appear to work very well.

We found the forms tractor a necessity for feeding pin feed paper. Unfortunately, the tractor is difficult to install and remove. It is also unfortunate that the forms tractor cannot be left in place when sheet feeding is desired. These are minor flaws, however.

The documentation is a collection of typewritten, photocopied pages. There are several useful diagrams and charts. Nearly everything one needs to know to successfully interface this printer can be found in the documentation. First-time users may find it a little confusing. Considering the wide variety of features offered on this printer, the documentation could be slightly more complete, and better organized. There is no index and no table of contents.

If you are not in a big hurry, this is an excellent, low-cost printer.

RATINGS:

Overall Value ..., ...9	Performance 10
Ease of Use 8	Documentation 8

DP–6500
Anadex

Approx. Retail Price.................................$2995
Type ....dot matrix
Interface.................................serial/parallel

This is a very rugged printer. It is also very fast, versatile, easy to use and even relatively quiet, considering its capabilities. The DP–6500 is the best office printer we have ever tested.

The DP–6500 reaches speeds of up to 500 characters per second (roughly 200 lines per minute). Seven international character sets are available. Custom fonts can be downloaded from the host. Character printing in double width, bold, italic, shadow, enhanced, condensed, and proportional spacing can be selected, as can pitches of 10, 12, 15, and 16.4 characters per inch. Paper widths of up to 16 inches are possible.

The standard Anadex graphics modes (72×72 dots per square inch and 144×144 dots per square inch) are provided, an Epson compatible graphics option is available. It is even possible to order options like UPC and 39 bar code printing. Both Centronics-style parallel and RS–232C serial interfaces are standard. A 4K print buffer is standard. It can be expanded to 16K in 4K increments. Paper can be sheet-fed or tractor-fed (the optional forms tractor is great, it snaps on and off quickly). The printer weighs 55 pounds and is 29.5×18.4×8.9 inches. It needs a heavy-duty stand or desk. Chances are, if you need a feature, the Anadex DP–6500 has it.

Even in the high-speed (draft) mode the print quality is excellent. The multipass "correspondence modes" are first class. Ribbons are large and easy to change. There is a self-test mode, and an effective automatic

Prices may vary; shop for discount prices.

paper thickness setting feature. The DP–6500 is relatively quiet when compared to other high-speed office printers. Anadex claims a noise level of less than 60 dBA.

A loud beeper responds to every switch depression, and there is no way to turn it off. The automatic paper thickness setting feature smudges the paper. It is possible to cause the head to move under its own power when the cover is open, so it is a good idea to turn the power off before you reach inside to change ribbons, adjust rollers, etc. There is no lever for the bail bar, so sheet fed pages can be a little tricky if you intend to print near the top of the sheets. These are all minor problems, and worth putting up with if you need the other features offered on the DP–6500.

This is a fully featured printer, so installation may take an hour or two. The nontechnical user should consider having the dealer set up the printer. The only installation problem we experienced was a safety switch that needed adjustment. The manual's troubleshooting section helped us find it right away.

The 100-plus-page typeset, bound manual is complete, easy to read and helpful. There are plenty of photos, diagrams, and quick reference charts. It contains the phone number for a customer hotline that is answered quickly by helpful, informed people.

The DP–6500 is well worth its hefty $2,995 retail price. If you do a lot of printing, or if you are always in a hurry, take a close look at this printer.

RATINGS:

Overall Value	9	Performance	10
Ease of Use	7	Documentation	10

DYNAX DX–15
Dynax, Inc.

Approx. Retail Price	$599
Type	daisy wheel
Interface	serial/parallel

There is a flood of low-cost, low-speed, letter-quality daisywheel printers. We think the Dynax DX–15 is one of the best.

The DX–15 is available with a choice of serial or parallel interfaces. Its rated speed is 13 characters per second. Proportional spacing, 10, 12, and 15 pitch modes are offered. There is a cassette-style black ribbon with an optional red spool ribbon making two color printing possible. The DX–15 has a 13.5 inch wide inch platten, however, there is only an 11-inch printing area. The maximum number of characters per line in the 15 cpi is 165 characters. There is a 3000 character buffer, which can be expanded to about 5000 characters. Optional forms tractors and cut sheet feeders are available.

Features include the ability to underline, bold print, strike-over (for legal work), and shadow print. A variety of daisywheels are available. They have 96 petals and are encased in a cassette to minimize the possibility of damage. American English, UK English, German, French, American Spanish, Dutch, S. Spanish, Italian, Canadian, Portuguese, and other print wheels are available.

There is an optional forms tractor and sheet feeder. Both of these options are restricted to 11-inch paper. The internal 3K buffer is used to free up the computer, and it is also possible to use this buffer for making multiple copies of the same document. There are color-coded operating buttons and indicator lights for on-line alarm and power indication. There is also an

Prices may vary; shop for discount prices.

audio trouble alarm. The left-handed platten knob will please left-handed operators.

This is a fairly easy printer to install. DIP switches are used to select language, page length, skip features, and serial configuration when appropriate. No cable is provided with the DX–15. You will either need to purchase one or make your own. Since you may find the documentation inadequate for cable-making tasks, you should consider purchasing a tested cable from a dealer.

The documentation for this product is fair to good. It is a reasonable translation from Japanese. There are many fine photographs, diagrams, and charts that make the text almost unimportant. There is plenty of meat for technical users, but novices will also find it helpful.

This is a slow printer. The characters are clear and crisp, and since both single and multistrike mylar ribbons are available, the quality is difficult to beat. The fabric ribbons work fine for draft printing as well. We found the printer to be fairly quiet in our tests and all features performed as advertised.

This is an excellent letter-quality printer if you don't mind lack of speed and mediocre documentation. If you purchase the DX–15, be certain to have the dealer show you how to operate and install it.

RATINGS:

Overall Value	10	Performance	9
Ease of Use	9	Documentation	8

GEMINI 10X DOT MATRIX PRINTER
Star Micronics, Inc.

Approx. Retail Price ..$399
Type ....dot matrix
Interface......serial/parallel

The Gemini 10X is one of the most fully featured, low-cost dot matrix printers available. That may be one reason for its popularity. Its simple operation and excellent documentation have no doubt added to the printer's success.

The Gemini 10X prints at 120 characters per second, comes with a built-in adjustable tractor feed, has a parallel or (optional) serial interface and is shipped with an 816 byte buffer that can be expanded to 8K. Bi-directional, logic-seeking printing is standard. It prints superscripts, subscripts, 9×9 dot matrix characters with true descenders, and provides three graphics modes: 62×72, 120×144, and 240×144. There are 96 standard characters available, along with italic and six international fonts. Pitches offered include 10, 12, and 17 cpi. Maximum characters per line are 80 to 136, depending upon the font selected. It is possible to download special fonts. There is a self-test mode. The printer supports software selectable tabs. Variable vertical line spacing is programmable. The minimum paper size is three inches, the maximum is ten inches. The manufacturer claims the printer can make up to three acceptable carbon or carbonless copies. A roll paper holder is provided at no extra cost. The replace-able printhead is rated at 100 million characters. Ribbons can be reversed (flipped) to double their life.

Installation was quite simple considering the variety of options on this printer. Everything except the necessary cable is provided.

We found changing the typewriter-style spool ribbons slightly messy, particularly when compared with many of the popular cartridge changing schemes in use today. Otherwise the printer performed flawlessly with a noise level similar to that of other printers in this speed category.

This is an excellent 266-page manual using down-to-earth descriptions of the printer concepts with few of the buzz words that frequently confuse first-time users. There is a helpful index and interfacing notes for Apple, Atari, Commodore, IBM, Osborne, and Radio Shack computer owners. Star even provides listings of sample programs to demonstrate the various features and interfacing techniques available on this printer. Ample diagrams, charts, and photos illustrate most sections of the spiral-bound manual. Three or four pages of the manual are devoted to each particular computer interface. This is one of the few universal printers that even a novice could quickly connect, configure, and use without technical help, due to the manual's excellence.

This printer is an exceptional value. You will not find more features for this price anywhere. If you don't mind messy ribbon changes, and are looking for a low-cost printer, this is it.

RATINGS:

Overall Value	10	Performance	8
Ease of Use	8	Documentation	10

HP2225C THINKJET
Hewlett-Packard Company

Approx. Retail Price ..$495
Type ....ink jet
Interface..............parallel

As the name implies, ink jet printers spray droplets of ink onto surfaces to create characters and/or graphics. HP's Thinkjet products are no-nonsense office printers for microcomputer users. The one we tested weighs less than six pounds, is 11.5 inches wide, and only 8.1 inches deep. It is also very quiet.

Paper widths of up to 9.5 inches can be accommodated. Both sheet and continuous paper feeding is possible. The paper feed pins are not really adjustable, so you will not be able to pin feed continuous labels, Rolodex cards, and other narrow stocks. Also, like all ink jet printers, the Thinkjet uses a nonimpact technology, so you will not be able to use multipart (carbon and carbonless) forms.

The Thinkjet's ink and nozzle cartridge assembly is disposable. Replacements sell for $7.95, and last for about 500 pages of text, according to HP. They snap in and out easily.

There is no platen knob, and no "official" way to move paper backward. The line feed button moves paper up, but not back. If you accidentally feed past the per-

Prices may vary; shop for discount prices.

foration you must waste the sheet, or remove the paper, or break a rule in the manual. You are not supposed to force the paper feed mechanism by hand.

Ink jet printers work best with specially finished paper that accelerates drying and minimizes ink bleeding, the causes of fuzzy and smeared looking characters. The Thinkjet comes with a sample package of this paper; HP dealers sell it by the carton. It does make a considerable difference in print quality—we found the print quality on regular paper to be lighter than that on the HP stock. We experienced more smearing on standard paper, too. It is annoying to write on the HP Thinkjet paper with felt markers. This type of ink spreads rapidly, and soaks through to pages below. Ball-point pens and pencils work fine.

Order plenty of extra ink cartridges. The same is true of the special paper—if you decide you need it.

Although the printer takes 9½-inch paper, it only prints lines that are about 6½ inches long. This makes for "mandatory" one inch (minimum) left and right margins. Characters printed in the condensed mode will be very small, no surprise when you consider that 142 of them fit on one 6½ inch line.

The HP printer comes with superb documentation. There are clear, well-labeled photos, great diagrams, and a complete index. The writing style is crisp and professional, and there are code charts for the technically inclined.

RATINGS:

Overall Value 10	Performance 10
Ease of Use 10	Documentation 10

LQ–1500 DOT MATRIX PRINTER
Epson America, Inc.

Approx. Retail Price .$1490
Type ....dot matrix
Interface..............parallel

Epson may be one of the largest manufacturers of dot matrix print mechanisms in the world. Besides selling their own popular line of printers, they provide IBM with its dot matrix printer for the IBM personal computers. The LQ–1500 is Epson's latest entry into the "correspondence quality" dot matrix printer war.

The LQ–1500 prints on 4- to 16-inch wide paper with its optional bi-directional forms tractor, or on cut sheets ranging from 7 to 14 inches in width with its optional, automatic, single or dual bin cut sheet feeders. An upright paper guide improved the manual loading of sheet paper, too. The 24 pin dot matrix print head provides a wide variety of beautiful 96 character ASCII type faces and 11 different international character sets. They offer 9×17, 15×17, and 37×17 matrices.

A variety of bit image dot matrix graphics modes are available as well, including a 2448×24 dots per line mode. Normal, enlarged, condensed, condensed-enlarged, elite, elite-enlarged, elite-condensed, proportional, and proportional-enlarged printing sizes are offered. This provides a range of 5 to 20 characters per

Prices may vary; shop for discount prices.

inch, and up to 272 characters per line. Double strike, italic, and underlining are all standard; superscripts and subscripts are supported. It is possible to download your own 128 character font sets. Cartridge ribbons are used.

Bi-directional, logic-seeking printing is standard in the text mode, the graphics modes utilize uni-directional printing. Variable line spacing is standard in $1/180$ of an inch increments.

Everything should take between 15 minutes and half an hour at the most to install. It is important to understand that printer cables and interfaces must be ordered separately for this product.

We found the quality modes slightly less pleasing on the LQ–1500 than on some of its competitors. The edges of the characters appear to be slightly more ragged than those on the Toshiba P1340, for example.

Nonetheless, this is a quiet, capable printer. It is very flexible and offers outstanding graphics capabilities. The plastic sheet feeding paper guide is a very useful attachment. It is easy to switch fonts and modes while printing via software commands.

The LQ–1500 offers above-average quality and performance, at a price comparable to its closest competitors. Be certain that the price quotes you get include the interface and cable required to make it work. If you are considering this printer primarily for its high-quality printing mode, be sure to compare the output from it to that offered by its competitors.

RATINGS:

Overall Value	7	Performance	7
Ease of Use	8	Documentation	9

ML 92
Okidata Corp.

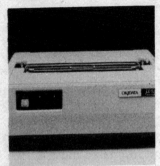

Approx. Retail Price ..$699
Type ....dot matrix
Interface......serial/parallel

Those in the know rate the ML 92 as one of the best values in the crowded printer market. Okidata is a large Japanese electronics manufacturer with a well-earned reputation for quality products, reliable designs, and helpful technical people based here in the United States to answer your questions. When looking for a printer, you should be sure to see the Okidata ML 92.

This is a 160 character per second printer with a 40 character per second dual pass mode. Switches on the front select forms length, top of form setting, forms feed, and line feed. The 9×9 dot matrix characters are formed with true descenders. There is a 96 ASCII character font set with an alternate set available. And 10, 12, and 17 pitch printing is offered, providing 80 to 136 characters per line. True superscripts and subscripts are standard. The printer underscores, supports tabs, and has bi-directional, logic-seeking printing. There is a standard 2000 character buffer that can be expanded to 4K. The ML 92 can friction feed 8.5-inch sheets and pin-feed stock from 2 inches to 9.5 inches wide can be handled with the optional forms tractor. A roll paper stand is available. There is a self-test mode. For those

Prices may vary; shop for discount prices.

needing complete IBM or Apple graphics compatibility, plug 'n play "personality ROMs" are available for IBM and Apple printer emulation.

Installation is quite straightforward, although the case does need to be removed to accomplish DIP switch settings. Since this is normally done only once, it is not a terrible inconvenience.

The dual pass, quality mode on this printer is among the best we have seen. It is better than dual pass modes we have seen on printers costing two to three times as much as the ML 92. The draft mode is excellent as well. The unusual draft typeface is much easier to read than many other fonts found on similarly priced dot matrix printers. This is a very reliably built machine. You will find metal in places where most other printers are made of plastic; there is considerable attention to detail. Unfortunately, we found the printer slightly noisier than other printers in its class, and ribbon changing can be messy since spool ribbons are used.

The ML 92 comes with a fine, clearly written manual. Rather than bombarding first-time users with buzz words, printer concepts are explained clearly in lay terms. There are tip sheets available for typical installation and operation problems.

This is one of eight Okidata models. We feel it may be a better buy than the comparable Epson unit. If you are looking for a good, heavy-duty dot matrix printer, you should consider the Okidata family.

RATINGS:

Overall Value	10	Performance	10
Ease of Use	9	Documentation	10

SPIRIT 80
Mannesmann-Tally

Approx. Retail Price ..$399
Type ....dot matrix
Interface......serial/parallel

Mannesmann-Tally is not as well known as Epson and some of the other popular printer manufacturers. But in many ways, their products offer superior performance and value when compared to those of most competitors, and the Spirit 80 is a perfect example of that.

This low-cost, dot matrix printer contains unique, overlapping square hammers in the print head for better horizontal and vertical line creation. It creates beautiful 9×8 characters using a snap-in, mylar ribbon cartridge. The mylar cartridges give blacker, sharper images than do fabric ribbons. The Spirit 80 offers bi-directional printing, dot addressable graphics, and Epson-compatible printer control codes. Friction feed and tractor feed are both standard. The maximum paper width accepted is 10 inches, the minimum 2½ inches. Pica and elite fonts are standard. Boldface, italic, superscript, and subscript printing are included. Underlining is also possible.

There is an optional "quiet pack" that further reduces the sound from this already quiet printer. The quiet pack sells for about $38.00. The only other two options available are an RS–232C interface ($98), and a roll paper holder. With the exception of a cable, everything else on this printer is standard.

Considering its performance, we found this to be an unusually small, nice looking printer as well. Its 80 character per second speed is acceptable for many business applications.

This printer is very simple to install. Even the optional quiet pack (consisting of foam rubber, a new cover, and other items) is also easy to install. It was up and running in less than 15 minutes. As is usually the case with printers these days, you will need to purchase or make a cable to interface the printer with the computer.

The first thing you notice with this printer is the quality of its output, and it is actually very quiet as well. We found the sheet tearing feature somewhat awkward, and except when we used it right on paper perforations, we had trouble getting a clean sheet break. The graphics modes are compatible with those offered by Epson. Overall, this printer performs beautifully.

There was plenty of attention paid to detail in the manual, right down to full-size outlines of the foam pieces needed for the quiet pack. This prevents any confusion when identifying and installing these small items. Diagrams, photos, and other technical information is complete and well organized.

This is one of those printers that will be as comfortable at home as it is at the office. Its low cost and excellent quality make it a true value.

RATINGS:

Overall Value	10	Performance	10
Ease of Use	9	Documentation	10

	Alphacom 81	**Bytewriter Praxis 35**
Manufacturer	Alphacom, Inc.	Bytewriter
Print Type	thermal dot matrix	typewriter
Speed	80 cps	12 cps
Paper Feed Mechanism	NA	NA
Interface	RS–232C serial, Centronics parallel, IEEE–488 parallel, and cables for specific computers	NA
Graphics	dot matrix, printed one dot-row at a time	none
Approx. Price	$170	$500
Other Features	requires specially treated off-white paper	can be used as a standard typewriter as well as a printer

Canon A–1210	CGP–220 Color Ink Jet	DMP–110 Dot Matrix
Canon USA, Inc.	Radio Shack	Radio Shack
color ink jet	color ink jet	dot matrix
40 cps	37 cps	25 cps or 50 cps
friction feed, requires roll paper	friction feed	tractor feed
Centronics parallel	serial or parallel	serial or parallel
dot matrix, 80 dots per inch	dot matrix, 640 dots per line	dot matrix, 960 dots per line
$795	$699	$399
provides seven colors: yellow, blue, red, green, cyan, magenta, black	seven colors: yellow, violet, red, green, cyan, magenta, black	mono- or proportional spacing

	DP-6500 Dot Matrix	DTC Style Writer
Manufacturer	Anadex, Inc.	Data Terminals and Communications
Print Type	dot matrix	daisy wheel
Speed	100–540 cps	10–32 cps
Paper Feed Mechanism	friction feed or tractor feed	friction feed
Interface	serial or parallel	Centronics parallel
Graphics	dot matrix, two resolutions provided	limited to vertical and horizontal lines
Approx. Price	$2995	$899
Other Features	multimode, alternate character sets	two colors (red and black), 35K spooling buffer

Prices may vary; shop for discount prices.

DX–15 Daisy Wheel	Daisywriter 2000	Epson FX–80
Dynax, Inc.	Computers International	Epson America, Inc.
daisy wheel	daisy wheel	dot matrix
13 cps	40 cps	160 cps
friction feed	friction feed or tractor feed	friction feed and tractor feed
serial or parallel	RS–232 serial or Centronics parallel	RS–232C serial, Centronics parallel, IEEE–488 parallel
none	none	dot matrix or graphics characters
$599	$1495	$699
3000 character printer buffer	16,000 character printer buffer	definable characters, reverse line feed

	Epson MX–80	Epson RX–80
Manufacturer	Epson America, Inc.	Epson America, Inc.
Print Type	dot matrix	dot matrix
Speed	80 cps	100 cps
Paper Feed Mechanism	tractor feed	tractor feed
Interface	parallel	parallel
Graphics	dot matrix	dot matrix, 240 dots per horizontal inch, 216 dots per vertical inch
Approx. Price	NA	$399
Other Features	supported by many software packages	alternate character sets, quiet printing mode

Prices may vary; shop for discount prices.

Gemini 10X	HP 2225C ThinkJet	HP 7475A Graphics Plotter
Star Micronics, Inc.	Hewlett-Packard	Hewlett-Packard
dot matrix	ink jet	six pen plotter
100 cps	150 cps	15 inches per second
tractor feed or friction feed	tractor feed	friction feed
RS–232C serial or Centronics parallel	parallel	RS–232C serial
dot matrix, 240×144	dot matrix, 96 dots per inch in both directions	color line graphics
$399	$495	$1895
functions exactly like the Epson MX–80	foreign character sets	compatible with many popular software packages

	Imagewriter Printer	**Inforunner Riteman**
Manufacturer	Apple Computer, Inc.	Inforunner
Print Type	dot matrix	dot matrix
Speed	120 cps	120 cps
Paper Feed Mechanism	tractor feed or friction feed	tractor feed or friction feed
Interface	parallel	parallel or serial
Graphics	dot matrix	dot matrix, 72 dots per vertical inch, and 60, 72, or 120 dots per horizontal inch
Approx. Price	$695	$399
Other Features	foreign character sets, proportional spacing	

LQ1500 Dot Matrix	ML92 Dot Matrix	P1340 Dot Matrix
Epson America, Inc.	Okidata Corporation	Toshiba America, Inc.
dot matrix	dot matrix	dot matrix
67–200 cps	40 cps or 160 cps	54 cps or 112 cps
friction feed or tractor feed	friction feed or tractor feed	friction feed or tractor feed
serial, parallel, or IEEE–488	serial or parallel	NA
2448 dots per line	NA	180 dots per inch in each direction
$1490 (parallel)	$699 parallel $799 serial	NA
many different typefaces	IBM and Apple emulation ROMs available	letter quality proportional spaced mode available

	Smith–Corona TP–1	Spinwriter 2000
Manufacturer	SCM Corporation	NEC Information Systems
Print Type	daisy wheel	thimble
Speed	12 cps	20 cps
Paper Feed	friction feed	tractor feed or friction feed
Interface	RS–232C serial or Centronics parallel	parallel
Graphics	none	none
Approx. Price	$595	$995
Other Features	uses Typetronic typewriter ribbons	wide variety of typefaces available

Prices may vary; shop for discount prices.

Spirit 80	TI855 Dot Matrix	Watanabe MP1000 Plotter
Mannesmann Tally Corporation	Texas Instruments, Inc.	Western Graphtec
dot matrix	dot matrix	six pen plotter
80 cps	160 cps	6 inches per second
tractor feed or friction feed	tractor feed or friction feed	friction feed
serial or parallel	RS–232C serial	RS–232C serial
dot matrix	dot matrix	color line graphics
$399	$995	$1190
Epson compatible	interchangeable font cartridges	optional metal nib pens

MISCELLANEOUS

This chapter covers many useful and unusual peripherals that can answer specific needs you may have. Even if you don't think you need any more peripherals, a quick look through these reviews will give you a good idea of the variety that is available.

If you need to use the same peripheral with more than one computer, take a look at the AMPS–25 ASCII Switch review. This is a device that allows up to four computers to share a printer or other output device. It has built-in circuitry that monitors the computers to see which one needs to use the peripheral next, so that you don't even need to manually switch anything when a different computer begins printing.

Another interesting product is the Kodak CRT Camera System. It creates instant prints or 35mm slides from the images on your computer display. This is a boon for anyone who has to prepare presentations and slide shows from data stored on a personal computer.

The Helix PC Bubble Disk is a 512K bubble memory for the IBM PC. Bubble memory is very fast (like RAM), but it retains information when the power is turned off. A bubble memory can greatly speed up execution of programs that do a lot of reading and writing on a floppy disk.

The KB 5151 Professional Keyboard is also reviewed here. It is one of the most popular after-market keyboards for the IBM PC and compatibles. The standard IBM PC has an unusual layout that frustrates experienced typists, but the KB 5151 is more like a regular electric typewriter. This can greatly increase your typing speed while using the IBM.

Prices may vary; shop for discount prices.

Another good add-on product for your personal computer is an uninterruptible power supply. As reliable as they are, power companies do sometimes have problems. And if the power fails while your computer is updating a directory track, you could lose all of the data stored on a floppy or hard disk. Two uninterruptible power supplies are reviewed here, the Topaz and the Datashield. These units will keep your computer up and running even during a power failure.

Several graphics tablets (or touch tablets) are also reviewed in this section. These devices allow you to enter graphics information by drawing on a tablet. With a graphics tablet, entering graphics can be fun; with a keyboard, this chore is usually tedious.

These are only a few examples of the types of peripherals covered in this chapter. As you can see, there are many ways to improve the versatility and performance of your personal computer by adding peripherals.

ASCII SWITCH MODEL AMPS–25
Advanced Systems Concepts, Inc.

Approx. Retail Price $540
Type ....RS-232 switch
Available for ....IBM PC and compatibles

Frequently computer users with RS–232C (serial) devices want to share them with more than one computer. For example, expensive modems, plotters, or printers can be used by many computers in an organization. One way to share these resources is through RS–232C switching arrangements. They permit a number of computers to be hooked to the same peripheral. Some switches are simple manual devices. Others are electronic in nature and offer a variety of sophisticated features. The Advanced Systems Concepts Model AMPS–25 is an example of one of the more sophisticated switches offered today.

This switch accepts inputs from up to four different devices (typically computers) and selectively sends the output from one of those computers at a time to the device being shared (a modem, plotter, or printer, for instance). Unlike manual switching arrangements, this appraoch permits computer users to send information from their computer without manually switching the switches. The Advance Systems Concepts' box "watches" its four inputs for requests to use the shared device. These requests are sent by the user over the same RS–232C cable used to send the data. If the shared device is not already in use, the switch box connects the requesting user to the shared device. If, after a specific period of time, no more data is sent from the current user, the ASCI switch "times out" the device, freeing up the shared peripheral for use by other users in the system.

The ASCII Switch contains front panel controls that make it possible to override the remote seizure of the shared device. Light-emitting diodes on the front panel show which user has control of the shared peripheral.

The ASCI switch operates at any one of eight different switch selectable BAUD rates from 150 bps to 19,200 bps. Normally all devices in the system must be set to the same speed.

Those experienced with RS–232C device installation will have little or no trouble setting up the ASCI switch. Novices may find themselves troubled by the "nonstandard" standards surrounding the RS–232C interface.

This manual is a small, no-nonsense, typewritten, photocopied document. It contains several useful diagrams and some operational and troubleshooting tips. Technical users will have no problem getting the system running with this documentation. Novice computer users may need some help. Knowledge of the RS–232C interface standard and its quirks is very helpful, since the manual does not spend much time dealing with these subjects.

We found the performance of this product to be fine under most circumstances. It is difficult or impossible to mix devices of different BAUD rates with this switch, something that can be an annoyance if the shared device is a multispeed modem, for instance.

The AMPS–25 deserves your consideration, particularly if you work in a multicomputer environment.

RATINGS:

Overall Value	9	Performance	9
Ease of Use	8	Documentation	7

ATARI TOUCH TABLET
Atari, Inc.

Approx. Retail Price .... NA
Type ....touch tablet
Available for ....IBM PC and compatibles

The Atari Touch Tablet is similar to the Koala Pad. Both have powerful software included in the price and both have small drawing surfaces. However, the Atari Touch Tablet may be somewhat superior for the Atari computers since the program comes on cartridge, and provides some slightly different features (including "rainbow" for creating a moving rainbow pattern in place of a solid color). Also, the Atari system uses a pen with a built-in pushbutton that allows you to save what you're drawing.

RATINGS:
Overall Value.................9 Performance.................9
Ease of Use....................10 Documentation............8

CRT CAMERA SYSTEM
Eastman Kodak Co.

Approx. Retail Price $190
Type..color copier
Available for ....IBM PC and compatibles

The Kodak Instagraphic CRT Imaging Outfit is one of a growing number of low-cost ways to make color photographic copies of computer displays. It creates instant prints or 35mm slides from images on your computer display in regular room light.

This is a complete, inexpensive package for photographing images from CRT's with *diagonal* measurements of 12 to 13 inches. The cone shuts out room light making it possible to shoot without turning out the lights.

The kit contains a light shielding hood; small rubber bumpers; an assortment of brackets; foam strips; spacers; an Instagraphic camera (with closeup lens installed); two packs of Instagraphic color print film; a Wrattan gelatin filter; a cable release; a carrying strap; 12 pages of instructions; a stick-on, quick reference guide, and a business reply card offering an article reprint on computer-generated slides.

Actual installation will vary depending on the design of your monitor and other considerations. Some monitors have recessed CRTs to minimize glare, others have knobs and switches located close to the screen, and others have automatic illumination sensors that must be dealt with. Even the thickness of the display's glass has an effect. In order to obtain properly focused images, the distance between the CRT's phospor dots and the camera's focal plane must fall within acceptable ranges. Moreover, side-to-side and up-and-down hood positioning must be correct.

The brackets, bumpers, and foam spacers are used for these adjustments. "Systematic" trial and error is required. You simply install bumpers, cut some foam, try a shot, cut or add some more foam, shoot again, etc. In extreme cases, according to Kodak, you may need to use "a small coping saw" to modify the hood. Once you have installed the proper foam spacers, bumpers, and brackets you will not need to adjust them again unless you change monitors.

The instant prints lack some of the snap and definition seen on the RGB monitor, and there is color shift. In some cases the images from the cheaper Commodore monitor looked better than those from the more expensive RGB display. Overall the results are pleasing enough though, and usable for most applications. Color slides look better than the instant prints.

Once the setup is complete, "aim and shoot" is all there is to it. Because the instant prints emerge from the bottom of the camera they may hit the table or keyboard on their way out. You may need to raise the monitor or move it to the edge of the desk if this is a problem.

Kodak provides a simple, comprehensive, 12-page instruction manual. There are 14 diagrams and many helpful hints. It is very well done. We couldn't find any phone numbers listed anywhere in the Kodak documentation. Users with problems are advised to "contact a dealer in Kodak audiovisual products listed in the Yellow Pages."

It is always a pleasure to find products that work, are carefully designed, documented, and packaged. This is one.

RATINGS:

Overall Value	10	Performance	9
Ease of Use	9	Documentation	10

Prices may vary; shop for discount prices.

HELIX PC BUBBLE DISK
Helix Laboratories, Inc.

Approx. Retail Price $1495
Type ....bubble memory
Available for ....IBM PC and compatibles

The random access memory (RAM) in most popular personal computers can only store information when the computer's power is turned on. Removal of the power, even for an instant, causes the computer to lose stored information. Floppy diskettes and hard disks are the most popular ways to store information when computers are turned off. New technologies, including bubble memory, offer an alternative.

The Helix board holds half a megabyte of bubble memory for the IBM PC. It is formatted as a fixed disk. It is nonvolatile, and can't lose data during power interruptions. It has no moving parts, and is maintenance free. MTBF is up to 180,000 hours of continuous use. The board is immune to dust, dirt, humidity, and temperature extremes. It can withstand vibration and shock up to 200 G's. There is built-in error checking and correction plus power-failure protection circuitry.

The board can plug into any available I/O card slot requiring no hardware or software modifications. It is expandable to 2 megabytes in half megabyte intervals, while appearing as a single drive to the operating system. A rear-mounted write-protect switch is provided.

The silent board operates up to 8 times faster than a floppy disk. It can be moved to another PC for file transfers.

The bubble memory board operates programs supporting floppy and hard disks. It has special hard disk commands and partitioning to hold multiple operating systems, including PC–DOS 2.0, Softech Pascal IV.13, and CP/M–86. Special hard disk commands such as RESTORE and BACKUP as well as partitioning are available to the user.

Helix bubble memory expansion boards are available for the Apple II and IIe as well.

Installation is quite simple. The board is plugged into any available empty slot. A driver file called "bubble" may need to be added to the boot disk on older IBM systems. The Helix board comes from the factory with jumpers preset for most applications. It is possible to partition the disk for more than one operating system. Once installed, the board must be initialized as though it was a small hard disk. Users with newer PCs can configure the board so that the system boots from the bubble memory.

The board performs as advertised. Database searches that took 68 seconds on a floppy disk took about 20 seconds using the bubble memory. Sorts that took 180 seconds on a floppy took about 60 seconds when using the bubble board. We never experienced any data loss even when power was removed while the board was being updated.

A 20-page user's manual accompanies this product. It is quite technical, but contains complete installation, partitioning, jumper options, and appendixes sections. Much of this manual will be confusing to first-time users who may want to have the board installed and formatted by a competent dealer.

RATINGS:

Overall Value	8	Performance	10
Ease of Use	10	Documentation	8

234

KB 5151 PROFESSIONAL IBM PC KEYBOARD
Key Tronic

Approx. Retail Price $255
Type...keyboard
Available for ....IBM PC and compatibles

The nonstandard layout of the IBM PC keyboard frustrates many touch typists, and others familiar with standard selectric keyboards. The most noticeable changes for many people are the locations of the shift keys and the labeling of the tab and return keys. Companies like Key Tronic market keyboards with standard key locations and labels. These keyboards can be purchased as replacements for your IBM PC, or can be ordered in place of the regular keyboard when you purchase your PC from many dealers.

There are two versions of this keyboard for the IBM PC. There is also a detached replacement for Apple II keyboards. Key Tronic offers other keyboards for Radio Shack users too. Finally, a line of special keyboards is available for the handicapped. This review will focus on the Key Tronic's top of the line IBM PC keyboard.

The shift keys are in standard typewriter positions and the labels for the tab and return keys are similar to those found on regular typewriters. The cap lock and numeric keypad lock keys have light emitting diodes to tell the operator when these functions have been selected. Pause and reset keys have been added. A separate cursor/editor key cluster has been included to further simplify operation. Touch typists will like the feel of the F and J keys, designed for easy homing. The most pleasing feature, in our opinion, is the relocation of the ten special function keys (F1–F10) on the Key Tronic product. They are arranged along the top of the keyboard instead of at the left-hand side. This arrangement corresponds with the displaying of special function key functions on the CRT, a frequently used software feature. The order of the special function keys is much more logical, and they are arranged in two clusters of five keys each, further simplifying access.

There is one version of this (5151) keyboard for the IBM PC and XT. The second one (5151J) is offered for the PCjr.

Installing the keyboard is very simple. It is plugged into the standard IBM keyboard jack on the rear of the machine. Owners of "compatibles" (Compaq, Panasonic, etc.) should check to see if their machines have a jack compatible with the Key Tronic keyboard before purchasing. Some, like the Compaq, do not.

This keyboard has a very nice feel. The additional features make the PC easier to operate. We particularly liked the reset key and the pause key. The separate editor/cursor key cluster is also a nice feature, once you have become accustomed to it. It prevents erroneous entries caused by accidentally placing the keyboard in the numeric mode. The location of the special function keys further speeds operation.

There is little documentation needed and provided with this product.

The best time to purchase the KB 5151 is when you buy the rest of the system. If you do lots of typing, or if the system is used by touch typists, it might be worthwhile to replace the keyboard(s) on your existing system(s) as well. These Key Tronic keyboards are so popular that some compatible systems are shipped with them as standard equipment.

RATINGS:
Overall Value ....9 Performance 10
Ease of Use ....10 Documentation 8

Prices may vary; shop for discount prices.

KOALA PAD
Koala

Approx. Retail Price .... NA
Type .... touch tablet
Available for .... IBM PC and compatibles

The Koala Pad is an excellent touch tablet with versions available for the Commodore 64, Apple, Atari, and IBM PC computers. It comes with a powerful graphics program that includes a barnyard scene and many farm animals. Some versions of the Koala Pad require a joystick port.

Koala Pad allows you to create images and store them to disk. Perhaps the only shortcoming is the easily lost plastic stylus that comes with the Koala Pad, and the small size of the tablet, which makes it somewhat difficult to draw finely resolved pictures without going into a magnify mode. On the whole, however, the Koala Pad is an excellent product.

RATINGS:
Overall Value .... 10 Performance 9
Ease of Use .... 10 Documentation 8

POWER MAKER UNINTERRUPTIBLE
POWER SUPPLY
Topaz Electronics Division

Approx. Retail Price $750
Type ....uninterruptible power supply
Available for ....IBM PC and compatibles

The UPS continuously monitors the power coming from the outlet. As long as the voltage is within acceptable standards, the UPS stays out of the way, simply passing power from the utility company along to your equipment. The *instant* the line voltage dips too low, the UPS begins generating power for your system.

In as little as 3 milliseconds the Topaz UPS detects a power problem and steps in to take over. When power is restored to the wall outlet, the UPS switches the computer back to the wall outlet.

The Topaz UPS has a built-in transient suppressor and filter networks designed to help protect your system from high voltage transients caused by lightning, motor surges, and other nasties. This feature operates even when the UPS is not providing the power.

There is a beeper to notify you that the power at the wall outlet has failed. There is no way to tell when the battery is running low.

Installation is easy. Unplug your computer, plug it into the Topaz UPS and plug the UPS into the wall. Switch on one switch and go back to work. The UPS can be placed under a desk or in any out-of-the-way location since there are no knobs, dials, or other items that need attention.

The manual is quite simple, but helpful. It is nicely

Prices may vary; shop for discount prices.

illustrated, and contains nearly everything you need for installation and operation.

Shortly after the Topaz 84864 was installed in our offices it got its first "real world" test. Someone flipped every circuit breaker in the building while trying to locate the one that needed resetting. The two computers and two printers protected by the UPS didn't even blink.

We later tested the Topaz UPS under load to determine if it would deliver as promised. The no load voltage, full load voltage, and output frequencies were all well within spec. Rather than run the time test under full load conditions, we tried with a "typical" small office configuration. The test set-up included two computers, a printer, and a desk lamp. Total power consumption was about 5 to 6.5 amps (600 to 780 VA) depending on what the printers were doing.

We started a stopwatch and pulled the UPS plug from the wall. We then went on with business as usual, printing, saving, and recalling disk information. More than an hour after the Topaz UPS started supplying power to the computers and printers, everything was still operating flawlessly. This is plenty of time to finish (or abort) printing projects, save memory contents to disk, and power down the systems. We don't recommend that you continue to work when emergency power comes on. If you work too long, the UPS batteries will discharge to the point where the UPS will shut itself off causing a system crash similar to the one you were hoping to avoid.

RATINGS:
Overall Value............ 10   Performance............. 10
Ease of Use............... 10   Documentation.......... 9

SHUFFLE BUFFER
Interactive Structures Inc.

Approx. Retail Price $349
Type..print spooler
Available for ....IBM PC and compatibles

Printers are usually the slowest devices in a computer system. Frequently the computer must wait for the printer to finish its printing task before it can start something else. Printer buffers have been developed to solve this problem. Most buffers are simply memory devices where text is temporarily stored until the printer has a chance to print it. These buffers make it possible for the computer to dump material to be printed and then begin working on other projects. Some printers contain internal buffers, others do not. The Shuffle Buffer is an example of an external buffer that can be used with printers that don't have buffers as well as with those that do.

The Shuffle Buffer can contain a minimum of 32K to a maximum of 128K of memory used to store information before it is printed. Most competitive buffers have similar capabilities. The Shuffle Buffer does have many unique features however. For example, it is possible to connect the Shuffle Buffer to the computer's serial or parallel printer port. It is also possible to connect the output of the Shuffle Buffer to either a serial or parallel printer. This means that the Shuffle Buffer can be used for parallel to parallel, parallel to serial, serial to serial, or serial to parallel interfaces. This makes it possible to use it as an interface converter as well as a print buffer.

The front panel of the Shuffle Buffer contains all of the necessary controls and indicator lights used to operate the "basic" buffering system. Other (fancy) operational commands are sent from the computer to the

Prices may vary; shop for discount prices.

Shuffle Buffer through the interface cable itself.

There is a bypass mode that removes the buffer from the system, connecting the computer directly to the printer in cases where that is desirable. There is a copy feature, permitting users to make multiple copies of the same text without tying up the computer.

Perhaps the most unique feature is a data compression technique that maximizes use of the buffer's memory. This data compression feature "strips out" multiple spaces, and other repeated characters, replacing them with "shorthand" representations that take less space in memory. When the information is sent to the printer, these shorthand representations are replaced with the actual characters themselves.

This product performs as advertised. It *does* free up the computer for other tasks, and the RAP features work well, too. It is possible to have some data lost with certain memory overflow conditions. It is also possible to lose some data when switching from the RAP to the bypass mode and when switching from certain other modes. Users with printers containing buffers may find operations a little confusing at first, since the Shuffle Buffer sends its information to the printer buffer, leaving the user feeling somewhat out of control.

If you are considering a printer buffer you should look carefully at Interactive Structure's Shuffle Buffer. It is one of the best we have seen.

RATINGS:
Overall Value 10   Performance 10
Ease of Use 9   Documentation 10

UNINTERRUPTIBLE POWER SUPPLY (UPS) 200 WATT
Datashield

Approx. Retail Price $359
Type ....uninterruptible power supply
Available for ....IBM PC and compatibles

Smart computer owners are adding uninterruptible power supplies to their systems. These devices take over when power from the power company fails, even briefly. Uninterruptible power supplies (UPS) prevent loss of data in memory, or data on disks.

The Datashield 200 WATT UPS provides between 5 and 30 minutes of standby electrical power to small computer systems. Within 4 milliseconds of a brownout or a complete power failure the Datashield UPS uses its backup batteries and its inverter circuitry to provide the 110 volt, 60 cycle AC required to power small personal computer systems. When the Datashield UPS takes over, an audible alarm informs the user that standby power is being generated. In addition, there is a low battery indicator light to warn the user that standby power will soon cease to be generated. The Datashield UPS also provides remote power failure indication, making completely unattended order system shutdowns possible on computer systems designed to use this feature. The Datashield UPS also provides noise and spike filtering, even when it is not generating standby power.

Installation is quite simple. Once removed from the carton, the UPS is plugged into a regular electrical outlet. All elements of the computer system are then plugged into the UPS. Datashield recommends that the UPS batteries be charged for 10 to 12 hours prior to the first generation of emergency power. Charging takes place automatically when the UPS is plugged in.

Prices may vary; shop for discount prices.

We found the performance of the Datashield to be as advertised. Standby power was generated for a slightly longer period of time than specified by the manufacturer.

This product comes with an eight-page, photocopied document. It contains useful information about installation, testing, and care of the UPS. There is also a list of 16 computer systems that have been tested with the Datashield UPS. One piece of bad advice is given in the instructions. Datashield does not recommend powering printers, modems, or other items that it deems "noncritical" parts of the system. Unfortunately, many software packages "lock-up" when printers, modems, and other peripherals fail to operate properly. The result can be an unrecoverable system crash, like the one UPS users hope to avoid. We recommend that you purchase a UPS system large enough to power all of the elements of your system temporarily. This is the only way to assure orderly shutdowns without loss of data in the event of power failure.

This is an excellent, low-cost UPS. Be certain that it is powerful enough to handle all of your current and future computer needs.

RATINGS:

Overall Value.............. 9	Performance.............. 10
Ease of Use.............. 10	Documentation.......... 8

SOFTWARE

Over the following pages, you'll find reviews of many different types of software: communications programs, database management programs, educational programs, finance programs, game programs, integrated software packages, utilities, languages, operating systems, word processors, and a variety of one-of-a-kind programs for handling specialized tasks. In looking through these reviews, there are a few things that you should keep in mind.

First, pay careful attention to the Ease of Use comments and ratings. This may be the most important consideration of all, no matter what type of software you're looking for. Most of the programs reviewed here are fairly easy to use, but some programs—particularly the most capable ones—require you to learn specialized, obscure commands. With one of these programs, you will not only spend more time doing the same amount of work, but you may find yourself avoiding using it altogether. It is often better to choose a program that you're sure you will use than to choose a very powerful program that you may never be able to figure out.

Another thing to watch for is software compatibility. In other words, try to choose programs that can use files created by the programs that you already own or use. For example, if you use WordStar and are looking for a spreadsheet, it would be best to find a program that stores spreadsheets in the same format that WordStar uses for document files. This gives you the option of using WordStar's editing capabilities to modify your spreadsheets, which may come in handy some time in the future.

Prices may vary; shop for discount prices.

Finally, as with all computer equipment purchases, you should try using the software yourself before buying. If possible, use the program in the same way that you will use it in your work. This is the only way to be sure of what you're getting—if you just watch a salesperson's demonstration of the program, you may be surprised at how difficult it is to actually do anything with it yourself.

Buying Floppy Diskettes

Nothing is more important to your software's continued well-being than the media it is recorded on. And you have a number of choices when it comes to choosing disks for your computer. There are dozens of names in the disk business, all vying for your dollar. Does it make a difference where you spend that dollar? Possibly, yes. While most floppy diskettes are comparable in quality, there are some differences. And prices vary greatly; you'll want to be able to choose a good quality diskette at the most reasonable price possible.

We sampled diskettes from seven common vendors: Datalife (by Verbatim Corp.); Memorex; Janus; Dysan; 3M; TDK; and IBM. We found all of the disks in this sample to be reliable in repeatedly recording and reading various files.

In the construction of the actual jackets that enclose the disks, we found some minor differences. The Memorex jacket was most resistant to abuse, with a stiff jacket and fully sealed edges around the entire edge of the jacket. The IBM and Janus diskettes showed good resistance to physical abuse, with still jackets and seals in multiple locations. The TDK, Dysan, 3M, and Verbatim diskettes were average to good in jacket quality, with the least number of seals at the edges (and in the case of the Verbatim, a thin, not-so-stiff jacket).

All the diskettes with the exception of the Verbatim contained a hub ring; that's a ring around the hole in the center of the diskette that adds strength to the diskette. Verbatim makes disks with hub rings. Look for "HHR" on the box. And in terms of prices, here is what we paid per diskette, purchasing through local computer stores in a major southwestern U.S. city:

Verbatim Datalife	$4.00
Memorex	4.50
Dysan	5.00
TDK	5.25
Janus	6.00
IBM	6.50

The Verbatim diskettes are clearly a good deal if you treat your diskettes gently and put them away when not in use (as you should). If you tend to abuse your diskettes by leaving them strewn around the computer desk haphazardly and writing on the labels with ballpoint pens (not recommended), you should opt for the Memorex, Dysan, or TDK variety; they may hold up better against such abuse. In our opinion, the Janus and IBM versions didn't provide any apparent improvement that was worth the noticeably higher price.

We also tested some no-label, generic diskettes, and found that you often get what you pay for. We found a high number of bad sectors on the inexpensive diskettes, and errors in reading data resulted on a few occasions. For these reasons, we advise steering clear of the bargain-basement diskettes, if you value your data. If you do purchase disks with bad sectors, return them to their source for replacement or a refund.

It is possible to buy quality diskettes in bulk, thereby saving money. Boxes of 50 or 100 DSDD 3M diskettes with envelopes can be purchased for as little as $2.50 per disk. Get together with a friend and share the savings.

COMMUNICATIONS

If you have a modem, the right communications software can give you access to more on-line information than you'll ever have time to look at. New electronic bulletin boards and information services are being announced almost daily, and there are probably several of these that cover your interests.

Most communications software can access any of these services. The important consideration in communications software is making sure that it will work with your modem; always ask if it supports your specific modem before buying communications software.

The following section provides an overview of some of the most popular on-line information services, followed by reviews of many popular communications programs.

On-Line Computer Services

CompuServe is one of the most popular remote computing services being used by personal computer owners. It allows you to do computer-assisted research, play games, or correspond with other computer users via regular telephone lines. CompuServe contains over 100 databases on 500 or 600 different specific topics. For example, it is possible to find out about the nutritional value of various kinds of food, national and local news, and banking information. Weather reports and airline schedules can also be accessed via CompuServe. It is even possible to use your computer and telephone line for shopping when you connect with CompuServe. You read a catalog on your display, place the order on your terminal, and it is delivered. Luggage, computer products, and books are a few of the many things you can buy this way.

Prices may vary; shop for discount prices.

There are movie reviews, sports statistics, and financial and business information as well. Users are billed by the hour, the basic charge being approximately $5 per hour. There are also storage charges for people wishing to create and maintain files on CompuServe's computer. The address is: CompuServe, 500 Arlington Centre Blvd., Columbus, OH 43220. The phone number is (614) 457-8650.

Dialog, a service of Lockheed, is perhaps the largest collection of databases in common use today. But Dialog is comparatively expensive. Connect time averages $40 to $100 or more per hour, depending upon the database selected. Some databases also include a per-record printing charge. These charges range from less than 5 cents to more than $100 per record. Obviously it is important to understand Dialog's billing methods and obtain training in the efficient use of this powerful service. For this purpose, Dialog has a series of local classes. Many manuals are also available, as are "training files," which allow users to experiment with various Dialog commands at a very low cost. Practically any subject in the Universe is covered on Dialog. There is an entire database containing nothing but information about coffee. There are other databases about advertising, chemistry, law, child abuse, insurance, even computer software. Using the computer software database, it is possible to search for descriptions of software packages meeting your specific requirements. Anyone needing research for business or scholastic purposes should look into Dialog's many services. For more information, write: Dialog Information Services, Inc., Marketing Dept., 3460 Hillview Ave., Palo Alto, CA 94304. Call (800) 227-1927. In California call (800) 982-5838.

EasyLink is Western Union's entry into the electronic mail services market. EasyLink subscribers can use their personal computers or terminals to access the TWX/TELEX network. Instant electronic mail can be sent to other EasyLink users and messages can be sent to those with TWX/TELEX machines. It is also possible to generate mailgrams using EasyLink. Western Union charges for its excellent, well-indexed operator's manual. It contains nearly everything both experienced and first-time users need to know to get the most out of a powerful new communications tool. Price varies with services used. Contact the Western Union Telegraph Co., EasyLink Instant Mail Service, 1 Lake Street, Upper Saddle River, NJ 07458. (800) 222-1288. In Texas call (713) 363-4476.

MCI Mail is a service similar to EasyLink, which actually hit the market before Western Union's. In some ways it is much more sophisticated than the EasyLink system. For example, in addition to instant electronic mail, it is possible to send laser printed documents via MCI Mail to recipients who do not have a personal computer. The laser printer can even reproduce your company's letterhead and individual's signature on paper. For those in a hurry, it is possible to have these paper copies hand delivered in most cities within four hours of their creation. MCI users also have access to the Dow Jones Databases through the MCI network. Fees range from one dollar for electronic mail to $24 or more for hand delivered mail. Prices vary somewhat depending on the length of the document. A measurement called the "MCI ounce" is used. In many cases it costs $2 or $3 to send a typical message. For overnight delivery via MCI Mail, the service is reasonable and reliable. Unfortunately, MCI's documentation is not as complete or well organized as that offered by Western Union. It is very difficult, for instance, to find out how to send documents containing underscores, bold print, and other formatting features offered on so many of today's word processing software packages for personal

Prices may vary: shop for discount prices.

computers. This subject is thoroughly treated in the Western Union documents and only hinted at in the MCI manuals. To sign up for MCI Mail, contact MCI Mail, 200 M Street NW, Washington, DC 00036. (800) MCI-2255.

NEWSNET is founded on an intriguing principle. The NEWSNET database contains the complete text of newsletters on a wide variety of subjects including advanced office concepts, African news, church information, tax shelters, television reviews, travel information, sports, the environment, and much more. Users can have the computer quickly scan individual newsletters or the entire newsletter collection for information on specific topics. It is even possible to set up an automatic system that continually monitors newsletters as they are added. Whenever new information on the topic(s) of your choice is added to the database, reports containing this information are automatically generated for you using NEWSNET's "News Flash" feature. There is a $15 minimum monthly charge for NEWSNET subscribers, and individual newsletter charges depending upon your usage. In many cases, people that subscribe to the paper versions of these newsletters receive a discount when searching the electronic versions. NEWSNET's subscription includes a monthly newsletter (which you receive in the mail) regarding NEWSNET services. For more information contact NEWSNET, 945 Haverford Rd., Bryn Mawr, PA 19010. Phone (215) 527-8030.

Nexis, a service of Mead Data Central, has been advertised as "the world's most powerful information system." While it is hard to substantiate a claim like that, Nexis certainly is one of the most powerful services available. Until recently, Nexis users required special terminals. Now Nexis is making the service available to personal computer users as well.

Owners of Apple Macintosh, IIc, IIe, IBM PC, and a variety of other systems are now able to use Nexis. If in doubt about your computer, contact Nexis before signing up for their services.

Lexis, a companion service of Nexis, also offered by Mead, is aimed at people in law offices. It is a well known and respected legal research tool. For more information about Nexis, Lexis, and other Mead Data services, contact Mead Data Central, 9393 Springboro Pike, P.O. Box 933, Dayton, Ohio 45401, or phone 1 (800) 865-1608. Ohio residents phone (513) 865-6958.

Plato Educational Services can also be accessed over telephone lines. Until recently these fine educational tools were only available to owners of special terminals. These terminals were usually found in better equipped high schools and colleges. Now, owners of IBM PC and compatible systems with graphics capabilities can access Plato services in their own homes and offices. A wide variety of programs are available including flight instruction, math tutorials, history lessons, and hundreds of other subjects. Special communications software is required, since some of the lessons even include animation displayed on your screen. It is available from the Plato people and is called Plato HomeLink. Contact the Plato people via Control Data Corp., 8100 34th Ave. S., Bloomington, MN 55420.

Finally you should know about The Source, billed as America's Information Utility. Like CompuServe, The Source has a variety of consumer and business services. You can send and receive electronic mail via The Source, join special interest groups, buy and sell things, read movie and book reviews, and much more. There is business news, sports news, and information from a variety of local newspapers. There are business programs and employment services

Prices may vary; shop for discount prices.

offered. For those interested in stocks and financial news, a wealth of information on these subjects can be obtained via The Source. There are even abstracts from articles written in a wide variety of popular computer magazines. Like CompuServe, The Source allows game playing, and it is possible to download games from The Source (and CompuServe) for later use on your computer after you disconnect from the phone line. For information about The Source write: The Source, 1616 Anderson Rd., McEan, VA 22102 or phone (703) 734-7500.

All of the above services cost money. While a number of free services have been set up, many of them by individual personal computer owners, these small systems usually only permit one user at a time. They are commonly known as electronic information systems or BBS (Bulletin Board Systems). Since they are virtually all not-for-profit, they tend to appear and disappear with some regularity. Most computer stores can give you the phone numbers of some of the more popular local bulletin boards. Once you have accessed one of the local boards, you will probably be able to print a list of other phone numbers. Bulletin board systems often support special interests. Some cater to particular computer owners (ie: IBM, Osborne etc.) while others share different interests like photography or dating. There are even adult (X-rated) bulletin boards. There is also at least one publication that tries to track small bulletin board systems, their phone numbers and general areas of interest. It is called the On-Line Computer Telephone Directory, and is available from OLCTD, P.O. Box 10005, Kansas City, Missouri 64111.

DATA CAPTURE 4.0
Southeastern Software

Approx Retail Price $65
Available for .... Apple
Features: simple and easy to use

DATA CAPTURE 4.0 doesn't do everything that a communications program can do, but what it does it does very well. It lets you communicate with any other computer that transmits and receives asynchronous serial data, which includes almost every computer of interest to Apple computer users. All of the program options are available from a single menu, making DATA CAPTURE 4.0 very easy to use.

After you have configured the program properly, it will place you in Enter mode whenever you start running it. In this mode, you can enter text into a capture buffer and then save it or transmit it. If you're hooked up to another computer, any data you receive will also be entered into the capture buffer (hence the name of the program).

In addition to the main menu, there is a simple setup menu that you can use to change specifications like the baud rate (110 or 300), the duplex setting (full or half), and the capture buffer status (on or off).

DATA CAPTURE 4.0 is a simple, elegant terminal program that can be learned in about half an hour. It takes the confusion out of computer telecommunications and is very highly recommended for Apple owners with no previous experience in this area.

RATINGS:
Overall Value	 8	Performance	 6
Ease of Use	 9	Documentation	 8

Prices may vary; shop for discount prices.

SMARTCOM II
Hayes Microcomputer Products, Inc.

Approx. Retail Price $149
Available for .... IBM PC and compatibles
Features: automatic dialing and logon, macros, on-screen status messages

Smartcom II manages remote communication for IBM PC and equivalent systems equipped with the Hayes Smartmodems. Menus and function keys are used. Smartcom II works with both external Hayes modems, and the internal, 1200B model. Modems with Hayes-compatible command sets will also work.

Smartcom II automatically originates and answers telephone calls. Automated dialing and logon features are provided. Telephone numbers may be stored in a personal communication directory or entered from the keyboard. Keyboard macros can be stored on disk to save time rekeying commands or information. Up to 26 macros can be defined for each remote system. Communication parameters such as BAUD rate, duplex character delay, and special keyboard characters can be selected and stored for each remote system. Up to 25 systems can be defined in this way. Smartcom comes preconfigured for many information services, including CompuServe, The Source, etc.

The software will transfer command and formatted files. It can also process them to conform with conventions of DOS and standard data processing techniques. Files can be sent using one of three data transfer protocols: Stop/Start, Send Lines, and Verification. Smartcom will also route incoming data to a disk or printer concurrent with its display on the screen. A buffering technique minimizes connect time. The user can create, display, print, erase, and rename files, even while connected with another computer. It can be used on both hard disk and floppy disk. DOS path features are supported.

On-screen status messages keep the user informed of both program and modem action, showing certain keyboard definitions, displaying error messages, and displaying the condition of the program's disk and printer capture buffers.

Smartcom II works flawlessly. In many, many hours of use there have been no surprises or disappointments. Smartcom "watches" your activities and provides default selections based on what you did previously. Many times its assumptions are correct, speeding operation.

Smartcom II is accompanied by a 210-page printed manual. Although the manual contains no index, its other sections are quite complete and well written. It contains sections on troubleshooting, macros, user support information, and even a section listing popular communications services and bulletin boards. The organization may confuse some people. It is important to understand Hayes terminology (i.e.: sets, macros, parameters, etc.).

Smartcom is not copy protected, and DOS commands can be used for backup.

There are packages with more features than Smartcom II, and packages that sell for less, but none match the value offered here.

RATINGS:

Overall Value	9	Performance	9
Ease of Use	9	Documentation	8

SUPERTERM
Midwest Micro, Inc.

Approx. Retail Price $90
Available for . . . . Commodore 64
Features: emulates many terminal types, user-definable keys

SuperTerm, one of the best terminal programs available for·the Commodore 64 includes virtually every feature offered by other terminal programs, and adds some of its own. Its manufacturer prefers to call it a terminal emulator, because it can mimic even elaborate minicomputer terminals.

SuperTerm supports file uploading and downloading, using both the PET bulletin board and CompuServe methods. SuperTerm can also receive programs from nonstandard systems and, with some minor adjustments, convert them into Commodore programs.

SuperTerm also does the usual things, such as capturing a copy of information received. This can be edited later, with the usual word processing commands, and then printed or saved.

To further simplify communicating with other computer systems, any key can be redefined to act like another key, troublesome characters can be filtered out, and special codes needed to get into large computer systems can be given with only a couple of keystrokes. Further, these and all other options of the program can be stored on disk once and do not have to be typed again.

RATINGS:
Overall Value 8   Performance 10
Ease of Use 8   Documentation 5

TELE–TALK
Datasoft Inc.

Approx. Retail Price $50
Available for . . . . Atari
Features: automatic billing computation for
timesharing services

This very complete telecommunications program for
the Atari is not only easy to use but easy to understand. Tele-Talk includes a clock feature that keeps
track of elapsed time and automatically computes the
time spent in dollars, which is helpful with services
such as CompuServe or The Source.

A bar graph indicates the status of the memory buffer,
and data received over the phone can be saved to a
disk or printed when the buffer is full. Uploading
(sending a file to another computer) and downloading
(receiving a file) are fully supported. The display
screen can be split so a user can type in a transmission
while data is still being received and displayed on the
other half of the screen. This is useful for CB-type
networks where a group of users communicate simultaneously.

Baud rate is selectable from 300 to 9600, although
recommended settings range from 300 to 1200. Input
and output parity can be checked to ensure that
nothing is lost or garbled during transmission.

Tele-Talk was written specifically for the Atari. It's a
good and practical telecommunication program that
requires little training or special knowledge to operate.

RATINGS:
Overall Value	8	Performance	7
Ease of Use	8	Documentation	7

TRANSSEND PC
Transsend Corp.

Approx. Retail Price $189
Available for . . . . IBM PC and compatibles
Features: easy to use

Transsend is a flexible communications software package that manages to maintain some degree of ease-of-use. Transsend lets you create, send, and organize messages. The program can also send and receive files, such as the files created by applications software like VisiCalc or Lotus 1–2–3. Transsend imitates a desktop, with several in-baskets and out-baskets that represent information. You set up a page in an electronic address book for every person or service that you will be communicating with. This address contains that person's phone number, so that Transsend can use your automatic modem to dial that person's phone number. A similar "services" basket contains logon information such as I.D. numbers and passwords for videotex services like The Source. Transsend works with automatic modems that use the standard Hayes 'Smartmodem' commands. The program can be used with manually operated modems, but you must then make all the calls. Extensive use of on-screen menus and clearly defined function key uses combine to make Transsend an easy package to use. At the same time, you don't give up power in the interests of gaining ease-of-use.

RATINGS:

Overall Value	8	Performance	8
Ease of Use	9	Documentation	8

DATA MANAGEMENT

This chapter covers programs that allow you to sort and organize information. Along with word processing and spreadsheets, this is one of the most common uses of personal computers.

Database managers are versatile programs that can sort information in many different ways. Information is entered in the form of records; each record contains all of the information concerning one item in the database. After you have entered all of the information you need to work with, the database manager program can selectively rearrange records or generate lists.

There are two common modes of operation for database managers: menu-driven and command-driven. Menu-driven programs display a menu of your options at all times, and you can select any of the currently available options. With command-driven programs, you must enter commands to specify what you want to do; this means you must know the commands, whereas in the menu-driven program you can always look at the screen for your options. Menu-driven programs are better for occasional users who may not remember the available commands, and command-driven programs are popular with experienced users who don't want to be slowed down by the displaying of menus. Whichever approach you prefer, this has no effect on the power or versatility of the program—it only affects how you use it.

n reading the reviews of database management rograms, you will notice references to Ashton-Tate's Base II. This was the first widely used data management program, and it has become something of a tandard by which others are judged. You should now, however, that dBase II is very powerful and ery difficult to use. If a manufacturer claims that heir program is more powerful than dBase II, that is npressive. But if they claim that their program is asier to use than "dBase II, the industry standard," his is misleading—almost every data management rogram is easier to use than dBase II.

ome good features to watch for in data management rograms are: the ability to link more than one file or atabase together; the ability to read records of information from files created by other programs; help creens, which will make the program much easier to se; extensive formatting options for generating reorts from existing data; and intuitively obvious ommands that will be easy to remember.

CONDOR
Condor-3

Approx. Retail Price $65
Available for . . . . IBM PC and compatible
RAM Required 128K
Features: command-driven

Condor is a relatively powerful database manager that
rivals offerings like R:base 4000 and dBASE II in
power, yet has a surprising number of user friendly
features built in. Condor lets you create files of information, and generate printed reports based on those
files. You have separate commands for viewing specific information that is in the database, and these
commands can be used in specific ways (to enable you
to locate all persons named Smith that live in Los
Angeles, for example).

When creating reports, you have a large amount of
flexibility over how you want the reports to look.
There is one minor drawback to Condor—the program does not offer a menu-driven approach, as you
will find in programs like PFS:File or Friday!, so you
will have to learn a few programming commands to
use Condor. But those commands are clear and relatively simple, and you get greater flexibility with Condor's programming-like approach.

RATINGS:

Overall Value	8	Performance	
Ease of Use	7	Documentation	

Prices may vary; shop for discount price

DBASE II
Ashton-Tate

Approx. Retail Price $495
Available for . . . . most systems
RAM Required 64K
Features: Programmable, very powerful

Designed for personal computers, dBASE II is probably the most popular database manager ever devised. It is a complex and powerful relational database manager that resembles a programming language in more ways than one. It's not an actual applications package that's ready to use; instead, dBASE II is more accurately described as a development tool that you can use to file information in a number of ways.

It uses a command structure to operate. By typing in the various commands, you tell dBASE II to perform different actions. First, you design your database, using the CREATE command. It will ask you for the specific information regarding the fields, which are the locations used to store your data. After you've designed the database, you then enter the information with the APPEND command. Later, you can use the INSERT and DELETE commands to add or remove information that's in the database. The DISPLAY command lets you examine information, and you can search for information by using the SORT and INDEX commands. It has the flexibility to search for and locate information in any field within the database.

Its faults lie primarily in the ease-of-use area. Because dBASE II borders on being a programming language, you must be familiar with the commands, and how they work, to make effective use of the program. If, as an example, you wanted to know the locations of all homes that were priced at less than $80,000, you might have to use commands like this:

```
USE HOMES
INDEX ON PRICE TO B:PRICES
USE PRICES
DISPLAY ALL FOR PRICE < 80000
```

To most persons, this is not exactly a normal means of communicating with a computer. To make matters worse, dBASE II is very unforgiving of improper command structure.

Still, once you get past the initial learning curve, dBASE II will handle the majority of information-filing needs that most persons will run across. And the program is well supported with dozens of tutorial books and cassette tapes, and classes and seminars available from many computer stores. An upcoming improved version, called dBASE III, is reported to be considerably easier to use than dBASE II.

RATINGS:

Overall Value	7	Performance	9
Ease of Use	5	Documentation	6

Prices may vary; shop for discount prices.

DB MASTER
Stoneware Inc.

Approx. Retail Price $350
Available for . . . . Apple
RAM Required 256K
Features: supports DIF files, includes report
generating program

Several features are incorporated into DB Master to
make data entry quick and easy. Common data formats—social security numbers, telephone numbers,
and dates—can be selected as special fields.

While the database portion of this program is the best
available, the report-generating section is a labyrinth
of menus. The powerful report writer is able to arrange
data in virtually any format, but a detailed study of the
manual is required before use.

With DB Master, applications are designed on a disk
separate from the program disk. Data files are kept on
a third disk.

RATINGS:
Overall Value 9   Performance . . . . . . , ...8
Ease of Use 8   Documentation 8

FRIDAY!
Ashton-Tate

Approx. Retail Price $295
Available for . . . . IBM PC and compatibles
RAM Required . . . . 64K (CP/M)
Features: menu-driven

Friday! is a simple to use database manager with some limits. The program uses a series of menus that provide you with multiple choices.

Friday! sets up a standard screen layout that can be changed for custom applications. Entering data is fast and simple, and Friday! has flexible search options. You can scan single records, or groups of records, and you can search on any one of a number of different criteria. Friday! creates standard column-type reports, customized reports, or mailing labels.

As for the limitations, Friday! is slow in searching for and retrieving data. At times, the number of menu choices you must step through to get from one part of the program to another becomes tedious. And you can enter a maximum of only 32 characters per field; for some applications, this may not be enough. Still, Friday! is very simple to use, includes outstanding documentation, and is well supported by the manufacturer.

RATINGS:

Overall Value	7	Performance	7
Ease of Use	8	Documentation	8

Prices may vary; shop for discount prices.

PC–FILE III
ButtonWare

Approx. Retail Price $49
Available for . . . . IBM PC and compatibles
RAM Required . . . . NA
Features: sound-alike searches, repairing of damaged databases

How can so much software be sold for $49? The answer is low-cost documentation, word-of-mouth advertising, and a new concept in software marketing called "user supported software." The author of PC–File invites you to try it at no cost, and send him a check for $49 if the software pleases you. You are further encouraged to make copies for your friends in the hopes that they too will like it and send their $49 "donation." We hope the concept works. This is first-class, low-cost software at its best. We tested the July 1984 (2.0) version of PC–File III.

PC–File III is a general purpose database manager program. It will allow sorting in almost any sequence. It allows rapid access to any record in the database, with a sophisticated search technique allowing comparison searches, soundex searches, or generic searches on any field in the record. For example, you can display all employees over a certain age, all customers with last names sounding like "Schwartz," or all items that are not in a certain category. Global changes can be made. PC–File III offers in-text and in-string searches as well.

The maximum field length is 65 characters per field, the maximum record length is 1430 characters, and up to 9999 records per database are possible, disk space permitting.

Reports can be printed from the database, listing all or some of the fields, from all or some of the records, in many different sequences, with subtotals and totals on the numeric fields. Report fields can be calculated based on information in other fields in the database. Reports can be sent directly to the video screen, printer, or disk for later use with a word processing program.

Entirely new databases can be created from existing databases. The new database can be in a different format, and can be a subset of the database from which it was "cloned." New fields can be added, old fields can be deleted, field positions can be rearranged, and field sizes can be lengthened or shortened. Masks can be used to assure proper data entry.

Version 2.0 comes with a printed, 64-page booklet. Further documentation for this product is also provided in a text file on the disk.

The author encourages users to make backups for themselves and others, as long as no fee is charged. The master copy is not copy protected.

If you can live without having an 800 telephone number to call for support, check out PC–File III.

RATINGS:

Overall Value	10	Performance	10
Ease of Use	9	Documentation	9

Prices may vary; shop for discount prices.

PFS:FILE
Software Publishing Corporation

Approx. Retail Price $140
Available for . . . . most systems
RAM Required 64K
Features: menu-driven, works in conjunction with
PFS:Report

If you're seeking a fairly powerful, straightforward
database manager that's a snap to use, consider
PFS:File. There are versions available for a variety of
computers. This program is relatively inexpensive and
handles many types of information.

PFS:File makes extensive use of forms. You enter data
according to the way that forms are laid out, and you
can retrieve the data by asking for specific information, or by printing reports in tabular form. Additional
report options are provided by PFS:Report, a companion program.

Most versions of PFS:File can hold just under 4000
characters per record, and up to 32,000 records can be
contained in a single disk file. There are upper limits to
file sites on a computer equipped with a hard disk
drive. Files on the MS–DOS version of PFS:File cannot
exceed 4 million bytes.

PFS:File is perhaps best-likened to an electronic
version of a filing system using 3×5 cards. Like all
programs in the PFS series, it is menu-driven, adding
to its ease of operation. It has its limits, but it can meet
the needs of many at a reasonable cost.

RATINGS:
Overall Value 8   Performance 7
Ease of Use 9   Documentation 7

PLEASE
Hayes Microcomputer Products, Inc.

Approx. Retail Price $349
Available for . . . . IBM PC and compatibles
RAM Required 128K
Features: help screens, many input options

Please is a middle-of-the-road database manager; not overly powerful, but reasonably so, and fairly simple to use. It compares favorably with similar products like Ashton-Tate's Friday! and Software Publishing's PFS:File.

Please can handle up to 99 characters per field and has a limit of 2000 characters (or 99 fields, whichever comes first) per record. Please gives you the flexibility of entering your data in several different ways; by using prearranged layouts, by creating your own layout, or by transferring data from other programs, such as WordStar, Lotus 1–2–3, VisiCalc, or dBASE II. Information can be extracted from Please in the form of lists, mailing label forms, or files on disk that can be used by other programs. There is also an extensive set of help menus to guide you through the use of the program.

RATINGS:
Overall Value	8	Performance	7
Ease of Use	8	Documentation	9

PROFILE III PLUS
Radio Shack

Approx. Retail Price $199
Available for TRS-80
RAM Required 48K
Features: easy screen set-up

Profile III Plus is the latest version of Radio Shack's time-tested Profile database management system for the Model 3 and Model 4 line. Profile III Plus is simple to use, although we also found the program somewhat limited in terms of power. You first define the way that you want your screen laid out, placing categories for the various information (names, addresses, and so forth) at different places on the screen. From then on, it is a simple matter of entering the data and printing the desired reports.

Profile III Plus is flexible in the ways it lets you search the database; you can choose from dozens of different criteria to hunt for specific information. The biggest limitation was the program's inability to handle more than 700 records on a two-disk drive system. This limitation can be overcome by adding more disk drives or by upgrading to a Radio Shack Model 12, but these are rather expensive solutions. Profile III Plus is also available in a hard disk version.

RATINGS:
Overall Value 8   Performance 7
Ease of Use 8   Documentation 8

R:BASE 4000 WITH CLOUT
Microrim, Inc.

Approx. Retail Price $690
Available for . . . . IBM PC and compatibles
RAM Required 64K–256K
Features: command-driven, user-defined syntax

R:base 4000 is a powerful relational database manager with the power of a top-notch filing system, along with extensive help screens that aid the novice user in learning the use of the program. As is common with this type of software, R:base 4000 uses a command-driven method of operation. The commands are all plain-English words like BUILD, DELETE, EDIT, JOIN, and SHOW. You can add algebraic operations to many of the commands, increasing their usefulness. And you can view a list of all available commands at any time, by using the help features of R:base 4000.

This program is also extremely powerful; according to the manufacturer, R:base 4000 can handle up to 100 billion records, with a maximum of 40 files per database. In actual practice, you will run out of disk space long before you use 100 billion records. But it's nice to know that the power is there. R:base 4000's error handling is good, and the program is fast in operation.

One unusual aspect of R:base 4000 takes some getting used to. The program refers to a collection of data as a *relation*, which is made up of *rows*, that are further divided into *attributes*. Virtually every other database manager on the market defines these concepts as *files*, which are made up of *records*, divided into *fields*. Since R:base 4000 uses its names throughout the command structure, you may find it confusing if you have worked with other databases before.

Prices may vary; shop for discount prices.

R:base 4000 comes with an excellent tutorial diskette that's divided into six lessons detailing the use of the program. The tutorial shows you how to search for specific information, how to create your R:base files, how to generate reports, and how to sort your information. One advantage of this tutorial over many others is that it doesn't lock you into a specific lesson plan. You can use the normal R:base commands at any point in the lesson to try out various features.

R:base 4000 can use information created by other programs, including dBase II, Lotus 1–2–3, VisiCalc, Multiplan, and most word processors. And one useful option called CLOUT lets you use ordinary language with the R:base program. With CLOUT, you could define sales representatives who didn't meet their quotas as "losers"; thereafter, typing the plain-English sentence "show me the losers" would result in a display of all sales reps who failed to meet their quotas. The CLOUT option can be very helpful if you're devising a database for untrained novices.

RATINGS:

Overall Value	9	Performance	9
Ease of Use	9	Documentation	8

EDUCATION

Educational programs can provide a nice combination of the benefits of self-instruction and classroom learning. Like self-instruction with books, educational software usually allows you to set your own pace. And like classroom instruction with a teacher, good educational software can provide specialized help in response to your individual progress.

Until recently, most educational programs were little more than text games. Recent releases, however, are much more sophisticated. They use the computer's graphics and sound capabilities to hold your interest and are available for almost any subject. These programs can be used to continue school instruction at home or provide supplemental instruction on new subjects.

There are several different approaches that can be used in education software. One of the simplest and most effective is drill and practice. In this type of program, a variety of problems requiring the same basic skills are presented, and the user must solve them as quickly as possible. Some drill and practice programs monitor the length of time required for each problem. With drill and practice programs, the user must already understand the basic concepts.

Prices may vary; shop for discount prices.

Another common approach is the tutorial program, which helps the user acquire new skills. These programs present new concepts one step at a time, and you can progress at your own rate. Tutorial programs have become very popular in bundled computer systems. Many bundled software packages include a tutorial program that teaches how to use the computer and software.

Although much of the software reviewed in this chapter is intended for children, there are also programs that can be helpful for adults, such as those that teach touch typing and the programming tutorials.

DELTA DRAWING
Spinnaker Software Corp.

Approx. Retail Price $50
Available for . . . . Apple IIe, II Plus
Type . . . . drawing

Delta Drawing is a graphics program for children. Children just think it's a fun way to draw, but at the same time they are learning something about programming.

The Delta cursor will move only at the user's command, but when it moves, it can draw! Learning the commands for moving the cursor is easiest when using the Delta Drawing Command Summary card included in the package. This card quickly tells how to draw, move without drawing, turn, erase, select color, and fill a shape.

In addition to the Delta Drawing Command Summary card, several other practical items are included. There are seven other cards with sample programs and pictures for the user to try, directions on saving programs to a separate disk, and many other useful tidbits of information. The plastic-coated cards should stand up well to use by children.

RATINGS:
Overall Value 8   Performance 8
Ease of Use 7   Documentation 9

Prices may vary; shop for discount prices.

DUCKS AHOY
CBS Software

Approx. Retail Price	$38
Available for	NA
Type	learning game (ages 3-6)

Ducks Ahoy is a very cute game for young children. It requires the player to plan strategies and keep track of many moving objects (ducks). Although the suggested age range is 3 to 6, older players (including parents) can enjoy the game.

The action takes place in a stylized Venice, Italy. Mandolins are strumming in the background. The player must maneuver a gondola through the waters surrounding four structures, and pick up ducks, dropping them safely on shore. The object is to pick up as many ducks as possible before losing all your boats.

The real challenge of the game is anticipating which of the ducks will make its way to the edge of the landing and jump in next. With more than one duck moving around, you have to plan a route that will pick up as many ducks as possible, as efficiently as possible. Complicating matters is a purple hippo who swims under the water, waiting to turn the gondola over. Successful game play involves charting the best route to get the ducks while simultaneously avoiding the hidden hippo.

RATINGS:

Overall Value	8	Performance	6
Ease of Use	10	Documentation	7

FACEMAKER
Spinnaker

Approx. Retail Price . . . . $3[5]
Available for . . . . Apple[
Type . . . . recognition game[

FaceMaker is really three games in one. The first game[
is a Face Construction Kit, which lets the user con-
struct a face by choosing appropriate parts and putting[
them together. The next game lets the child ente[r
instructions to make the face do certain things—blink[
smile, etc. The third game shows a sequence of faces[
The child must recreate the faces generated by the[
computer. Spinnaker claims that these games help to[
improve a child's memory and concentration.

However, there is some question about interest to[
children over nine years old. If your child falls in th[e
9–12 age range, you might be wise to let your child try[
the game before buying it.

RATINGS:
Overall Value 9   Performance . . . . [
Ease of Use 9   Documentation . . . . [

HOW ABOUT A NICE GAME OF CHESS?
Odesta

Approx. Retail Price $35
Available for .... Apple II, IIe, IIc
Type .... chess simulation

How About a Nice Game of Chess? is a program that teaches you how to play chess, and also plays the game at many different skill levels. It is presently available on disk for the Apple II series of computers, with a special version (with improved graphics) for the Apple IIc.

How About a Nice Game of Chess? guides the student through a series of lessons in the fundamentals of Chess Play, explaining rules and then illustrating using actual game play examples. When you actually want to get into a real game, How About a Nice Game of Chess? will be a willing opponent, able to assist with advice if you get stuck.

How About a Nice Game of Chess? does have disadvantages. It may not be challenging enough for really good players, and for those just learning, the lessons may move along at too slow a pace. Still, How About a Nice Game of Chess? is well worth the price for anyone who wants to learn and/or improve their game of chess.

RATINGS:
Overall Value 7   Performance 7
Ease of Use 8   Documentation 9

I AM THE C–64
Creative Software

Approx. Retail Price $30
Available for .... Commodore 64
Type .... computer tutorial

I Am The C–64 is a tutorial program that does a commendable job of showing the new Commodore 64 owner just what the machine is all about. It's well done, and it is a better way to learn the machine's features than plowing through the documentation that comes with the computer.

The program is divided into six lessons that are contained on two diskettes. Lesson one provides a quick and entertaining look at the graphics and sound capabilities of the computer. Lesson 2 introduces you to the use of the keyboard, while the third lesson provides a graphically illustrated introduction to BASIC programming. Lesson 4 continues the BASIC tutorial with coverage of more complex BASIC commands, while Lessons 5 and 6 describe how to bring out the 64's music and graphic capabilities in more detail.

The documentation is rather weak, but the software is so simple to use that the documentation really isn't necessary. I Am The C–64 is recommended for the new Commodore 64 owner.

RATINGS:
Overall Value 8   Performance 7
Ease of Use 9   Documentation 5

KNOW YOUR APPLE
Muse Software

Approx. Retail Price $35
Available for . . . . Apple II Plus
Type . . . . computer tutorial

Know your Apple helps a brand new Apple computer user begin understanding the machine. This is not an introduction to computer programming, but rather a setup instruction course. No prior computer knowledge is required. Clear, high-resolution pictures display the many parts of an Apple. The area under discussion flashes for easy recognition.

Every important part of the computer is highlighted and clearly explained. The two best sections of this program deal with the inside of the Apple and the mystery of the disk drives. The owner is guided in the proper placement of different internal boards, the place to plug in the joystick, and even the correct location for a lowercase adapter. The section about disk drives clearly explains how to operate the drives. It also explains how to format a disk and how to record data.

Packaged in the shape of a miniature Apple computer, Know Your Apple includes a manual that is simple, clear-cut and printed in large type for nonstrain reading. It also contains a five-step photo outline for the initial setup of the hardware.

RATINGS:
Overall Value 8   Performance 7
Ease of Use 9   Documentation 9

MASTERTYPE
Scarborough Systems

Approx. Retail Price $40
Available for . . . . most systems
Type . . . . typing drill

MasterType presents you with a spaceship in the middle of the screen. Each corner of the ship is protected by a shield. At each corner of the screen an invader (actually a word or series of characters) appears and moves toward the spacecraft. By typing the required characters, you can shoot down the attacking invader. Any corner of the ship can only be hit once during a game—the single hit destroys the shield. The second hit causes the spaceship to explode.

After you have conquered one screen, the game shows your typing speed and the suggestion that you move up to the next lesson. The lessons range from simple "home row" keystrokes, through large words and numeric characters.

MasterType does a pretty good job of establishing the eye-to-hand-to-key identification that is required for touch-typing. The game aspects are an added extra that provide more interest to the player.

RATINGS:
Overall Value 8   Performance 8
Ease of Use 9   Documentation 6

Prices may vary; shop for discount prices.

MUSIC CONSTRUCTION SET
Electronic Arts

Approx. Retail Price $40
Available for .... Apple, Atari, Commodore
Type .... musical notation aid

Music Construction Set teaches basic musical concepts through a technique that gives the user a great degree of control over most aspects of musical composition. It is available in disk-based versions for the Apple, Commodore 64, and Atari computers.

Music Construction Set is a music generation program that is somewhat similar to the MacDraw program used in Macintosh computers. The principal tool used is the joystick. Using the joystick, you move a hand that picks up and places notes, rests, and other symbols onto two musical staffs. Tempo can be speeded up and slowed down, different musical voices are available (on the Commodore and Atari computers), and a wide range of variations are provided.

The instruction booklet guides the user through the basic concepts of music theory. Hours of enjoyable learning can be had using Music Construction Set. It is indeed a bargain as a tool for learning the basics of music composition.

RATINGS:

Overall Value 9   Performance 10
Ease of Use 9   Documentation 8

ROCKY'S BOOTS
The Learning Company

Approx. Retail Price $50
Available for . . . . Apple II
Type . . . . logic tutorial

Rocky's Boots is a widely acclaimed educational game that teaches basics of logic, reasoning, and circuit design. It is available on disk for the Apple computers, with an enhanced version available for the IIc.

Rocky's Boots is an electronic construction set, similar to Electronic Arts' Music Construction Set and Pinball Construction Set. But instead of moving around flippers or notes, you are moving around the basic elements of computer logic—AND gates, OR gates, wires, switches, clocks, and other components. It all sounds more difficult and confusing than it really is—even seven-year-olds quickly catch on to how the various parts interact.

Simple tutorials present the basic elements involved in the construction of these circuits. Increasingly challenging puzzles force the player to determine the correct logical structures required to solve more complex problems. Although the information is presented in an abstract manner, the skills gained by playing Rocky's Boots are useful in many different situations.

RATINGS:
Overall Value 8   Performance 9
Ease of Use 7   Documentation 10

SUCCESS WITH MATH (SERIES)
CBS Software

Approx. Retail Price $25
Available for . . . . Apple, Atari, Commodore
Type . . . . math tutorial

Success with Math is the title of a series of mathematical tutorials available on disk for Apple, Commodore 64, and Atari computers. Subjects range from simple addition/subtraction for grades 1–4, through quadratic and differential equations for high school grade levels.

These educational packages should actually be called tutorials, rather than games. They require the student to work through a series of self-paced problems illustrating the steps involved in successful problem solving.

These tutorials can provide a great deal of satisfaction as students grasp difficult concepts and their performance in school improves. The Success With Math Series is a bargain compared to the cost of private tutoring or games with less specific goals.

RATINGS:
Overall Value 9   Performance 8
Ease of Use . . . . , . 9   Documentation 9

TIMEBOUND
CBS Software

Approx Retail Price . . . . $33 (disk)
Available for . . . . Atari, Commodore, IBM
Type . . . . history drill

In Timebound, the player is in control of a time machine. You must search through time to find a character who is trapped in a time loop. On the screen, a particular event in history is flashed (this is where your quarry was last seen)—you must position your time ship in the right category and move forward or backward in time to find your goal.

Just knowing dates isn't always enough for this game —you also have to determine which category your target is hiding in, and maneuver your ship through time to that category. All this must be done within a certain time limit.

Timebound sounds more interesting than it actually is, however. Although it probably helps develop the skills it claims to, game play is somewhat cumbersome and uninteresting. This game will be fun for some players, but it isn't for everybody.

RATINGS:
Overall Value	6	Performance	7
Ease of Use	9	Documentation	7

286

TURTLE TRACKS
Scholastic Software

Approx. Retail Price $40
Available for . . . Apple, IBM, Commodore, Atari, TI
Type . . . . programming tutorial

Logo is one of the most popular languages for teaching beginning programming. It is preferred over BASIC because it is simple to learn, it is a powerful graphic tool, it makes learning logic fun, and it provides instant gratification (simple programs generate immediate graphic results).

Although the language used in Turtle Tracks is not standard Logo, it is very close. The excellent instruction book guides the user through the steps of "teaching" a turtle to draw. As the turtle moves around the screen, he can be told to leave symbols behind. The user has control over the colors and shapes that the turtle uses to draw with. All of the instructions used to move the turtle are Logo commands.

The user can also teach the turtle to play music. By teaching the turtle, the player gains many of the logic and reasoning skills that go into computer programming—and has fun doing it. With a minimum of practice, many of the major programming concepts (branching, subroutines, loops, etc.) can be easily learned.

Turtle Tracks seems to be as much fun for computer-phobic adults as it is for children. While there are other Logo training programs available, Turtle Tracks is inexpensive and one of the easiest to learn.

RATINGS:

Overall Value	9	Performance	7
Ease of Use	9	Documentation	8

FINANCE

The programs in this chapter fall into two general categories: spreadsheets and accounting packages. Spreadsheets, such as Visicalc and Multiplan, allow you to enter rows and columns of numeric information (usually dollar amounts) and then specify relationships between various rows or columns. If you change a value or a relationship, the resulting changes in other parts of the spreadsheet will be shown immediately. This makes spreadsheets valuable planning and forecasting tools, because the long-range effect of various changes can easily be seen.

Accounting packages are software systems (usually more than one program) that can be used to keep all of a business's financial records on the computer. They usually are built around a general ledger program, and include options for printing bills, checks, profit/loss statements, and balance sheets. Many large, customized accounting packages are available, but the packages reviewed in this chapter are more general. They're programs that can be used by anyone who needs to keep track of a small business's financial dealings.

There are a few things to keep in mind when you look for a spreadsheet program. First, check how fast it can recalculate a large spreadsheet after a change has been made. Some programs are very slow in this area, and you may want to avoid them.

Prices may vary; shop for discount prices.

Another thing to check is software compatibility—can the spreadsheet read files that have been created by other programs? This is particularly important if you have both an accounting package and a spreadsheet, because you may want to read information from your accounting package records into the spreadsheet for forecasting and planning budgets.

Some spreadsheets use a mouse controller to move from location to location, while others use the cursor keys. Try both approaches yourself before you decide on a particular program, since there are many different opinions on which is faster and easier.

Templates are available for most popular spreadsheets, and these can save you a lot of setup time. A template program will automatically create common spreadsheet forms that you can customize to your specific application. Templates are available for things like annual budgets, inventories, and investment planning.

One final thing to think about when you look at spreadsheets—will your printer be able to handle the size of the spreadsheets you will create? If you create an annual budget with 12 monthly columns and a yearly totals column, for example, this could run to well over 132 characters, which is a common maximum for printers. This kind of problem is best resolved before you purchase a spreadsheet program.

BACK TO BASICS ACCOUNTING SYSTEM
Peachtree Software

Approx. Retail Price $95
Available for . . . . IBM PC and compatibles
RAM Required 128K
Type . . . . general ledger

This diskette-based system includes a General Ledger with a chart of accounts that permits trial balances, detailed General Ledgers, cash disbursement journals, cash receipt journals, cash sales journals, income statements, balance sheets, account activity reports, check writing, check registers, and cash reconciliation.

Each module creates a series of predefined reports. It is designed to run on IBM PC and compatible computers with at least 128K of RAM, 2 floppy disk drives, and either a monochrome or color monitor. An 80 column printer is required for reporting. Back to Basics is designed to be used with popular preprinted forms including those offered by the Deluxe Computer Forms Company.

The package comes with three disks (one for each function) and each disk must be installed and configured separately. The disks are copy protected, and come ready to use, so it is not necessary to transfer DOS system files to them. The installation feature is automated, and the user need only respond to screen prompts. A number of questions are asked, referring to the system configuration and to the user's business. The system creates data disks for each function at this time as well. The documentation describes this process in a confusing and ambiguous manner.

This is a relatively easy to use package. Since it is not designed to work with hard disks, there is a fair amount of diskette swapping. Nonetheless, owners of

290   *Prices may vary; shop for discount prices.*

small businesses will find this to be a fine performer and an excellent replacement for manual bookkeeping. A maximum of 254 accounts are permitted, and up to 1500 checks can be written per month. The practical limit to the number of actual General Ledger entries is about 2000 per month.

This software comes with a 374-page handbook, a 23-page hardware booklet, a 48-page sample report booklet and a Back to Basics Roadmap brochure. The handbook contains an overview of accounting procedures, in-depth analyses and references for the General Ledger, Accounts Receivable, and Accounts Payable procedures. An entire chapter is devoted to business situations, and it contains a full index. A small section is devoted to troubleshooting. This manual is nontechnical.

If you have a small business and plan to keep it that way, Back to Basics should be considered. Users with involved accounting problems, multidivisional organizations, or those planning to have transactions that exceed several thousand a month should look carefully at the size limitations of this offering. If you have little or no accounting experience, the manuals themselves offer one of the best tutorials we have seen on manual and computerized accounting. If you do nothing more than sit at a dealer and read the first part of the manual, you may find that this is time well spent.

RATINGS:

Overall Value 8	Performance 7
Ease of Use 8	Documentation 10

BPI ACCOUNTING SYSTEM
BPI Systems

Approx. Retail Price $395
Available for . . . . Apple
RAM Required 48K
Type . . . . general ledger

BPI Accounting System is a full-featured, comprehensive system for small business accounting. The various modules such as General Ledger and Accounts Receivable can be used separately or as part of a fully integrated accounting system. The documentation is superb and obviously written for the business user who has no prior experience with computers.

One unique and useful feature is the ability to queue commands (automatically execute a series of commands in the system). With the General Ledger package, the user can generate a profit and loss statement or balance sheet at any time. The BPI Accounts Receivable system includes invoicing and can be fully integrated with the General Ledger.

Due to the capacity limitations of Apple disk drives, the BPI system requires some disk-swapping. While some provision has been made to adjust file sizes, the system's capacity is generally limited. There is a provision for security codes to prevent unauthorized access to company records.

BPI Accounting System is a well-planned and comprehensive small business accounting system.

RATINGS:

Overall Value	7	Performance	9
Ease of Use	9	Documentation	8

Prices may vary; shop for discount prices.

CALC RESULT ADVANCED
Computer Marketing Services

Approx. Retail Price	$150
Available for	Commodore 64
RAM Required	64K
Type	spreadsheet

Calc Result is easy to use. A Help screen guides you, and the program protects you from accidentally erasing formulas. It can copy a screen to the printer at the press of a key, and the colorful manual only lacks a list of commands and an index.

Calc Result's special features include a choice of eight foreign languages to work in, a wide selection of colors, and full control of page formatting. Once set, these features are stored on a working copy of the program disk and don't have to be selected again.

What makes Calc Result unique is its ability to do three-dimensional spreadsheets of up to 32 pages and look at up to four parts of them at once though special screen windows. You can merge data from several pages into the one page—for example, to combine daily worksheets into a monthly summary. Calc Result's internal capacity holds two pages of information in memory at once, and up to 2000 cells of information.

Skilled users will appreciate Calc Result's IF-THEN-ELSE decision-making ability.

Calc Result Advanced is an excellent spreadsheet program, yet at a reasonable price.

RATINGS:
Overall Value	8	Performance	10
Ease of Use	8	Documentation	6

DOLLARS and SENSE
Monogram

Approx. Retail Price $180
Available for .... IBM PC and compatibles
RAM Required..NA
Type.........................general ledger/personal budget

Dollars and Sense is a financial management program that does much more than simply keep track of your checkbook balance and juggle a few bills. Dollars and Sense manages your budget, handles checkbook balancing, creates detailed financial reports, produces financial graphs, and even writes your checks (you must purchase special checks for this feature).

Dollars and Sense offers three sets of accounts that are defined by the program: business; household; and tax preparation. Plus, you have the ability to create your own sets of accounts with a maximum of 120 categories.

The program records checks and credit-card charges as liabilities, and deposits are treated as income. Dollars and Sense automatically keeps a running balance of your funds on hand.

The program is menu driven, and the menu clearly defines the steps needed to enter a transaction, as well as the steps for editing or deleting previous transactions. Dollars and Sense recognizes the human tendency to make mistakes, as the program lets you change previous entries, which is not allowed with some accounting programs.

The graphics options of Dollars and Sense are extensive; if anything, they are probably more than you realistically need. You can build graphs to show trends in spending, to compare a planned budget against ac-

Prices may vary; shop for discount prices.

tual expenditures on a month-to-month basis, or to show the distribution of funds among the various categories, all with bar or line graphs. These graphs can be displayed on a monochrome or color monitor, and you can print the graphs.

The print checks option requires you to use special checks on fanfold paper that can be fed into a computer printer, so you may need to order these from your bank if you want to use this option.

The documentation that's supplied with Dollars and Sense is poorly organized and could stand improvement. Fortunately, there is a good tutorial disk that familiarizes you with the program.

In all other respects, Dollars and Sense is well done. If your finances consist of one income, a dozen checks per month or so, and a few bills, we honestly feel that you would be better served with a pocket calculator. But if you are juggling a number of expenses and multiple incomes, or perhaps have a small business operating out of your home, you'll find Dollars and Sense to be a good replacement for your dog-eared general ledger.

RATINGS:
Overall Value ....8 Performance 8
Ease of Use ...., ...8 Documentation 8

DOW JONES GENERAL LEDGER
Trademark Software

Approx. Retail Price $995
Available for . . . . IBM PC and compatibles
RAM Required 128K
Type . . . . general ledger

When the people at Dow Jones and Company, Trademark Software, and Arthur Young and Company got together to create new microcomputer accounting software, the goal was to provide exceptional capabilities, performance, and support. They may have succeeded, partially at least.

This double entry General Ledger Module has six journals: cash receipts, cash disbursements, sales, purchases, payroll, and a general journal. The user can maintain the chart of accounts, prepare a budget, make and post journal entries, close the books, and perform a number of utility functions. A wide range of reports can be created, including various types of balance sheets and income statements, detail and summary trial balance reports. Budgets, the chart of accounts, and changes in financial position can also be printed.

This software has a unique "full screen" editing feature, simplifying editing of entries. It has a "pencil" journal entry mode, allowing corrections without reversing entries, and allows "inking" of journal entries, which freezes the audit trail. The chart of accounts provides multilevel structuring and consolidation, more than 1000 accounts may be added at any time.

One new user per customer can attend a class conducted by trainers that have been "certified" by Arthur Young and Company. Other users can be trained at additional cost.

Prices may vary; shop for discount prices.

The General Ledger package performed as advertised. We found disk activity to be a little higher than with some comparable packages, slightly slower performance in some areas, but with no serious degradation in overall performance. Entries do not appear to be completely "bullet proof." For example, when we were asked to enter a file name at one point we entered a question mark instead, which caused the system to crash.

Since the other planned modules are not yet available for testing (order entry, inventory, etc.), it is not possible to comment on the General Ledger's integration with those future products.

A large, printed manual accompanies this software. It contains thorough descriptions of each feature this software offers. It has complete appendixes, index, and glossary sections, including troubleshooting, printer information data storage, and formatting information.

The manual devotes a chapter to the backup procedure. The software provides a backup option, allowing the user to make copies of data files without leaving the system. Specific periods or the entire year can be recovered.

If you are in need of a flexible, easy to use General Ledger package, and/or are willing to wait for additional elements (A/R, A/P, Payroll, etc.), the Dow Jones software is worth considering. It is easier to use and better documented than many others we have seen.

RATINGS:
Overall Value 9   Performance 10
Ease of Use...........10   Documentation 9

MULTIPLAN
Microsoft Corporation

Approx. Retail Price $195
Available for . . . . IBM PC and compatibles
RAM Required 64K
Type . . . . spreadsheet

Multiplan is a powerful electronic spreadsheet that we rated as a top-of-the-line product in the pure spreadsheet category. Multiplan provides a spreadsheet size of 63 columns by 255 rows.

While that may sound limited, in practice it isn't a problem due to Multiplan's ability to link different spreadsheets together. When multiple spreadsheets are linked, as you change information in one spreadsheet, the amounts in the other spreadsheet change automatically to reflect the new figures. This feature lets you create a worksheet that's limited only by the amount of space on a disk.

Multiplan also accepts names as a substitute for formulas; instead of cryptic cell formulas like C3=B2*A4, you can use formulas like "TOTAL=SALES * COST." Multiplan can use worksheets created by VisiCalc, and you can save Multiplan worksheets in a format that many other programs can use.

In short, if you don't need graphics or database management features, but you do want a full-featured spreadsheet, Multiplan will fit the bill.

RATINGS:
Overall Value	9	Performance	8
Ease of Use	9	Documentation	9

Prices may vary; shop for discount prices.

STATE OF THE ART GENERAL LEDGER
State of the Art, Inc.

Approx. Retail Price $400
Available for . . . . Apple
RAM Required 48K
Type . . . . general ledger

This accounting package is the most technologically advanced, practical business package available for the Apple. Eight modules make up the complete system. The General Ledger module is considered the heart of the system because it can be used alone or integrated with any of the other modules, such as Accounts Receivable, Sales Invoicing, and Accounts Payable.

General Ledger is based on a double entry accounting system. The program produces daily, weekly, or monthly reports, including the General Ledger Detail Report, Trial Balance, Income Statement, and Balance Sheet. It provides control reports that are necessary for a complete audit trail and requires that you print copies of all of them before updating permanent files. This results in a deluge of paper and can be annoying at times.

State of the Art General Ledger is ideally suited for a small business. Even when working with very large files, the requested information appears on the screen in a fraction of the time that other accounting programs take. Highly recommended for those who need a powerful accounting system.

RATINGS:
Overall Value 7   Performance 9
Ease of Use 7   Documentation 9

SUPERCALC2
Sorcim Access

Approx. Retail Price $295
Available for . . . . CP/M, MS–DOS
RAM Required 64K
Type . . . . spreadsheet

SuperCalc2 is a worthwhile improvement over its predecessor, SuperCalc. SuperCalc2 uses the familiar row-and-column format, and a series of commands are chosen by pressing the slash key. The column widths in SuperCalc2 are adjustable, an important improvement over the original VisiCalc. SuperCalc2 also has a series of comprehensive "help" screens that provide information on the use of the program.

You can combine multiple spreadsheets into a single large spreadsheet, and you can transfer information from the spreadsheet to a disk to be used by other programs. As you might expect, you can insert or delete columns and rows, copy cells from one part of the spreadsheet to another, and protect cells from being changed accidentally. SuperCalc2 also lets you arrange rows or columns in ascending or descending order. This is a limited kind of database power, but it is a nice feature to have.

On an overall basis, SuperCalc2 is a reasonable choice for a spreadsheet.

RATINGS:
Overall Value 7   Performance 8
Ease of Use 8   Documentation 7

VISICALC IV
VisiCorp.

Approx. Retail Price $250
Available for .... IBM PC and compatibles
RAM Required 64K
Type .... spreadsheet

VisiCalc is the program that legitimized the personal computer in the office. And VisiCalc IV adds much-needed improvements to the capabilities of the Visi-Calc spreadsheet. VisiCalc IV provides a spreadsheet that measures 63 columns by 254 rows. The spread-sheet is fast in operation, but its size is limited when compared to some of the competition.

VisiCalc IV lets you enter text and formulas in spread-sheet fashion, into any cells that you choose. A unique keysaver feature lets you save commands and other keystrokes for later use. With the REPLICATE com-mand, you can copy information from a cell or a group of cells to another place on the worksheet. VisiCalc IV lets you print an entire worksheet, or a small part of a worksheet. A sideways printing feature is provided for wide documents. You can also save worksheet infor-mation in a format that can be used by many other programs on the market.

With a graphics display, VisiCalc IV can create bar, pie, and line charts based on the information that you've stored in the worksheet.

There is one limitation of VisiCalc IV—you cannnot perform any database functions, as you can with Lotus 1–2–3 or Supercalc3.

RATINGS:
Overall Value 7   Performance 6
Ease of Use 8   Documentation 8

GAMES

Games are the most popular form of computer software, consistently outselling all other categories. There are hundreds of games available, and this chapter reviews many of the best of them.

There are two major categories of computer games: arcade games and strategy games. Arcade games are usually played with a joystick or other special controller, and they simulate the play action and graphics of popular coin-operated video games. The computer versions of most of these games are not as realistic or responsive as their arcade counterparts (because the arcade machines are designed specifically for the games they play), but they are still entertaining and challenging. Zaxxon and Frogger are two typical arcade games reviewed in this chapter.

Strategy games come in many different types. In text adventure games, for example, a written description of a scene is provided, and the player specifies what action he or she would like to take. The program then responds with a new scene that is the logical consequence of the player's actions. A final goal, such as finding a treasure, guides the player through all of the scenes. Infocom's Enchanter is an excellent example of this type of game.

A variation on the text adventure is the graphic adventure game. These games play very much like text adventures, but a graphic description of each scene is provided, either along with or instead of the text description.

Prices may vary; shop for discount prices.

In addition to these types of games, there are many simulations of board games and sporting events available for personal computers. Chess and poker are popular subjects for simulation games, and several new games feature athletic events. HES Games, for example, is a new game from HesWare that simulates several Olympic events.

Another type of simulation that is very popular is the flight simulator games. These games have the same type of controls as an airplane, and you try to fly to a destination or land the airplane. Microsoft's Flight Simulator is not only a popular game, but it has become a standard test of IBM software compatibility because of the way that it uses the IBM PC hardware and operating system.

AIR TRAFFIC CONTROLLER
CBL Marketing

Approx. Retail Price $35
Available for . . . . IBM PC and compatibles
Type . . . . simulation

If you like to work while you play, or if you are interested in sharpening your ability to juggle up to 26 tasks at the same time, Air Traffic Controller may be just the game for you.

This game simulates the conditions faced by an air traffic controller in a radar approach control environment. The computer screen is used as a radarscope with some additional displays. Communication to aircraft is done via the keyboard. The computer itself acts as pilot and neighboring controller.

As an air traffic controller, the user has the responsibility for the flow of aircraft within an area of 15×20 miles from ground level to 5000 feet of altitude. Within this area are various airports, navaids, airways, and fixes. During the course of a session a certain number of aircraft will enter this airspace. The player is to guide them all to their predetermined destination within certain safety and time constraints.

At the beginning of the game, the player can choose his or her starting conditions. Any number of aircraft from 1 to 26 can be chosen, and the player can choose the length of time to play, from 99 minutes (easy) to 16 minutes (nearly impossible). A choice of two maps is offered. Each map has two airports, each with only one active runway. The controller must guide planes in and out of these airports. The map also contains fixes. These are points through which aircraft enter and exit the air space.

Prices may vary; shop for discount prices.

Factors to be considered by the player are the airplane's speed, altitude, heading, and fuel. Both jets and propeller craft use the airspace, jets flying twice as fast as propeller planes. The game is over when the player has successfully landed all arriving aircraft, and guided all departing aircraft out of the airspace. However, the game is also over if a plane crashes, runs out of fuel, enters the mountain range too low, or the user runs out of time. Two planes in conflicting airspace will also end the game.

Two versions of Air Traffic Controller are provided on the disk, one for color displays, the other for monochrome displays. BASIC or BASICA are required to run the game. It can be loaded easily on a hard disk if you so desire.

Besides learning the air traffic rules, it is important to remember that only upper case letters can be used for commands. This gem of wisdom can be found on page 10 of the 12-page manual. This is one of those games that can give you sweaty palms and requires considerable concentration. It will give you additional respect for real air traffic controllers once you have played it. It is a very habit-forming game.

This software comes with a 12-page printed manual that describes the game strategy in detail.

As this is not a copy protected disk, backups are made in the usual easy fashion.

There are a number of air traffic control games on the market. We think this is one of the best. But if you are looking for something mindless to help you relax, this is not it.

RATINGS:
Overall Value 9   Difficulty 10

BILL BUDGE PINBALL CONSTRUCTION SET
Electronic Arts

Approx. Retail Price $34
Available for . . . . Atari, Apple, Commodore
Type . . . . pinball simulation

Pinball Construction Set is exactly what the title suggests. Available in disk format for Atari, Apple, and Commodore computers. Pinball Construction Set is a program that allows you to design and play your own computer pinball game.

Compared to such games as David's Midnight Magic and Slam Ball, where you are stuck with a single playfield, this game gives you control of numerous components that go into the design of a pinball game. Using your joystick, you design the playfield by moving icons representing such elements as flippers, bonus gates, and most other components of modern pinball machines. You can also control the amount of gravity, the speed of play, the elasticity of bumpers, and other features. The program allows you to store your masterpiece on disk so you can play the same game again.

There are some problems. The first, and most obvious, is that you can't just load the disk and expect to play pinball—you have to remember how to load the games you've stored on the disk or take the time to build a new game. Joystick control is confusing, with the left flipper being controlled by either moving the joystick to the left or hitting the fire button. The trade-off, however, is that you can use the fire button and move the stick to the right to move both flippers up.

RATINGS:
Overall Value 10   Difficulty 8

Prices may vary; shop for discount prices.

ENCHANTER
Infocom

Approx. Retail Price $50
Available for . . . . IBM PC and compatibles
Type . . . . text adventure

Infocom has made some of the very best adventure games. Such titles as Deadline, Suspended, and Witness are classics of the genre. Enchanter is another in the line of Infocom adventures and is currently available only on disk for the IBM PC.

Unlike adventure games from most other software manufacturers, the Infocom adventures are text only —they don't have any graphics. Also unlike most other adventures, Enchanter (and the Infocom titles) respond in a much more understandable manner. With most adventures, you have to do a lot of random guessing to come across the right combination of words needed to make your next move. Enchanter, however, understands whole sentences. This ability makes Enchanter easier and less frustrating to communicate with, but no less easy to solve.

Studying the manual is essential to playing this game. However, once the instructions are learned, you should be prepared to lose countless hours trying to win. At around $49.95, you'll get a lot of good playing value from Enchanter.

RATINGS:
Overall Value 9   Difficulty 9

**FLIGHT SIMULATOR, and
FLIGHT SIMULATOR II
by Microsoft and subLOGIC**

Approx. Retail Price $50
Available for . . . . most systems
Type . . . . flight simulation
Flight Simulator is available on disk for the IBM PC,
and Flight Simulator II is available in disk versions for
the Apple II series computers, Radio Shack computers, and the Commodore 64.

Both versions of Flight Simulator actually simulate
what is involved in flying and landing an airplane—
reading the instruments and controlling throttle,
flaps, and landing gear. The view of several actual
airports has been built into these packages.

Both simulators come with large manuals—full of required reading—you can't just load the game and
play. Learning to use this package involves *really*
learning to use it—working through the instructions
and practicing on the screen. To make the package
more attractive as a game, all versions include a World
War I dogfight program.

Depending on the machine, the graphics run from
poor to fairly good. Controls are relatively easy to
learn. But don't buy this program if you expect a
game—you'll be disappointed. However, if you want
to get a feel for actual flying, Flight Simulator and
Flight Simulator II are a good substitute for the real
thing.

RATINGS:
Overall Value 7   Difficulty 9

Prices may vary; shop for discount prices.

HES GAMES
Human Engineered Software

Approx. Retail Price $35
Available for . . . . Commodore 64
Type . . . . sports simulation

HES Games give the player the opportunity to compete in 6 Olympic-type events—hurdles, springboard diving, weightlifting, 100 meter dash, long jump, and archery. It is available on disk for the Commodore 64.

Unlike some earlier athletic games, the events in HES Games involve a variety of skills. For example, the running events require rapid right-left movements of the controller. To do hurdles and long jump, precise timing of the jumps (upward movement of the joystick) is necessary. The weight lifting requires exact timing of the up-down movements involved in performing the lifts. The other events require similar control techniques.

Top scores, rankings, instant replay, fan noises, and world records are features of the game, which is best played competitively by more than one player. On the minus side is the slow disk access that is built into the Commodore 64, switching events is a time consuming process. The game can also be rather hard on controllers.

If you like arcade games like *Track and Field*, you should like HES Games.

RATINGS:
Overall Value 8   Difficulty 7

JUMPMAN
Sierra On-Line

Approx. Retail Price $40
Available for .... Atari, Commodore
Type .... ladder game

Jumpman can be considered something of a leap beyond Donkey Kong. Although the basic object of both games is to maneuver your player through a series of obstacles involving elevators, ladders, ramps, and other devices while simultaneously avoiding deadly pursuers, Jumpman gives you 30 completely different game screens to conquer. Jumpman is currently available in disk-based versions for the Commodore 64 and Atari computers.

Jumpman is loaded with many excellent features—good graphics and sound, 30 game screens, a high score screen, the option of selecting the speed that Jumpman moves, and even a variety of difficulty levels (easy, moderate, and very difficult), or a random mode that mixes them all up. Jumpman can be played by up to four players (although you'll have to pass the joystick around for all to play).

At a suggested price of $40, Jumpman can provide many hours of challenging fun. If you liked Donkey Kong, but wanted more screens, more challenges, and a lot of fun, Jumpman is a good choice.

RATINGS:
Overall Value 9   Difficulty 9

MINER 2049ER
Microfun, Big Five Software, Roklan

Approx. Retail Price $50
Available for .... most systems
Type .... ladder game

Miner 2049er is a game that resembles a souped up Donkey Kong. It is also one of the most heavily licensed original games yet. Big Five Software developed the game in cartridge for the Atari computers (and the 5200), then licensed disk rights for the Apple computer to Microfun (a subsidiary of MicroLab), the cassette rights for the Commodore 64 to Roklan software, and most other rights to Tiger Electronics, which has a TI/99-4A cartridge available.

The object of Miner 2049er is to maneuver your character through increasingly difficult game screens. As you do this, the playfield changes—once all areas of the field have been passed over, you progress to the next screen. This isn't, of course, anywhere near as easy as it sounds. Along the way, your player must avoid the numerous obstacles that litter his path.

Miner 2049er is a very good game. Depending on the version you get, there are between 10 and 13 game screens to conquer (compared to Jumpman this number is small, but it's still quite a challenge). The biggest problem is that you must progress through the screens in numerical order. If you want to practice screen 9, for example, you must go through all the earlier ones, even though you may have already mastered them. Providing a way to work on a specific screen would have been a nice touch.

RATINGS:
Overall Value 7   Difficulty 9

MR. ROBOT AND THE ROBOT FACTORY
Datamost, Inc.

Approx. Retail Price $35
Available for . . . . Commodore, Apple, Atari
Type . . . . ladder game

Mr. Robot and the Robot Factory is a Miner 2049er-type game that outdoes the original. The game requires the player to pass through an increasingly challenging playing field that includes ladders, conveyors, slides, and elevators.

The game consists of 26 increasingly difficult game screens. Mastery of the game screens requires lots of practice, in addition to memorization of the techniques required to overcome each of the challenges, precise timing, and a bit of luck.

The player is given the option of playing the game with the screens in a random order or in increasing levels of difficulty. You can start at easy, medium, or top difficulty levels, and you don't have to play through the easier levels once you've conquered them.

The designers have included a feature that could keep the game from becoming obsolete—Mr. Robot's Robot Factory is a powerful editor that allows users to build their own game screens, using a large selection of game elements. These new games can then be saved onto disk. In effect, you can create your very own, original version of Mr. Robot at any time you want. Mastery of all the elements, in the numerous possible combinations, could make this game one that remains interesting for years.

RATINGS:
Overall Value 9   Difficulty 10

Prices may vary; shop for discount prices.

NEUTRAL ZONE
Access Software

Approx. Retail Price $40
Available for . . . . Commodore 64
Type . . . . space game

Neutral Zone is a space game available on disk for the Commodore 64. Although it's been around for some time, it still approaches state of the art in game graphics.

The object is to maneuver your space ship through a very well drawn, high resolution background, complete with stars, planets, and comets. As you maneuver through this scene, you must use your indicators to track the enemy ships that try to destroy your space station (located in the middle of the scrolling background). These ships move away from you and shoot blazing fireballs at you.

Game play is challenging, and graphics and sound are excellent. In fact, Access Software suggests that you hook the audio output from your computer into a high quality stereo amplifier, in order to get the full impact of the game's sounds.

There are a few weaknesses in the program. Game play can be *too* challenging (and, perhaps, a bit boring), and the cassette version takes *nine minutes* to load However, if you want a stand-out graphics program, Neutral Zone, for about $39.95, is a strong entry.

RATINGS:
Overall Value 7   Difficulty 10

OIL'S WELL
Sierra On-Line

Approx. Retail Price .... $30 (disk)
Available for .... most systems
Type .... digging game

It's been said that the secrets to a good game are to make one that is easy to learn, but hard to master. Oil's Well follows that rule very well. Versions are available on disk for Apple and Commodore 64 computers, and a cartridge version is available for Atari Computers. An IBM PC version is being planned.

The object is simple—maneuver your drill bit through all levels of an underground mine, picking up all the loot that's distributed there. While you do this, you must avoid the underground creatures that try to bite through your drilling line. You can drill through them, but they can destroy your drill. As you drill down into deeper levels, you must keep a sharp eye on the action near the top.

The only problem with Oil's Well is that it's extremely addicting. If you don't want to lose hours playing the game, don't buy it.

RATINGS:
Overall Value 8   Difficulty 9

Prices may vary; shop for discount prices.

PAC-MAN
Atari, Inc.

Approx. Retail Price $45
Available for . . . . most systems
Type . . . . maze game

Pac-Man is the most famous (and most imitated) arcade game ever created. Several versions have been released by Atari and numerous similar look-alike games have been offered by other manufacturers. The versions vary somewhat among themselves, but the essentials are the same.

Pac-Man is a round, yellow character who (under the direction of the player) grazes through a maze, eating dots as he goes. Four hungry ghosts chase Pac-Man, and they have him for dinner if they can catch him. The game ends when Pac-Man has been caught three times.

Pac-Man is not always a helpless victim because he can eat power dots on the screen for energy to kill his pursuers. Each dot eaten by Pac-Man adds to the score and extra points are awarded for devouring ghosts and nabbing occasional bonus prizes.

Pac-Man is a very simple but challenging test of hand-eye coordination. Some rudimentary strategy planning is required. Of all video games, this is the most popular. Pac-Man has gobbled up many hundreds of thousands of quarters in arcades.

RATINGS:
Overall Value 9   Difficulty 5

QUEST FOR TIRES
Sierra On-Line

Approx. Retail Price $40
Available for . . . . Apple, Atari, Commodore
Type . . . . obstacle game

Quest for Tires is a clever scrolling game employing the characters from the BC comic strip. It is available on disk for Atari, Commodore 64, and Apple computers.

The object is to help Thor, who is riding his wheel, get through the prehistoric obstacle course (by jumping boulders, ducking under trees, hopping over turtles, etc.) to save Cute Chick, who is being held prisoner in a cave at the end of the course. To do this takes good timing and a lot of practice.

There are some problems with this game. The Apple version is not as good as the other formats, since the Apple isn't really able to scroll smoothly.

At around $39.95, Quest for Tires is a cute game that will appeal to players who are tired of violent simulations.

RATINGS:
Overall Value 7   Difficulty 7

SPACE TAXI
Muse Software

Approx. Retail Price $30
Available for . . . . Commodore 64
Type . . . . space game

If you can imagine, for a few minutes, that you are driving a taxi somewhere in outer space, you'll probably do quite well with Space Taxi, a game on disk for the Commodore 64. The object of this game is to maneuver your taxi through a variety of progressively difficult obstacle courses.

The taxi controls provide close approximations of space motion (moving in a vacuum with minimal gravity) but you can travel in only four directions—up, down, right, or left. Maneuvering your joystick will fire thrusters that produce appropriate movement.

Making the game more interesting is the taxi's passengers, who actually *speak*, hailing your cab with a "Hey taxi!" You have to land near (but not on top of) your passenger, who will enter the cab and ask to be taken to his destination ("pad nine, please"). The object is to deliver your fare as quickly as possible.

The primary weakness of Space Taxi is that the controls are unique and difficult at first. The other shortcoming is that each new screen loads from disk, and on the Commodore 64 this is a slow process. However it's usually well worth the wait.

RATINGS:
Overall Value 8   Difficulty 8

STAR WARS
Parker Brothers

Approx. Retail Price $40
Available for . . . . Atari, Coleco, Commodore
Type . . . . space game

If you liked the arcade version of Star Wars, you'll be happy with any of the cartridge versions for the Atari, Commodore, and Coleco Adam versions. Although the arcade version used vector graphics (composed of connected lines on a special screen), the Parker Brothers version simulates the vector display extremely well.

The object is to maneuver your spaceship through a series of screens, destroying tie fighters, flying through (and destroying) towers, and finally flying through the cavern in the death star. The game gives you three difficulty levels and is challenging for players at all levels. Graphics and sound are very good, and game play is also excellent.

Perhaps the only major difference between the Parker Brothers version and the coin-op model is that the home version doesn't have the voices of the movie's characters talking to you. Once you play the game, you won't miss them; at about $39.95, Star Wars is a very faithful reproduction of the arcade title.

RATINGS:
Overall Value 9   Difficulty 10

Prices may vary; shop for discount prices.

ULTIMA SERIES
Sierra On-Line

Approx. Retail Price $60
Available for . . . . most systems
Type . . . . adventure game

The Ultima Series is three adventure-type games en-titled, appropriately enough, Ultima I, Ultima II, and Ultima III. Because of the months that could be in-volved in playing them, these games are a definite value (the entertainment per dollar is very high). You should check with your dealer regarding availability of the Ultima series titles for your computer. At press-time, Ultima I was available on disk for the IBM PC, Ultima II on disk for IBM PC, Apple, Commodore 64, and Atari computers, and Ultima III available only for the PC. This is likely to change.

The general object of the series is to solve the many puzzles, and win the many battles involved in getting your player (whose attributes you select) through to the completion of the game. The game is something like one tremendous puzzle, requiring careful guesses, good strategy, and a great deal of luck.

The Ultima adventures are excellent entertainment, capable of tying a player up for countless hours. Don't be surprised if you get hooked on Ultima games—also don't be surprised if you spend every evening for weeks or months trying to solve the game.

The Ultima series also comes with complete instruc-tions and a game map to try to keep track of your players. At around $59.95 each title of the Ultima series is a good value.

RATINGS:
Overall Value 9   Difficulty 10

INTEGRATED

Integrated software (programs that combine more than one function, such as word processing, a spreadsheet, and data management) has become very popular. Lotus 1-2-3 was the first popular integrated product, and it topped the software sales charts every week for nearly two years. There are now many imitations of Lotus 1-2-3 on the market, as well as original integrated packages that offer more features or entirely different approaches.

The advantage of an integrated program (over buying all of the features in separate programs) is that the same information can be used in all of the different sections of the program at the same time. When you make a change in a spreadsheet, for example, that change will be incorporated into the letter you're creating in the word processing program and a bar chart being displayed by the graphics program.

When shopping for an integrated software package, expect to spend much time comparing features and testing individual programs. With an integrated package, you are actually buying several programs at once, and you should look at each of those programs separately. Compare the word processing, spreadsheet, data management, communications, or graphics section of an integrated package to other single-purpose programs, to see what compromises were made when they were all combined into a single integrated product.

Because of the high cost of this type of software, you should also make certain that you have the hardware required to make full use of an integrated package before you buy. Find out whether the program you are considering is compatible with your printer, and if the program displays graphics, check whether it is compatible with your monitor.

Another consideration is memory. Integrated packages use great amounts of RAM; usually 256K or more on the IBM compatibles. The minimum RAM requirement should be clearly marked on any integrated packages you look at, and you will probably want to have more RAM than the minimum. Extra RAM will allow you to generate and use more information, such as bigger spreadsheets.

If you can't find an integrated package that offers the features you need, you might want to consider an operating environment, such as Desq or VisiOn. Operating environments allow you to combine various individual programs into an integrated system. Desq allows you to use the applications programs that you already have, while VisiOn uses applications modules designed by VisiCorp. Operating environments usually have extra hardware requirements like a hard disk or more memory, but they may be the best approach for some users.

CONTEXT MBA
Context Management Systems

Approx. Retail Price $695
Available for . . . . Hewlett-Packard
RAM Required 256K
Functions: word processing, database, spreadsheet, graphics, communications

Context MBA uses the common spreadsheet format for both spreadsheet and database functions. The MBA spreadsheet provides 999 rows by 95 columns. The spreadsheet lets you work with financial data easily; you can choose a range of cells to move or copy around the worksheet.

Context MBA provides database capabilities by letting you store information in the form of records, within the horizontal rows of the worksheet. You can add, remove, and change your records, and you can use Context MBA's sort commands to arrange the database in the order of your choice. Although Context is fairly fast in its operations, it does not have the speed of Lotus 1–2–3 or Ashton-Tate's Framework.

Word processing is reasonably flexible with Context MBA; you can use a full screen for entering text, and you have the use of some word processing functions, such as search and replace and the control of margins. It's no substitute for a fully featured word processor.

Graphics capabilities to handle bar, pie, and line charts, and communications capabilities for sending Context data to other computers round out this integrated software package.

RATINGS:
Overall Value 8   Performance 7
Ease of Use 7   Documentation 9

Prices may vary; shop for discount prices.

DESQ
Quarterdeck Office Systems

Approx. Retail Price $399
Available for .... IBM PC and compatibles
RAM Required 256K
Functions: any MS-DOS applications

Desq is an operating environment for your software that creates an electronic desk with a big plus. That plus is, Desq is designed to use your existing familiar software. Instead of having to dispose of your expensive software and learn new programs. Desq lets you run popular software like WordStar, dBASE II, and Lotus 1–2–3 on a single screen.

Desq creates windows on the screen for each applications software package that you use, and lets you transfer information between these windows. For example, you might have one window open, using WordStar to process a letter, with another window showing a Lotus 1–2–3 spreadsheet. You can quickly and easily mark a section of the spreadsheet and copy it into the window containing the letter. Desq can handle up to 10 of your favorite applications programs, which you select by pressing function keys.

There is a price that you pay for all of this speed and power; Desq—like VisiOn—is 'hardware hungry.' You'll need at least 256K of memory and a hard disk drive to use Desq.

RATINGS:
Overall Value ....10 Performance 9
Ease of Use .... 9 Documentation 9

ELECTRIC DESK
Alpha Software

Approx. Retail Price $345
Available for .... IBM PC and compatibles
RAM Required 256K
Functions: word processing, database, spreadsheet, communications

Electric Desk is an integrated software package that falls midway between the more powerful offerings, like Symphony and Framework, and low-end software like the PFS series. This program offers word processing, an electronic spreadsheet, database management, and communications in one package. The word processor section of Electric Desk provides complete editing and deletion capabilities.

Electric Desk automatically rearranges (reformats) text as you make major changes. You also get full search-and-replace text features, variable line spacing and tabs, and underlining and character bolding. The database manager feature does not have the power of a dedicated database management program like dBASE III, but it will do fine for simple filing of many types of information, like mailing lists. The spreadsheet measures 255 rows by 255 columns, and data from within the spreadsheet can be shared with the other parts of the program (like the word processor function). A communications feature lets you communicate with other computers or videotex services. The only feature that's missing from Electric Desk is the ability to do any types of graphics. If you don't need this feature, Electric Desk may meet all your needs while saving you money.

RATINGS:

Overall Value	10	Performance	10
Ease of Use	9	Documentation	10

FRAMEWORK
Ashton-Tate

Approx. Retail Price $695
Available for . . . . IBM PC and compatibles
RAM Required 256K
Functions: word processing, database, spreadsheet, graphics, communications

Ashton-Tate's Framework is an integrated software package with a number of unique features. Framework provides fully featured word processing, spreadsheets, database management, business graphics, and communications features in a single, well-integrated package. But there is more to Framework than the usual applications offered by integrated software packages. Framework provides an outline processor that lets you organize your thoughts in outline form before expanding the outline into text that can be used in a document. And, as its name implies, Framework provides a series of frames that let you use more than one feature of the program at the same time. You can open one frame to use word processing to work on a document, while another frame shows the contents of a spreadsheet, with a third displaying a database. You can place as many frames on the screen as you can visually keep up with, and you don't have to stop performing one application to begin using another.

Framework has a universal set of commands, so that many of the commands in the database or the spreadsheet are the same commands that you use for the word processor. This design, along with a simple menu-style structure, make Framework relatively simple to get started with, considering the power it offers. The word processing function provides a full set of word processing commands, including multiple margins in a single document, automatic justification and reformatting, headers, footnotes, page numbers, block move and copy, search and replace, underlining, boldface, and italics. The spreadsheet can use algebra or plain-English names in its formulas, and you can link multiple spreadsheets together. The database manager uses a spreadsheet-like format, and has full sorting and searching capabilities. Graphics support provides six different types of graphs, and works on a monochrome or color monitor. Framework's communications feature lets you link to mainframe computers or videotex services, and a built-in programming language called Fred lets you develop your own specialized applications.

Framework can be a good buy, if you regularly use most or all of its features. If you were to buy the capabilities of Framework as separate programs, you could spend over $1,000, and you still wouldn't have the simple, common commands and well-done integration that Framework offers.

RATINGS:
Overall Value .... 8 Performance 10
Ease of Use .... 8 Documentation 8

Prices may vary; shop for discount prices.

LOTUS 1–2–3
Lotus Development Corp.

Approx. Retail Price $595
Available for . . . . IBM PC and compatibles
RAM Required 192K
Functions: word processing, database, spreadsheet, graphics

Lotus 1–2–3 has sold more than any other business software package for personal computers, and for good reason. Lotus 1–2–3 handles many of the tasks that managers and professionals need to perform on a daily basis, and it does so without requiring you to change programs. The integrated capabilities of Lotus 1–2–3 give you a powerful spreadsheet, average database management capabilities, and limited word processing in a single package. (An upgrade to the Lotus 1–2–3 package, called "Symphony," adds a full-featured word processor and communications software to the 1–2–3 package.)

Everything that 1–2–3 does for you is modeled around the spreadsheet concept. The information that you're working with, whether it's figures for a cost analysis, a collection of names that you want to sort, or a memo to the staff, is entered into the 1–2–3 spreadsheet.

If you're working with figures, the spreadsheet operates like any electronic spreadsheet. You can perform a full range of calculations on the numbers entered into the spreadsheet, and 1–2–3 provides a huge spreadsheet size of 256 columns by 2048 rows. That's a total of over a half million cells available for your use. Besides entering your own numbers and formulas, 1–2–3 lets you choose from among a number of built-in common financial formulas.

When you use Lotus 1–2–3 for database management, you again use the spreadsheet format. But this time, the horizontal rows become records, and the vertical columns become the information fields inside each record. When creating a database, you might, for example, place first names in column "A," last names in column "B," addresses in column "C," cities in column "D," and so forth. Using the program's sorting commands, you can then search through the database for names or addresses meeting specific conditions, or arrange the data in alphabetical or numeric order. It's this ability to mold to your application that makes the database management capabilities of Lotus 1–2–3 so attractive. You also get graphics features that let you create bar, pie, and line charts based on information stored in a spreadsheet or a database.

The word processing features are limited; you can enter text into a spreadsheet; edit it; and print the text, alone or as part of a spreadsheet, database, or graph display. The amount of editing you can perform is limited, and does not include the features of a complete word processing package. Among 1–2–3's other strengths are its ease of use, due to its common command design and tutorial disk, and the program's broad base of support. Templates are readily available for a number of common applications such as simple general ledger, cost analysis, or profit and loss statements. This is a direct result of the popularity of Lotus 1–2–3.

RATINGS:

Overall Value	8	Performance	9
Ease of Use	8	Documentation	8

Prices may vary; shop for discount prices.

SUPERCALC3
Sorcim Access

Approx. Retail Price $395
Available for . . . . IBM PC and compatibles
RAM Required 96K
Functions: spreadsheet, database, graphics

SuperCalc3 is a flexible spreadsheet and graphics package, with a reasonable number of database functions thrown in.

SuperCalc3 is based around an electronic spreadsheet that stores information in the common row-and-column format. You can enter text, numbers, or formulas into any spreadsheet location. SuperCalc3 also provides limited database capabilities, by allowing searches for specific information and the sorting of columns in alphabetical or numeric order. Sorting information contained in a database can be done by pressing as few as two keys; this is much easier than the procedures needed to produce graphs with most similar products.

Where SuperCalc3 really shines, however, is in its graphics capabilities. You can create seven different kinds of graphs, including bar, pic, line, and stacked-bar graphs, whether your computer has a color or monochrome monitor. And unlike Lotus 1–2–3, you do not have to swap disks to prepare your graphs. Entering information is easier with SuperCalc3 than with the older versions of the SuperCalc program. SuperCalc3 is also priced more reasonably than its main competitors, Lotus 1–2–3 and Context MBA.

RATINGS:
Overall Value 9   Performance 8
Ease of Use 9   Documentation 8

Information accurate at time of printing; subject to manufacturer's change.   **329**

SYMPHONY
Lotus Development

Approx. Retail Price $695
Available for . . . . IBM PC and compatibles
RAM Required 256K
Functions: word processing, database, spreadsheet, graphics, communication

Symphony, Lotus Development's encore to its popular Lotus 1–2–3 software package, is an integrated offering with five popular applications—a spreadsheet, graphics, word processing, database management, and communications—in a single program. As with Lotus 1–2–3, Symphony uses its familiar spreadsheet concept as the basis for all its applications. Symphony offers a huge spreadsheet that, in theory, measures 255 columns by 1892 rows. (In practice, you will run out of memory in your PC long before you can use all of this space. But Symphony was designed to support newer machines with additional memory, such as IBM's upcoming PC II.) Although a few of the commands differ between Lotus 1–2–3 and Symphony, you still get all of the powerful spreadsheet functions that Lotus 1–2–3 was noted for. Symphony also has the ability to create bar, line, and pie graphs. Added to the graphic features are options for high, low, and closing graphs (useful for following the stock or commodity markets) and exploded pie charts. Unfortunately, as with Lotus 1–2–3, you must still exit the spreadsheet and insert a separate disk when you want to print a graph. The database manager features of Symphony use the rows and columns of the spreadsheet for the storage of your database fields, such as names, addresses, or zip codes. You can search through a database for specific information, sort columns of information in ascending or descending order, and print reports based on the qualifications that you choose for specific data. You can also create

Prices may vary; shop for discount prices.

data entry screens that occupy an entire screen. That wasn't possible with Lotus 1–2–3, and it makes use of the database easier for a novice user.

Symphony's word processing mode is a substantial improvement over the limited text editing found in Lotus 1–2–3. With Symphony, you get all of the features of a full word processor including the ability to move and copy blocks of text, search for and replace specific words, change margins, and vary tabs and line spacing. You can also open a number of windows on the screen, and examine or work with different documents in each window. The communications feature is also a full-fledged program. It allows communications with public bulletin boards, videotex services, and many company mainframe computers. The communications software also supports the popular "XMODEM" protocol, which is used to transfer files from most public bulletin boards.

Symphony is a powerful software package, aimed directly at the "power" user of a personal computer. It has many commands to learn, and it will take an investment in time for one to grow familiar with the package. If you have that time, you'll find that Symphony is a likely candidate to meet most or all of your personal computer software needs.

RATINGS:

Overall Value	8	Performance	9
Ease of Use	7	Documentation	8

T/MAKER III
T/Maker Co.

Approx. Retail Price $275
Available for . . . . IBM PC and compatibles
RAM Required . . . . NA
Functions: word processing, database, spreadsheet, graphics

T/Maker III provides word processing, spreadsheet, limited database functions, and graphics. But it doesn't use the familiar spreadsheet concepts for entering information. Instead, T/Maker III uses a "program editor," a kind of word processor, as the heart of all its functions. The program editor comes close to offering all of the features of a good word processor. You are limited—by the size of your computer's memory—in the length of a file that you can handle with T/Maker III. (The normal limit is about 44,000 characters.)

For spreadsheet-type calculations, you use T/Maker III's editor to create a series of tables containing the information that you are working with. You then add formulas to the tables to tell T/Maker III what you want to do with your data. The database functions are limited; you can find specific information in the tables, but you cannot perform detailed financial operations on that information while using the search features. T/Maker III doesn't have the power of Lotus 1–2–3 or Context MBA, but the program is simple to use, and carries a more reasonable price tag.

RATINGS:
Overall Value 7   Performance 7
Ease of Use 9   Documentation 8

Prices may vary; shop for discount prices.

VISI ON
VisiCorp

Approx. Retail Price $1365
Available for . . . . IBM PC and compatibles
RAM Required 512K
Functions: word processing, spreadsheet, graphics
(all not included)

VisiOn is known in the software world as an operating
environment. It's not exactly a program; instead, it
provides a working area on your screen modeled after
an ordinary desktop, and various programs can run on
the electronic desktop. VisiCorp provides applications
software for word processing, spreadsheets, and
graphics that can be used in the VisiOn environment.

The most common applications, word processing and
spreadsheets, require the purchase of Visi On Word
and Visi On Calc along with the basic Visi On package.
Visi On Word is a reasonably powerful word processor
that will measure up to all but the most demanding of
users. Visi On Calc is a capable spreadsheet with one
objectionable flaw; it is very slow in calculating, when
compared to other spreadsheets like Lotus 1–2–3 or
Multiplan.

VisiOn's other drawback is the expensive hardware
needed to use it. You'll need an enormous amount
(512K) of memory, color graphics capabilities, and a
hard disk drive to use Visi On, so the average PC
running Visi On represents a total investment of
$7,000 to $10,000. Not all IBM-compatible hard disks
work with VisiOn. Check with VisiCorp or a knowledgeable dealer before you invest.

RATINGS:
Overall Value 6   Performance 6
Ease of Use 6   Documentation 6

UTILITIES

Certain types of programs are only used to work on or with other programs. This includes compilers, interpreters, disassemblers, disk utilities, and operating systems. All of these are reviewed in this section.

Compilers are programs that help you create programs of your own. You can write a program as a standard text file, using a line editor or word processing program, and the compiler will turn that source file into a set of instructions that your computer can execute. Compilers are available for many different languages, including Fortran, Cobol, BASIC, Pascal, and assembly language. (Assembly language compilers are called assemblers.)

Interpreters are very similar to compilers, in that they turn instruction written in a programming language into instructions that the computer can understand. But while a compiler works on an entire program at once, an interpreter takes each individual command and tries to interpret and execute it immediately. Interpreters are available for many languages, but the most common are BASIC interpreters. The BASIC that comes built-in with many machines (in ROM) is a BASIC interpreter.

Disassemblers do the opposite of what assemblers do. They take a compiled program (in machine language instructions) and convert each instruction into an assembly language instruction. With a disassembler, you can often modify or debug a compiled program, even if you don't have the original program as it was written in a programming language.

Disk utilities are used for inspecting or modifying the data on a disk. There are many different types of disk utilities, but the most popular are programs that allow you to restore deleted or damaged files. When you delete a file, the information in that file will still be on the disk until you write something new over it—only the file's entry in the directory (the list of the contents of the file) has been removed. Disk utilities are available that allow you to restore that directory entry and recreate a file that you have accidentally deleted.

If all of this doesn't make any sense to you, then you probably don't need any of the programs listed in this section. You're probably using your computer to do specific tasks with applications programs, and utilities are used by experienced users and programmers to gain capabilities that are not provided by applications software. After you've used your computer for a while, though, you may want to come back and read through these reviews. After you've gained some experience and run into some of the obstacles that utility programs can help you over, you'll be ready to consider them once again.

BASIC COMPILER
Microsoft

Approx. Retail Price $395
Available for ....IBM PC and compatibles
Type ....compiler

The BASIC Compiler is a worthwhile, albeit rather expensive tool for those who are serious about developing programs in BASIC. It gets around the speed limitations of the standard BASIC that's provided with the IBM PC and similar machines.

Using the BASIC Compiler, you can speed up programs that run slowly when written in the standard BASIC. Using the BASIC Compiler isn't necessarily a simple process, though. You must first use a word processing program (or the editor that's built into the standard Microsoft BASIC) to write your program. Then, you load that program into the BASIC Compiler, which will produce a program known as the "source" program. After this step, you use a linker (included in the package) to produce several program files called "object" files. Finally, you use the compiler on the object files to produce a file that can be run by the IBM PC; this is the actual program, ready for use on the machine.

If all of this makes no sense to you, you're better off without the BASIC Compiler. After all, the standard Microsoft BASIC will do virtually everything that the BASIC Compiler will do, just in a slower fashion. But if you insist on maximum speed from a high-level language like BASIC, then the BASIC Compiler is your kind of tool.

RATINGS:
Overall Value 7   Performance 8
Ease of Use 7   Documentation 8

Prices may vary; shop for discount prices.

THE COMPLETE GRAPHICS SYSTEM
Penguin Software

Approx. Retail Price $80
Available for .... Apple IIe, II, II Plus
Type .... programmer's aid

Complete Graphics System is a professional-quality utility for graphics programmers. It allows the user to create designs or character fonts, which can then be edited or saved to disk. It also has a three-dimensional graphics capability.

Keyboard commands are used to draw images, although the Apple II game paddles can also be used if desired. Figures can be drawn freehand and then filled in with over 100 different colors and shades. Images are stored in high-resolution color shape tables that can be used by other programs.

The 3D graphics module will create and edit three-dimensional images. Once an image has been defined, it can easily be rotated to be viewed from any angle. Images can even be scaled to look larger, for inspection of details.

A font editor is also available. It provides the ability to create and save entire character sets for use in other programs.

Complete Graphics System is a must for both serious and novice Apple II graphics programmers. Although the keyboard is a little awkward for creating and editing images, the capabilities provided by this package are worth the trouble.

RATINGS:
Overall Value 9   Performance 10
Ease of Use 9   Documentation 9

CP/M 2.2
Commodore

Approx. Retail Price $20
Available for . . . . Commodore 64
Type . . . . operating system

The Commodore 64 version of the widely used CP/M (Control Program for Microcomputers) operating system is usable but incomplete. It is sufficient for learning and simple applications.

One good feature of this version is its ability to handle a second disk drive via an IEEE-488 dual drive, or imitate one within a single drive by swapping disks. On the other hand, having a second disk device is not permitted.

For full CP/M, 80 columns are almost a must, but this version has only 40 columns. Also with this version, the disk drive is somewhere between relatively and painfully slow. With only 44K of available memory, it is too small for some common applications, and certain standard CP/M capabilities (such as the I/O byte) are not provided.

CP/M 2.2 worked with most CP/M programs tested, and includes a modern program to get them into your computer. The manual, however, is too complicated for novices to use.

If you want to learn CP/M, this package will let you do so very inexpensively. On the other hand, if you want to make serious use of CP/M, you should consider buying a computer designed to run CP/M.

RATINGS:

Overall Value	7	Performance	7
Ease of Use	5	Documentation	6

MACRO ASSEMBLER
Microsoft–IBM

Approx. Retail Price $100
Available for ....IBM PC and compatibles
Type...assembler

For the advanced programmer who needs to dig beyond the normal levels of programming languages and into the inner parts of the computer, IBM's Macro Assembler is the tool for the job. You can use the Macro Assembler to produce assembly-language programs that will run directly on the IBM PC and on most PC compatibles.

The process of using the Macro Assembler isn't painless, but it is about as simple as assembly-language programming will ever get. You first create the program, using a text editor or word processor. You then load the program into the assembler, which produces a listing of the program, along with a new file called a "translated object" file. You must then use the Link utility (provided with PC–DOS) along with the object file to create a final version of the program that will run on the PC.

We found the Macro Assembler to be relatively compatible with some non-IBM computers; we used it on a Compaq and an Eagle PC with no ill effects.

The documentation is good for reference, but rather poor for learning. If this is your first experience with assembly-language programming, you should find a good book on the subject to accompany the IBM Macro Assembler.

RATINGS:
Overall Value 9	Performance 9
Ease of Use 9	Documentation 6

MICROSOFT BASIC
Microsoft

Approx. Retail Price $350
Available for .... most systems
Type .... programming language

Microsoft BASIC (MBASIC) is the programming language of choice for many applications on dozens of different models of computers. The IBM versions are supplied free with the PC–DOS operating system. Other computers may require you to purchase BASIC, or it may be included with the machine.

MBASIC operates in one of two ways: in a "direct mode," which lets you enter BASIC commands that are immediately processed; and in an "indirect mode," which stores a program in memory and takes no action on that program until you issue the RUN command. MBASIC automatically switches between the modes, which are dependent on whether or not you precede a BASIC statement with a line number.

This is a well-documented, complete version of BASIC that supports a large number of commands and statements. Some of the more flexible commands and statements that aren't included in other, less powerful BASICs include: CHAIN and COMMON, to pass program control over to a different program; ERR and ERL, for providing error-handling routines in your programs; INKEY and ONKEY, for monitoring and using the keyboard; PEEK, POKE, and CALL, for executing machine-language routines from BASIC; and TRON and TROFF, trace features that are very helpful when you must find the bugs in a program.

All disk-based versions of MBASIC provide full disk routines for transferring files to and from disks. MBASIC lets you do more than just save programs;

340

you can perform file maintenance, such as viewing the files on a directory, and erasing files. And some versions of MBASIC, including those offered on the IBM PC and compatibles, provide commands for manipulating screen colors and graphic images.

On the IBM version, MBASIC makes good use of the keyboard to provide a number of programming shortcuts. The keyboard's function keys and a number of character keys combined with the 'alternate' key can be used to enter complete words like LIST, RUN, PRINT, and GO TO.

MBASIC also offers a flexible editor on all computers on which it is used. You can edit any lines in the program by typing the word EDIT. You have full cursor control during the editing process, eliminating the need to retype the entire program line.

MBASIC can accurately deal with single precision arithmetic (up to seven accurate digits) or double-precision arithmetic (up to 16 accurate digits).

MBASIC is moderate in execution speed. Its speed can't be compared to BASIC compilers, however, which operate much faster due to their design. The documentation for MBASIC varies from good to abysmal, depending on the computer you use MBASIC with. Microsoft provides MBASIC to computer makers, who usually write their own manuals. But there are plenty of good books written to help you learn to use this popular, well-done BASIC.

RATINGS:

Overall Value	9	Performance	8
Ease of Use	8	Documentation	7

NORTON UTILITIES
Peter Norton

Approx. Retail Price $80
Available for .... IBM PC and compatibles
Type .... miscellaneous disk utilities

The Norton Utilities is a 'toolkit on a disk' for the avid user of an IBM-compatible. The program's biggest claim to fame is its file recovery utilities. Using the file recovery utilities, you can often save files that are on damaged disks. You can also recover files that have been accidentally erased from a disk. The Norton Utilities also provide disk inspection routines; these will let you examine and modify the contents of a disk. The utilities are very useful for examining the insides of a specific program.

If all this sounds high-tech, it should. The Norton Utilities will, by nature, appeal to the advanced PC user or the programmer. But the ability to recover a damaged or erased file may be well worth the cost, even for the novice user who may never use the other tools provided. The documentation is clear, and will help explain the use of the utilities, some of which are admittedly rather complex.

RATINGS:

Overall Value	10	Performance	9
Ease of Use	8	Documentation	8

Prices may vary; shop for discount prices

ProDOS
Apple Computer, Inc.

Approx. Retail Price $40
Available for .... Apple IIe, IIc
Type .... operating system

ProDOS is a disk operating system for the Apple II series of computers. It requires 128K of memory and one disk to be used. And since it is different than the old reliable AppleDOS 3.3 that Apple users have put up with for years, many may wonder just why ProDOS is needed. It turns out that AppleDOS has its limitations. And ProDOS does a good job of overcoming those limitations. ProDOS allows the use of "tree-structured" directories. Without a long and boring explanation, this simply means that hard-disk users can keep up with their files much more easily with ProDOS. ProDOS can simulate a filing cabinet, with information filed in various "folders" that are called subdirectories. And if you don't care for such organization, you can choose not to use the subdirectories. ProDOS files are not compatible with information stored using AppleDOS 3.3. However, a utility is included with ProDOS that lets you convert files created with Apple DOS 3.3 or 3.2 to ProDOS format.

RATINGS:
Overall Value .... 9 Performance 9
Ease of Use .... 7 Documentation 7

RID (RECORDING INTERCHANGE DIAGNOSTIC)
Dymek

Approx. Retail Price $35
Available for . . . . IBM PC and compatibles
Type . . . . disk diagnostics

After six months to a year of use, one or more of your floppy disk drives may begin to occasionally misbehave. Symptoms frequently include data errors, unreliable program loading, and the inability of one disk drive to use diskettes created on a different drive. Until recently, the only solution was to take one or all drives to a repair facility for a checkup, which frequently costs between $15 and $65. The RID disk and some of its competitors help users isolate and even correct problems in their own offices.

RID is a disk drive diagnostic disk. It performs seven tests on a computer's disk drive, and will perform them on both sides of a double-sided drive. RID tests the rotational speed to determine if it is within specification. Noise tolerance is tested to determine if the drive can play back without error, on a worst-case data pattern with half the normal amplitude (signal strength).

It does a write/read test to make sure the drive being tested can write a record, read it properly, write over the record, and then read this second record without error. Track alignment is tested to determine if the read head is properly aligned for track position. It determines if head alignment is jeopardized by the direction of head positioner travel. Disk clamping is tested to evaluate the ability of the disk drive to center the disk onto the drive hub before it is clamped into position. Finally, it tests to determine if the level of erase crosstalk will cause degradation of interchange performance.

Prices may vary; shop for discount prices.

All that is necessary is to transfer two files from DOS to the program disk. RID has a file that does this automatically. All the user does is type "HI" and the files will be transferred. The disk is then ready to use.

We tried the RID disk with both good and "problem" drives. In every case RID made the proper evaluations. It even helped us locate a marginal disk drive controller board. The straightforward "English" assessment of drive performance even included suggested corrective activities that can be performed by the user (i.e.: clean diskettes and try again).

The software comes with a two-page instruction and specification sheet glued inside the disk holder, and a ten-page information brochure. The information brochure describes each test and discusses the results. The specifications section gives a more technical description of these tests, although none of this documentation will be easy for a novice to understand.

As the disk contains special recordings that cannot be copied, it is not possible to make a backup of this disk.

The first time the RID disk saves you a trip to a repair shop, it will more than pay for itself. Purchase one before you need it.

RATINGS:

Overall Value	10	Performance	10
Ease of Use	10	Documentation	9

WORD PROCESSING

Word processing is the most common use for personal computers in business and the home. There are many features to look for in a word processing program, depending on the type of work you expect to do with it.

If you're new to word processing, any word processing program will increase your writing efficiency. There are some limitations, however, that can be very annoying after you become more experienced with the program. It's best to understand all of the features before you buy, even those features that you won't be using at first. This will keep you from buying a program that you'll outgrow in a few months. Powerful word processing programs are available that are simple enough for beginners to use.

Menu-driven word processing programs are the easiest to learn, because you can always look to the menu for a list of your available options. With most menu-driven programs, there is an option that experienced users can choose to keep the menu from being displayed. This creates a larger working area on the screen.

One limitation that you should be sure to check on is the maximum number of characters in a line and the maximum file (or document) size. If the program is limited to 80 characters per line, you won't be able to work on spreadsheets or large tables with it. If the maximum document size is very limited, you'll have to break large documents into many smaller pieces, which can be time-consuming and confusing.

Prices may vary; shop for discount prices.

Although most word processors support special printing effects like underlining, boldface, and subscripts, there are many different ways to display these effects on the screen. If you want to see an exact replica of the final printed page on the screen, you need a word processor that can display those effects on your monitor. If you choose such a program, make sure that you know of any special hardware requirements it may have, such as a graphics adaptor or special monitor.

Another consideration, if you're a very fast typist, is whether the program can keep up with you. Type very fast for a few lines, and then check if the program missed any letters. This limitation can be particularly annoying, since word processing is supposed to make your writing faster and more efficient.

Finally, make sure that you check the features and capabilities of the word processing program as it runs your model of computer. Most word processing programs are available in versions for many different computers, and each version may offer slightly different capabilities and limitations. Advertisements for word processing software usually describe the most powerful version and then say "available for the following computers." This doesn't mean, however, that all of the features will work on all of the computers. As with all software purchases, you should ask specific questions and assume nothing.

APPLE WRITER 2
Apple Computer, Inc.

Approx. Retail Price $150
RAM Required 48K
Available for .... Apple II Plus, Apple IIe

One of the better word processing packages available for the Apple II series is Apple Writer 2, an improvement on the time-tested Apple Writer program. This program combines flexibility with user friendliness. It uses a series of menus that let you choose various options at the touch of a single key. Text entry is simple, and for the most part, painless; there is a small but noticeable delay when you reach the end of a line, as the software catches up with your typing.

To move the cursor around the screen, you use combinations of the cursor arrow keys and "Apple" keys, or various control key combinations. For example, control-B moves you to the beginning of a document, while control-E takes you to the end.

Apple Writer 2 handles form letter creation, a plus if you want to use the program in an office. This is not a visually accurate editing screen, so the appearance of the text on the screen may not resemble the appearance of the text that is printed. Apple Writer 2 comes with tutorials on disk that help you learn to use all the features of the program.

RATINGS:
Overall Value 7   Performance 7
Ease of Use 9   Documentation 8

ATARIWRITER
Atari, Inc.

Approx. Retail Price $100
RAM Required 16K
Available for . . . . Atari computers

AtariWriter is a reasonably powerful and friendly word processor for the Atari computers. It offers standard word processing features such as easy insertion and deletion of text from any point in a document, search-and-replace of selected text, and the ability to move and copy blocks of text from one place to another. AtariWriter comes in plug-in cartridge form, so you can use this software on any Atari computer, regardless of how little memory you have.

AtariWriter lets you choose from cassette or floppy disk as a method of storing documents. A command line at the top of the screen shows you the format of the document, including the line spacing, margins, and type of print used. AtariWriter can handle double columns of text, as well as form letters. Since the Atari screen displays just 40 characters of text at a time, the way that your document appears on the screen usually isn't the same as it will appear when it prints. This is due to a limitation of the Atari computers and not the AtariWriter software. There's even an "undo" command that lets you restore text that's accidentally been deleted.

AtariWriter offers a large number of professional features, and the program works well. It is one of the best word processing programs available for an inexpensive home computer.

RATINGS:
Overall Value 8   Performance 7
Ease of Use 8   Documentation 7

EASYWRITER II
Information Unlimited Software

Approx. Retail Price $395
RAM Required 96K
Available for .... MS-DOS,PC-DOS

EasyWriter II is a much improved word processor for the IBM PC and compatibles. It shouldn't be confused with EasyWriter I, an earlier program that gained a widespread reputation for having numerous problems. EasyWriter II is a page-oriented word processor. It divides your document into individual pages, and works with a page at a time.

Editing is done in an unusual way with EasyWriter II. The program considers text in the form of units, with the Function-9 and Function-10 keys moving the cursor forward or backward one unit. You can place the editing in a character mode, word mode, line mode, sentence mode, paragraph mode, or page mode; pressing F9 or F10 will then move the cursor by the appropriate amount.

EasyWriter II also gives you the standard word processing features of text move and copy, and the ability to copy text from other documents. A nice feature of the printing options is the ability to print a number of documents using a single print command.

The documentation is good, and includes a disk-based tutorial to teach you the ropes of EasyWriter II.

RATINGS:
Overall Value 8   Performance 7
Ease of Use 8   Documentation 8

Prices may vary; shop for discount prices.

MICROSOFT WORD
Microsoft Corporation

Approx. Retail Price $375
Available for . . . . IBM PC and compatibles
RAM Required 128K

Microsoft Word is one of the first of a new generation of word processors that outperforms many of the other products on the market. It is expensive, but it is heavy with features that approach those of office word processing machines.

Microsoft Word lets you enter and edit text inside of windows on the screen. You can use one window (the entire screen), or you can open multiple windows and edit different documents at the same time. You can edit up to seven documents at once with Word, although the screen gets a little cluttered with more than three windows open at once. You can copy or move text from any window to another window.

Word is intuitively simple to use, due to its unique command design. All of the commands use a one-letter abbreviation that represents what it is you are trying to perform. For example, once you press the escape key to enter the command mode, you could press P to print a document, C to copy text, D to delete a paragraph, or S to search for a specific set of words.

You can also choose commands or highlight text using a hand-held mouse. You roll the mouse around on a desk surface, and an arrow on the screen moves along with the mouse. By aligning the arrow with a command (or a portion of the text to be highlighted) and pressing a button on the mouse, you choose that command, or highlight that particular part of the text. You can use Word with or without the mouse, and the program can be purchased alone, or with the mouse.

Word produces text on the screen in a visually accurate format. Underlined text is underlined, and bold and italicized text appear on the screen as they would in print. If you're using a color monitor, you can set the windows in different background colors.

Word also excells in printer support, both now and in the near future. Word provides a full range of printer type styles, including proportional spacing, on a wide variety of printers.

Word is one of the few packages currrently on the market with the ability to fully support a laser printer. Such printers, based on office copier technology, are just coming on the market, and cost $3,000 and up. But a combination of Word and a laser printer will give you print quality rivaling an offset press.

Word has a built-in merge feature for creating and printing multiple form letters. And a glossary feature lets you store commonly used sentences or paragraphs, and call them up into a document at the touch of a key.

The documentation is pretty confusing in places and could stand improvement. But the program itself is a first-rate word processor that currently stands far ahead of most of its competition.

RATINGS:

Overall Value	8	Performance	9
Ease of Use	9	Documentation	6

MULTIMATE
Multimate International

Approx. Retail Price $495
Available for . . . . IBM PC and compatibles
RAM Required 256K

MultiMate is a top-notch attempt to make the power and style of a dedicated word-processor available on a personal computer. MultiMate combines speed, flexibility, and ease-of-use in one powerful package. You pay for all of this power, as MultiMate is not inexpensive, and requires a generous amount of memory installed in your computer. But if you need the power of a dedicated word processor at a reasonable cost, MultiMate deserves a close look.

MultiMate is modeled after the design of the Wang word processors found in many offices. So, if you've ever used a Wang, you'll find MultiMate to be very familiar. The program is totally menu driven. The menus give you numbered selections for each feature. Once you select a feature, additional menus appear to further define your options. MultiMate also provides instructions at the bottom of the screen that aid you in remembering which keys to use for additional choices.

MultiMate uses combinations of the keyboard's ten function keys, along with the shift, control, and alternate keys, to provide editing functions. You can move throughout the text quickly, and stick-on labels are provided for the keys to identify what functions they perform. You also get different ways to search and replace text, and move and copy text. MultiMate also handles multiple columns of text, a feat that many word processing packages don't deal with very well if at all.

Another big plus is the "document summary screen." This screen appears whenever you begin editing a document, and it lets you enter pertinent information, such as the author's name, a description, the date of creation, and the total number of pages. Built-in merge features let you create form letters, and an 80,000 word dictionary provides automatic spelling checker capability. MultiMate provides automatic spelling checker capability. MultiMate provides a variety of printing options; you can print one page, a group of pages, or the entire document. You can set margins, pitch (number of characters per inch), and you can even tell the computer to wait until a certain time or date to start printing the document.

Learning to use MultiMate is a snap, thanks to the tutorial-on-a-disk that steps you through all of the features of MultiMate's operation.

MultiMate clearly ranks among the high-end word processors for the IBM PC and compatibles. Not everyone can justify the expense, as there are capable, less expensive word processing packages on the market. But if you process words on a regular basis, and need the range of features, then MultiMate is an excellent choice.

RATINGS:

Overall Value	7	Performance	9
Ease of Use	9	Documentation	8

PEACHTEXT 5000
Peachtree Software

Approx. Retail Price $250
Available for . . . . IBM PC and compatibles
RAM Required 128K

As more than just a word processor, Peachtext 5000 is one of the better buys on the market. It's not as powerful as some of its competition, but it does provide the functions that most persons need in a word processor. And the advantages of Peachtext 5000 are in the additional programs that come with the package: a spelling checker; an electronic spreadsheet; Random House Electronic Thesaurus; and a list manager are included in the package.

Peachtext 5000 makes heavy use of control keys to perform commands. For editing, you simply enter text, and the usual cursor (arrow) keys and delete keys produce the expected result. You can move and copy chunks of text, or delete marked portions of text. Because this program uses a separate formatter to handle printing, the image on the screen isn't exactly what you'll see when your text is printed. Search-and-replace options, and automatic form-letter creation are also valuable features of the program.

The additional programs are a nice touch. While PeachCalc (the spreadsheet) doesn't measure up to a Lotus 1–2–3 or a SuperCalc3, it is still a capable electronic spreadsheet. The Random House Thesaurus is an easy-to-use, automated synonymfinder that operates within the PeachText 5000 word processor. The list manager is a simple database manager.

RATINGS:
Overall Value 9   Performance 8
Ease of Use 8   Documentation 7

PERFECT WRITER
Perfect Software

Approx. Retail Price $199
Available for . . . . CP/M, MS–DOS
RAM Required . . . . 128K (MS–DOS)

Perfect Writer, despite its name, is not perfect. But it does come close, offering full-featured word processing and some features that are hard to find among programs for the older, CP/M-based computers. Perfect Writer is actually two programs in one; a text editor, used for entering and editing your documents, and a text formatter, used for printing documents in various formats.

Perfect Writer uses "embedded commands," which are commands preceeded by a formatting symbol. The commands are numerous, and a bit confusing at first. But once you've learned them, you can quickly adjust the format of a document with a minimum of fuss. You can also edit more than one document at a time with Perfect Writer; this is a feature that's common in some word processors for the IBM PC, but not in other CP/M-based programs.

When editing multiple files, the screen splits into two sections, and each section contains a separate file. Perfect Writer supports numerous printers, and the program includes a utility that lets you change the arrangement of the control keys to your liking.

RATINGS:
Overall Value 9   Performance 7
Ease of Use 9   Documentation 8

PFS:PROOF
Software Publishing

Approx. Retail Price	$95
Available for	most systems
RAM Required	128K (MS–DOS)

PFS:Proof is a proofreading and spelling correction program that complements PFS:Write (a word processor by the same company). PFS:Proof also works well with files created by WordStar, or any standard text files produced by a word processor. PFS:Proof checks and corrects your documents in a fast, one-step process. PFS:Proof uses a 100,000 word dictionary; this is one of the largest dictionaries used by a spelling checker. A "guess" feature lets PFS:Proof search for what it thinks is the correct spelling of the word. You can customize a second, personal dictionary. Words can be added to the personal dictionary one at a time, or they can be added at once in the form of a list. A big plus of PFS:Proof is that the program shows misspelled words in context, or how they appear in the actual sentence. In fact, the entire document (or as much as will fit on the screen) appears, and the misspelled word is shown as a reversed image. PFS:Proof is, like the other programs in the PFS series, totally menu driven. The clear operation and simple menus make it hard to make a mistake when running this program.

RATINGS:
Overall Value	9	Performance	9
Ease of Use	9	Documentation	9

SCREENWRITER
Sierra On-Line

Approx. Retail Price $130
Available for .... Apple II
RAM Required 48K

ScreenWriter is a professional word processor that is easy enough for a beginner to understand. It has simple and straightforward commands.

There are two editing formats: INSERT mode and CHANGE mode. The INSERT mode allows you to insert text, moving other text forward. The CHANGE mode allows you to write over the old text, replacing it with new text. A single keystroke switches from one mode to the other.

One nice feature is that words or phrases can be assigned to certain keys. Then, when you need the desired word or phrase, you simply hit the appropriate key. This eliminates repetitive typing. Another good feature is generating form letters from a mailing list, with the option of personalizing any individual letter. Text centering, bold face, and underlining are all supported.

The cursor movement commands are extremely simple. A single keystroke can move the cursor one character, one word, one line, one page, or to the beginning or end of the file.

RATINGS:
Overall Value 6   Performance 9
Ease of Use 10   Documentation 8

Prices may vary; shop for discount prices.

SUPERSCRIPSIT
Radio Shack

Approx. Retail Price $199
Available for . . . . Radio Shack
RAM Required 48K

If you own a Radio Shack computer, SuperSCRIPSIT is a good choice for a word processor. It's a big improvement over the earlier SCRIPSIT program, which left much to be desired.

SuperSCRIPSIT lets you enter and edit text in a straightforward manner, and you can move and copy blocks of text just as easily. SuperSCRIPSIT uses control keys to implement its functions; by holding the control key while pressing other keys, you choose operations like setting margins and line spacing. SuperSCRIPSIT provides full underlining and bold-facing, and it supports proportional-space printing (assuming your printer can handle that option). There's also a $149 proofreading option that lets you perform automatic spelling correction of your text.

SuperSCRIPSIT does not support graphics of any kind, so you won't be using this program for any unusually shaped characters or for charts. Early versions of the program had a nasty habit of losing large amounts of text at inopportune times; but those problems have been cleared up in the latest version, making SuperSCRIPSIT one of the best word processors for Radio Shack computers.

RATINGS:
Overall Value 9   Performance 9
Ease of Use 7   Documentation 8

TI-WRITER
Texas Instruments

Approx. Retail Price $100
Available for . . . . TI 99/4A
RAM Required 32K

TI-WRITER offers all of the major functions that you would expect to find in much more expensive word processing software. It is flexible, easy to learn, and relatively powerful.

You can insert and delete lines of text, move or copy blocks of text, and rearrange words, sentences, and paragraphs. You can justify text, causing all right-hand margins to form an even edge. This program also has an attractive feature not found in most word processing programs; if you accidentally erase a character or line, you can press just one key to get back the erased text. In addition, you can set tabs and indents, and search for specified words or phrases.

It would be nice to have an optional spelling checker, which TI-WRITER doesn't, and some of the keystrokes are awkward and a little irritating. Still, despite these minor limitations, TI-WRITER gives you a lot for your money. It is almost comparable to Word-Star, a popular program for more expensive personal computers, and WordStar cost hundreds of dollars more than TI-WRITER.

RATINGS:

Overall Value	 9	Performance	 10
Ease of Use	 7	Documentation	 9

Prices may vary; shop for discount prices.

WORD JUGGLER
Quark Engineering

Approx. Retail Price $190
Available for . . . . Apple
RAM Required 64K

Word Juggler may be the best word processing pack-age we have tested. Its power, convenience, and com-mon sense approach to operation should be an in-spiration to programmers everywhere. We tested the Apple III version of this product, but an Apple IIe version is also available.

This fully featured word processing package also works with optional spelling checking software. A phototypesetting interface software package is also available. A combination of menus and special func-tion keys are used to speed operation. Both Word Juggler files and regular ASCII files can be edited or created. Plastic templates (or key caps) are provided to label the word processing function keys.

All editing takes place in memory, limiting the size of documents. Very logical key combination sequences have been created. For example, the right arrow key moves the cursor right one position. When the shift key is held down and the right arrow key is pressed, the cursor moves to the start of the next word. The control key/right arrow combination moves the cursor to the end of the current line. Many of the other func-tions operate in this same "three level" approach.

Word Juggler boots in the insert mode. Users desiring overstrike editing can change this. The usual array of find, replace, change, block save, block load, block move, header, footer, page numbering, and print fea-tures are offered. It is possible to display documents exactly as they will print, making it simple to modify page endings and make other format decisions. Specific pages of a document can be printed. Multiple copies of a document can be requested. An envelope feature makes it possible to quickly reprint inside addresses from letters in the proper position on envelopes (changing the left margin).

Specific formatting functions are spelled out on the screen rather than being represented by cryptic codes (i.e.: "double space" is displayed rather than ".sp2"). It is possible to merge addresses and other variables with text quite simply. Disk data and keyboard data can be combined. There is a sort routine, making it possible to create address lists, and then sort them. It is possible to use Word Juggler on hard disks.

The disks come almost ready to use. The user need only configure them for his or her printer.

The 72-page typewritten manual contains tutorial, reference, data file merge, backup, troubleshooting, file formats, printer filter, glossary, and index sections.

The package comes with a master diskette and a backup master. The disks are copy resistant. Quark charges $10 or $20 for replacements. A data disk backup procedure is not available through Word Juggler. DOS commands are used instead.

Except for the fact that you will need to create very large documents in sections, this is possibly the closest thing to perfect word processing available on microcomputers today. Unfortunately, no MS–DOS version is offered or planned.

RATINGS:

Overall Value 10	Performance 10
Ease of Use 10	Documentation 10

WORD PRO 3 PLUS/64
Professional Software

Approx. Retail Price $80
Available for . . . . Commodore 64
RAM Required 64K

Word Pro sets a standard for Commodore word processing software. Most competitors either use its file format or include the ability to convert Word Pro files to whatever they use instead. Word Pro 3 Plus for the Commodore 64 is adapted from one of the best known of all programs for Commodore's larger PET and CBM computers.

Part of the key to Word Pro's popularity is that it retains the commonly used cursor controls so popular with Commodore owners. Also, it is very simple for a beginner to type a letter into Word Pro. The result looks strange, with words broken in the middle at line ends, but it works even with a narrow screen like the Commodore 64's.

Before printing, formatting commands must be added; these remain visible in the text, making it easy to remember what commands were given. One weakness in this approach is that it is difficult to visualize the final document until it is printed, so you may waste some time and paper getting the format commands correct on complicated documents.

Apart from video output, the new Commodore 64 version of Word Pro has nearly every feature desirable in a word processor. The weakest part of all versions of Word Pro is the manual, which has a rambling style.

RATINGS:

Overall Value	 8	Performance	 7
Ease of Use	 6	Documentation	 5

WORDSTAR
MicroPro International

Approx. Retail Price $495
Available for . . . . most systems
RAM Required 64K

WordStar is often referred to as the standard by which other word processors are measured. The program's popularity stems from some good reasons. It was an early entry in the micro market. Thousands of copies were quickly sold, making many people familiar with it. Moreover, WordStar is powerful and flexible. WordStar performs all functions from a main menu, called the "no-file" menu. By typing various combinations of control keys, you can select commands in a number of sub-menus for functions like copying and moving blocks of text. WordStar also allows the use of "dot commands." These commands add a large variety of control over the documents' final appearance. With the dot commands, you can include or omit page numbers, control line spacing in small increments, change the pitch (number of characters per inch), and perform many other functions. The dot commands let you make the changes you desire at any point in a document, not just at the beginning of the document.

Printing a document is handled effectively from the main menu. You can select from a number of print options, such as the number of pages printed, and whether you are using continuous-form paper or single-sheet paper. You can also print one document and edit another document at the same time. Doing so, however, noticeably slows down the program's response on the screen. WordStar can be used with all commonly used printers on the market.

Prices may vary; shop for discount prices.

Two optional programs, MailMerge and SpellStar, can be used to add automatic form-letter creation and spelling correction capabilities. There are also dozens of programs offered by independent companies that add to WordStar's capabilities. These include more advanced spelling checkers, an electronic thesaurus, and grammar checkers.

Among WordStar's lesser traits are its lack of speed at times (because WordStar must often read the disk to perform functions, slowing down the program), and the confusing control keys used to perform different operations. Also, most versions crash if text is sent to a full disk. Frequently all data on the disk are lost when this happens.

In WordStar's favor are the program's reliability, extensive formatting capabilities, and broad support. WordStar can be used on most brands of personal computers available. And there are more spelling and grammar checkers, tutorial books, and computer classes available for WordStar than for any other word processing program.

RATINGS:

Overall Value	7	Performance	9
Ease of Use	5	Documentation	8

MISCELLANEOUS

This chapter covers a variety of software, including programs that answer specific needs or solve specific problems. Browse through the reviews, and you may find a program that can help you with a task that you haven't previously been doing on your personal computer.

Two project managers are included in this section. Project managers are a new type of software that is becoming very popular with supervisors and planners. These programs let you define a project as a group of activities with specific start and stop times. You can then specify which activities must be completed before other activities can begin. The program will calculate the times and dates that each activity can slide to without affecting the overall schedule, as well as the critical path. Harvard Project Manager, Microsoft Project, and VisiSchedule, the project managers reviewed here, are three of the best in this new area.

A handy program called Sideways is also reviewed here. Sideways does one simple task—it turns your wide spreadsheets sideways so that they can be printed on one continuous piece of fan-fold paper. In the spreadsheet section, we warned you about the possibility that your printer may not be able to print wide spreadsheets; with Sideways, you can get around that problem.

Prices may vary; shop for discount prices.

Some spelling checkers are also included in this section, while others appear in the word processing section along with the programs they were written for. The Word Plus, reviewed at the end of this chapter, will work with a variety of word processing programs and will automatically correct your spelling errors. These types of programs can be a great help if you are a poor speller or sloppy typist.

MacPaint, the graphics package for the Apple Macintosh, is also reviewed here. It is one of the most powerful graphics packages around for small computers. With it, you can create professional-looking diagrams and illustrations for reports, or simply draw pictures for your own enjoyment. This program was originally bundled with the Macintosh, but recent Macintosh buyers have to purchase it separately.

HARVARD PROJECT MANAGER
Harvard Software, Inc.

Approx. Retail Price $395
Available for . . . . IBM PC and compatibles
Type . . . . project scheduler

One of a number of software packages designed to help manage your company's time in a better fashion is Harvard Project Manager. This program takes two proven methods of management, known as PERT (Program Evaluation Review Techniques) and Critical Path, and it automates these tedious jobs.

The software lets you define projects as a group of activities, with specific start times and stop times. By adding descriptive tasks, you create a roadmap on the screen. This roadmap has times and dates by which each part of the project must be started and completed to meet the completion date for the entire project. Harvard Project Manager has the "what-if" capabilities common in spreadsheets, in that you can change a date and see what the effect on the entire project will be if that part falls behind schedule.

Harvard Project Manager is limited in the financial data it can handle; you can list total expenses for each task, but you cannot individually define separate expense amounts within each task. Barring that information, Harvard Project Manager does a fair job of automating the planning process.

RATINGS:
Overall Value 7   Performance 8
Ease of Use 7   Documentation 8

Prices may vary; shop for discount prices.

LETUS A–B–C
R. Nelson

Approx. Retail Price $30
Available for .... IBM PC and compatibles
Type .... computer magazine database

"I just read about that . . . Where was it?" The proliferation of computer information makes storing and finding computer-related magazine articles a real challenge. Letus A–B–C disks for use with the low-cost PC–File database management software makes finding the article you need a snap.

Letus A–B–C is a series of databases, summarizing articles and letters from magazines about IBM Personal Computers. It was created using PC–File III, a general purpose "database manager" program. Together, the Letus A–B–C database provides the IBM PC user with a tool for performing literature searches at a very nominal cost—in the office or at home.

The initial releases of Letus A–B–C disks cover the period 1982 through 1983 for the following five magazines devoted to the IBM PC: *Softalk, Personal Computer Age, PC Magazine, PC World,* and *PC Tech Journal.* The databases come on three double-sided, double-density diskettes.

An attempt was made to include every article of each magazine. This database extends the magazine's index by providing a "key word" field that can quickly be searched with PC–File. For example, one can search for all of the articles that make reference to a particular product or idea (e.g.: hard disks or user supported software.)

This database also contains "Letters to the Editor," "Questions and Answers," Helpful Hints," etc. In addition to the key word field and the identification fields (i.e., author, title, magazine issue, and page) there are three lines that give a general, terse description of the article. Names of products and manufacturers are given wherever possible.

Updates of Letus A–B–C will be provided on an annual or semi-annual basis. The 1984 update will be provided monthly for $15, or quarterly for $20.

As the documentation resides on the disk, the user must print this out before reviewing the databases. Otherwise, the disk is ready to use with PC–File.

Once you understand the organization of these files, they become very easy to use. It may be useful to print out the list of all of the key words used in the indexes on these disks. The searching process is quite straightforward. Using PC–File's reporting features, information about desired documents can be printed or displayed. Users with hard disks can combine multiple floppy disks into one large magazine database. This single large database can then be searched, sorted, and otherwise modified. The quantity and quality of article indexing varies from disk to disk, but is generally quite good. The information is more current than many of the more expensive time sharing systems (Dialog, The Source, etc.).

Backups can be made in the usual fashion through DOS. The authors encourage users to make copies for themselves and their friends.

RATINGS:
Overall Value	10	Performance	9
Ease of Use	10	Documentation	8

Prices may vary; shop for discount prices.

LEXICHECK
Quark Engineering

Approx. Retail Price $190
Available for .... Apple IIe, III
Type .... spelling checker

This spelling checker has been designated to work with Word Juggler word processing software. While it does not contain as many features as some competitive products, its simple integration with Word Juggler makes it the ideal choice for Word Juggler users. We tested the Apple III version.

Lexicheck is a high performance spelling checker designed for use with Word Juggler on the Apple III or IIe. Lexicheck comes with a dictionary of 30,000 words (a dictionary of legal terms is available at extra cost). When the user checks a document with Lexicheck, each word is compared against the words in the dictionary. The user is informed of any word not in the dictionary, and given the choice to change it, accept its spelling or add the word to the dictionary. The user can create personal dictionaries. A word is then checked against both the main dictionary and any other dictionary you specify. This is advantageous for those who need a dictionary of medical terms or a dictionary of computer terms, etc.

The disk comes ready to use. No installation is necessary beyond inserting the documentation into the Word Juggler manual, and making a backup copy of the program disk.

It is very easy to use. Most functions require only one or two keystrokes. Lexicheck does an adequate job of spelling checking. In the beginning, users may find it necessary to add properly spelled words to its comparably small (30,000 word) dictionary. This process is very easy. Unlike many of today's newer spelling checkers, Lexicheck does not offer guesses or suggested spellings. This is a very fast spelling checker, which can be speeded up even further by turning off the display while checking continues. When Lexicheck finds a repeated spelling error, every occurrence is corrected simultaneously. Users must remember to save the corrected copy to disk since this is not automatically done, nor is a backup copy of the uncorrected copy automatically made.

Quark includes a 19-page typed manual with this software. It is designed to fit in a section of the Word Juggler manual. It contains a small tutorial, a reference section, and an "errors and recovery section."

The Lexicheck disk may be backed up using the normal Apple III copy program. However, the master disk is the only one Quark will update should an update be required.

While Lexicheck is not the most fully featured or largest spelling checking program offered for microcomputers, it is an excellent choice for those using the superb Word Juggler word processing program.

RATINGS:

Overall Value 8	Performance 9
Ease of Use 9	Documentation 9

Prices may vary; shop for discount prices.

PFS:GRAPH
Software Publishing

Approx. Retail Price	$140
Available for	IBM PC and compatibles
Type	graphics

PFS:Graph is a business-graphics program that's very useful for business applications. Basically, what this program does is create graphs suitable for presentations. You can make bar graphs, pie charts, line graphs, or stacked bar graphs with PFS:Graph.

The program works with up to four sets of numeric data. You can enter the numbers directly, or they can be transferred from records created with PFS:File, a database management program. You have the ability to place names of your choice on the various parts of the graphs.

PFS:Graph makes full use of color if you're using a color monitor, although you cannot select the colors; the program chooses them for you.

The one noticeable limitation of this program is its inability to handle more than four sets of data. If you want to build a pie chart that breaks down the nation's population in a dozen ways, you're not going to do it with this program.

Like other programs in the PFS series, PFS:Graph is menu driven, making this graphics package simple to use.

RATINGS:

Overall Value	7	Performance	7
Ease of Use	9	Documentation	8

MICROSOFT PROJECT
Microsoft Corporation

Approx. Retail Price $250
Available for . . . . IBM PC and compatibles
Type . . . . project scheduler

Project is a well-done project planning package that borders on being a full-blown time and cost analysis tool for professionals. Project is relatively simple to use, and its power and flexibility are likely to surprise you.

Project uses a format that bears a strong resemblance to an electronic spreadsheet. Dates are laid out in your choice of days, weeks, months, or years across the top of the screen. The individual tasks of the project are outlined in the rows along the left-hand side of the screen. Project builds a time chart across the screen, by calculating all the start and stop times you provide for all of the individual tasks.

A very strong plus of this program is the ability to itemize costs in detail; in effect, the program doubles as a job-costing program, by calculating totals for individual departments based on the number of personnel and materials you assign to a given task. And due to Project's familiar spreadsheet-like design, many professionals who regularly use spreadsheets will find Project to be an easy package to adapt to.

RATINGS:
Overall Value 8   Performance 9
Ease of Use 9   Documentation 8

     Prices may vary; shop for discount prices.

SIDEWAYS
Funk Software

Approx. Retail Price .... NA
Available for ....IBM PC and compatibles
Type...spreadsheet rotation

Sideways is an ingenious program with a single-minded purpose in life—to turn your spreadsheets 90 degrees, so they will print on your printer in a vertical format. Since most spreadsheets are wider than they are long, Sideways can solve the problem of wide spreadsheets that normally print on multiple sheets, which then must be taped together.

Sideways requires you to first save your spreadsheet as a text file on disk. Since nearly all spreadsheet packages provide a way for you to do this, it shouldn't be a problem. You then run the Sideways program, and answer a few questions that are presented on a menu.

Sideways also works with text files produced by your word processor, but it's the avid spreadsheet user who will find this program most helpful. One caution: you will generally find Sideways printing to be slower than regular printing.

RATINGS:
Overall Value 7   Performance 6
Ease of Use 9   Documentation 9

VISISCHEDULE
VisiCorp

Approx. Retail Price $300
Available for . . . . Apple II
Type . . . . project scheduler

VisiSchedule from VisiCorp is a sophisticated project planner for professionals involved in tracking and scheduling complex projects from planning to completion. Manpower requirements, resource allocation, and cost ceilings can all be reliably tracked. As with VisiCorp's popular VisiCalc program (see separate review), predictions can be made based on various assumptions.

VisiSchedule employs critical path analysis, which means that complex tasks are broken up into smaller critical tasks. These simpler tasks can then be more effectively managed and controlled. Each subtask and its associated deadlines are graphically represented in the overall project schedule, and the system automatically takes holidays and slack time into account when calculating manpower requirements.

The 40-column Apple display screen cannot display an entire schedule at once, but scrolling is used to move the screen window to any part of the schedule. Project milestones are shown on the schedule, and a complete copy including calendar time charts and summary reports can be displayed or printed.

VisiSchedule is fully compatible with all programs in the VISI series. It is an excellent planning and management tool for any business or organization.

RATINGS:

Overall Value	9	Performance	9
Ease of Use	7	Documentation	9

Prices may vary; shop for discount prices.

THE WORD PLUS
Oasis Software

Approx. Retail Price $150
Available for . . . . IBM PC and compatibles
Type . . . . spelling checker

The Word Plus is a spelling checker that rates highly in comparison to many similar products. It automatically reads through files that have been created with your word processor, and checks the files for misspelled words. The program's big advantage over earlier spelling checkers is that The Word Plus will not only find the incorrectly spelled words, but it will also correct them.

The Word Plus has a 45,000 word dictionary, which greatly reduces the chances of the program indicating that a correctly spelled word has been misspelled. The Word Plus lets you view a questionable word "in context," or as it appears in the sentence. This is important in some cases, such as with synonyms like 'there' and 'their.' The documentation is poor and could stand much improvement. Fortunately, The Word Plus is fairly easy to operate. At its price, it represents a reasonable value in a spelling checker.

RATINGS:

Overall Value	8	Performance	7
Ease of Use	8	Documentation	8

PRODUCT INDEX

HARDWARE

PRODUCT INDEX

HARDWARE

PRODUCT INDEX

HARDWARE

PRODUCT INDEX

SOFTWARE

PRODUCT INDEX

SOFTWARE

PRODUCT INDEX

SOFTWARE

Explore the World of Computers with SIGNET

(0451)

☐ **THE TIMEX PERSONAL COMPUTER MADE SIMPLE: A Guide to the Timex/ Sinclair 1000 by Joe Campbell, Jonathan D. Siminoff, and Jean Yates.** You don't need a degree or have an understanding of computer language to follow plain and simple English in the guide that lets you quickly, easily, and completely master the Timex/Sinclair 1000—the amazingly inexpensive, immeasurably valuable personal computer that can enhance every area of your life. (121384—$3.50)*

☐ **51 GAME PROGRAMS FOR THE TIMEX/SINCLAIR 1000 and 1500 by Tim Hartnell.** Why spend money on expensive software? Here are easy-to-program, exciting to play games designed especially for your Timex/ Sinclair 1000 and 1500. Whether you like thought games or action games, roaming the far reaches of space or the ocean depths, drawing pictures or solving puzzles, you'll find something to challenge your game playing skills. (125983—$2.50)*

☐ **THE NEW AMERICAN COMPUTER DICTIONARY by Kent Porter.** If the words "Does not compute!" flash through your mind as you try to wade through the terminology in even a "simple" programming manual, or you're having trouble understanding this odd language your friends, family, and co-workers are suddenly speaking, then you definitely need this, your total guide to "computerese". Includes more than 2000 terms defined in easy-to-understand words, plus a wealth of illustrations. (125789—$3.50)*

*Prices slightly higher in Canada
